China's Foreign Trade Policy

China's rise as a major trading power has prompted debate about the nature of its involvement in the liberal international economic order. *China's Foreign Trade Policy* sheds light on this complex question by examining the changing domestic forces shaping China's foreign trade relations.

Specifically, this book explores the evolving trade policy-making process in China by looking at:

- China's WTO accession negotiations
- China's bilateral trade disputes
- the development of China's antidumping regime
- China's emerging trade disputes in the WTO.

In addition, Ka Zeng examines how lobbying patterns in China are becoming more open and pluralistic, with bureaucratic agencies, sectoral interests, regional interests and even transnational actors increasingly able to influence the process and outcome of China's trade negotiations.

Using case studies of China's trade disputes with its major trading partners, as well as China's participation in the dispute settlement process of the World Trade Organization, to present an in-depth analysis of China's trade relations, this book will appeal to students and scholars of international political economy, Chinese politics and foreign policy, and more generally Asian studies.

Ka Zeng is Associate Professor of Political Science at the University of Arkansas.

Routledge Contemporary China Series

China's Foreign Trade Policy

The new constituencies

Edited by Ka Zeng

 Routledge
Taylor & Francis Group

LONDON AND NEW YORK

First published 2007
by Routledge
2 Park Square, Milton Park, Abingdon, Oxon, OX14 4RN

Simultaneously published in the USA and Canada
by Routledge
270 Madison Ave, New York NY 10016

Routledge is an imprint of the Taylor & Francis Group, an informa business

Transferred to Digital Printing 2009

Typeset in Times New Roman by
Bookcraft Ltd, Stroud, Gloucestershire

British Library Cataloguing in Publication Data
A catalogue record for this book is available from the British Library

Library of Congress Cataloging in Publication Data
China's foreign trade policy: the new constituencies / [edited by] Ka Zeng.
    p. cm. – (Routledge contemporary China series; 22)
    Includes bibliographical references and index.
    1. China–Commercial policy. 2. China–Foreign economic relations.
    I. Zeng, Ka, 1973–HF1604.C4532 2007
382'.30951–dc22   2006100585

ISBN10: 0-415-77086-6 (hbk)
ISBN10: 0-415-54709-1 (pbk)
ISBN10: 0-203-94681-2 (ebk)

ISBN13: 978-0-415-77086-6 (hbk)
ISBN13: 978-0-415-54709-3 (pbk)
ISBN13: 978-0-203-94681-7 (ebk)

Contents

viii *Contents*

Tables and figures

Tables

Figures

Appendix

Contributors

Scott Kennedy is an Associate Professor in the Departments of Political Science and East Asian Languages and Cultures and director of the Research Center for Chinese Politics and Business at Indiana University. He is author of *The Business of Lobbying in China* (Harvard University Press, 2005) and several articles on various aspects of China's evolving political economy. His current project examines Chinese involvement in international economic regimes.

Yuka Kobayashi is a Junior Research Fellow and doctoral candidate in Law at the University of Oxford. She has taught public international law and Chinese law at Oxford, and has publications in the area of China and international law. Her research interests include Chinese law, international law, theories of compliance and cooperation, and international relations of East Asia.

Wei Liang is a visiting scholar at the Berkeley Roundtable on the International Economy (BRIE). She has previously taught in the Department of International Relations at Florida International University. Her research interests include international trade negotiations, international competitiveness in high technology industries, and transition economies' participation in the World Trade Organization.

Andrew Mertha is an Assistant Professor in the Department of Political Science and the Program in International and Area studies at Washington University, St Louis. He is the author of *The Politics of Piracy: Intellectual property in contemporary China* (Cornell University Press, 2005) and has articles appearing in *International Organizations*, *Comparative Politics*, and *The China Quarterly*. His most recent published research is on the political pluralization of hydropower policy in China. Currently he is working on a project on China's ultra-concentration of industry and its relationship with international trade. He has lived in China on-and-off for almost seven years, beginning in 1988.

Megumi Naoi is an Assistant Professor in the Department of Political Science at University of California, San Diego. Her research bridges international and comparative political economy with a focus on the politics of trade and compensation in East Asia. Her main research project examines how economic integration changed politicians' incentives to target transfers to sub-national provinces – to mobilize political support in Japan, Thailand and China. Her other research projects concern when states adopt GATT/WTO legal trade remedies as opposed to domestic or bilateral instruments, the impact of non-class based political alignments on trade-related compensation policies, and how multilateral trade liberalization mobilizes interest groups differently than either unilateral or bilateral liberalization.

Ka Zeng is an Associate Professor in the Department of Political Science at the University of Arkansas. Her publications include *Trade Threats, Trade Wars: Bargaining, retaliation, and American coercive diplomacy* (University of Michigan Press, 2004) and articles on China's involvement in the world economy. Her research interests include international trade negotiations, foreign direct investment and trade disputes and China's harmonization with international law.

Acknowledgements

We would like to thank the Institute for International, Comparative, and Area Studies (IICAS) and the Institute on Global Conflict and Cooperation (IGCC) at the University of California, San Diego (UCSD) for providing financial support for us to organize a conference on Chinese Foreign Trade Policy in August 2006. Susan Shirk and Peter Cowhey at IGCC generously offered additional funds to make this conference possible. Melissa La Bouff at IICAS provided able assistance with logistical arrangements. This conference provided a valuable opportunity for contributing authors to present their individual research and for us to collectively revisit the main arguments and evidence of the project. We are grateful to Barry Naughton at UCSD and Judith Goldstein at Stanford University for participating in this conference in the capacity of discussants and for offering many critical yet constructive comments which helped to visibly improve the final product.

We would also like to thank *Political Science Quarterly* for their kind permission to reprint a slightly modified version of "China's porous protectionism: the changing political economy of trade policy" by Scott Kennedy, originally published in Vol. 120, no. 3 (2005).

1 Introduction

Ka Zeng and Andrew Mertha

In the last two decades China has claimed itself a major center of global trade and manufacturing activities. The Chinese economy has demonstrated unprecedented growth through its national policy of reform and opening up to the outside world following Maoist isolationism and disarray stemming from the Cultural Revolution. But while this has led to tremendous social welfare gains in China and has contributed to global trade in significant ways, Chinese manufacturers have also had to confront their trading partners in the advanced industrialized world over a mounting range of trade disputes. For example, not only were Chinese manufacturers and authorities increasingly presented with antidumping suits initiated by China's major trading partners, they also have had to respond to Washington's pressure to revalue the Chinese currency, the RMB, and have clashed head to head with the United States over protective duties on products such as furniture, semiconductors and automobile parts. The tone of US trade relations with China seems to have harkened back to the height of US–Japan trade relations in the 1980s. It is not an exaggeration to say that China will become one of the main rivals of the United States in the area of trade policy and that China is likely to remain a central concern of US trade policy in the years to come. These growing causes of trade friction between China and the US raise important questions both about the sources of these conflicts and the future orientation of US–China trade relations. They also raise questions about the process of trade policy-making in China which, up until now, has remained rather opaque to outside observers.

Existing studies of China's interactions with its major trading partners have examined how China bargains with the US on the basis of the assumption of a unitary actor. They have also treated Chinese foreign trade policy as a case study of the making of Chinese foreign policy in general or focused on the implications of China's accession into the World Trade Organization (WTO) for the Chinese economy and society. Relatively little scholarly attention has been devoted to the domestic politics behind China's behavior in the world trading system.[1] This issue is nevertheless of vital importance as it directly bears on the future of China's role in regional and global trade relations. It is therefore important to address this lacuna in order to understand how China does and will continue to respond to trade challenges from abroad.

This volume represents a collective effort to unpack the domestic politics of trade policy-making in China and to tackle questions about the emerging forces shaping China's foreign trade policy. The emphasis on how domestic actors shape China's behavior in the international trade realm promises to offer a novel perspective on China's international economic relations. Specifically, this project addresses the following questions:

- What is the domestic political process of trade policy-making in China? Is it changing? If so, in what ways?
- What kind of formal institutional changes have been necessary for a formerly centrally planned economy such as that of China to make such a transition?
- What is the changing pattern of trade policy lobbying in China?
- How did institutional reforms such as decentralization and administrative reorganization affect China's trade policy-making process and outcomes?
- To what extent does domestic politics in China influence the outcome of China's bilateral disputes and China's activities in the rules-based international trading system?

While the processes and changes described in this book are still tentative and ongoing, they nevertheless capture some of the more important dimensions of the making of trade policy in China and provide us with a first cut into this critical issue.

Review of the literature

Existing studies have not explicitly focused on China's foreign trade policy. As discussed below, studies of Chinese foreign policy tend to pay marginal attention to trade, in particular, to the domestic politics underlying the agenda setting and outcome of trade negotiations and the implementation of trade agreements. Another body of literature discusses the effect of China's WTO membership on the Chinese economy and society. In addition, while there is a rich literature on the political economy of trade, scholars of China and its trade relations have yet to engage this literature.

In the first place, one strand of the literature focuses on China's foreign policy-making process or on the impact of China's integration into the international system on the country's foreign policy behavior (e.g. Economy and Oksenberg, 1999; Hamrin and Zhao, 1995; Jacobson and Oksenberg, 1990; Johnston and Ross, 1999; Lampton, 2001; Lieberthal, 2004; Lu, 1997). While these works have provided in-depth analysis of foreign policy-making institutions, structures and processes, they have either avoided discussing foreign trade policy or have treated it as a case study of the making of Chinese foreign policy in general. This work fills this gap in the literature and seeks to more systematically investigate the process of decision-making behind China's bilateral and multilateral trade disputes.

Another strand of the literature (Abbott, 1998; Cass, Williams and Barker,

2003; Panitchpakdi and Clifford, 2002; Alexandroff, Ostry and Gomez, 2003; Lardy, 2002; Drysdale and Song, 2003) focuses on the implications of China's entry into the world economy for China's society and economy. These works engage in an assessment of WTO membership in terms of such issues as income disparity, social welfare and industrial development in China. None of these works has specifically addressed the evolution of China's foreign trade policy in the shadow of WTO membership. The above scholarship therefore differs from this project in terms of its substantive focus.

Finally, there is a substantial body of work[2] that deals with the political economy of trade policy in open economies. For example, these studies emphasize the importance of such factors as the electoral system, macroeconomic cycles, interest group pressure or geographical concentration on trade policy. They also assess the influence of industry versus class conflicts, the impact of asset specificity on the choice between alternative models and avenues of interest group lobbying on trade policy. In terms of how political institutions aggregate and channel society demand for trade protection, the literature emphasizes the different consequences that electoral systems, party systems or regime type may have on trade policy and how political institutions privilege the interests of certain political actors over others.

Do models of trade policy derived from studies of open economies apply to a transitional economy such as China? How relevant is this body of literature for our understanding of China's trade policy? This volume seeks to broaden our understanding of the evolving nature of China's trade relations as that nation adapts to the requirements of the WTO. As relatively little is known about the trade policy-making process in a transitional economy such as China and the applicability of standard models of trade policy to the Chinese context, it is necessary, perhaps even imperative, for us to engage in a more detailed analysis of China's foreign trade policy process as that country becomes a more active member of the world trading system. The findings yielded by this volume are apt to be tentative, yet they should represent a first step in our understanding of Chinese behavior in the realm of China's international trade relations.

Themes of this volume

The chapters in this volume point to a number of common and interrelated themes that have been ignored, or, at the very least, under-explored, by the existing literature. First, given the fact that the WTO is understood as being a liberal institution, to what extent has China become more liberal in its trading regime? Second, given the rhetoric in the United States about "the China threat", to what degree does China actually "threaten" the US, and, by extension, the norms of free trade ostensibly espoused by the WTO? Finally, to what extent are China's strengths simultaneously its principal weaknesses when it comes to Beijing's ability to compete in this more liberal trading order?

Internalization of the WTO's liberal norms

On the first dimension – to what degree China has internalized the liberal norms of the WTO – the answer is complex and in flux. China's accession into the WTO in 2001 has prompted debate about its behavior in the multilateral trading system. Just as in the area of security affairs, scholars of China's behavior in the international economic system have asked questions such as whether China is a status quo power or a revisionist power.

In examining the initial years of China's presence in Geneva, Margaret Pearson (2006), for example, argues that Beijing is far from a revisionist power and has instead been a cooperative player under the WTO's institutional rubric. Citing China's support for the trade liberalization agenda of the Doha Round of multilateral trade negotiations and China's broad adherence to the rules of the organization, Pearson contends that with the exception of Chinese behavior on Taiwan, there is little indication that Beijing is challenging the rules and norms of the WTO. Robert Lawrence (2006) analyzes China's participation in the WTO (including the terms of its accession, current trade regime, and China's participation in the Doha Round negotiations and its involvement in the institution's regular activities) *and* Chinese initiatives with regard to Free Trade Agreements (FTAs), concluding that China's trade policies are by and large supportive of a rules-based multilateral trading system.

Revisionist accounts of China's behavior in the international economic system, however, postulate that China's membership in the WTO could potentially weaken the rules-based international system. Mallon and Whalley (2004), for example, raise the concern that as China is not yet a full market economy, it could resort to protectionist policy instruments that threaten to substantially increase the number of trade disputes for the WTO's dispute settlement mechanism (DSM), forcing other members to choose between the undesirable alternatives of neglect, which would promise to undermine the rule of law upon which the WTO operates, and trade retaliation designed to induce Chinese compliance. Related is the concern that following its accession to the WTO, China would seek to expand its influence and to change the rules of the WTO. Critics worry that as a large developing country, China would take up the leadership role in attempts to scale back the limitations faced by developing countries.

One approach to assessing the above debate about China's commitment to WTO rules and norms is to examine reputational concerns in Beijing's foreign trade behavior. The institutional changes that have taken place in China's foreign trade policy may help to shed light on this issue. During the pre-reform era, trade policy was centrally controlled as were other areas of economic policy. The Ministry of Foreign Trade and Economic Cooperation (MOFTEC, previously MOFERT, the Ministry of Foreign Economic Relations and Trade), which has now been transformed into the Ministry of Commerce (MOFCOM), was the primary bureaucratic institution responsible for designing China's foreign trade and economic aid strategies under the guidelines established by the central leadership. The decision-making process for foreign trade and economic affairs has traditionally followed the "fragmented authoritarian" framework (e.g., Lieberthal, 2004), a framework that has characterized China's domestic decision-making process in general.

In the "fragmented authoritarianism" framework, emphasis was placed on achieving consensus and narrowing the divergent policy goals of different ministries and agencies. Decisions are made in a top-down manner where the relevant bureaucracies and interests oftentimes engage in extensive bargaining and coordination. While the Standing Committee of the Politburo sets the basic policy orientation and direction, China's equivalent of the cabinet, the State Council, is charged with policy implementation. In this framework, the spirit and letter of policy are often altered to meet the parochial goals of those functional bureaucracies and local government actors necessary for the policy to be implemented successfully. That is, those agencies necessary to ensure the minimum degree of policy implementation success are able to change the contours of the policy by folding their demands into the policy package. Thus, the policy that is adopted bears little more than a passing resemblance to the original policy goals of the top leadership. Given the centrality of bureaucratic agencies in such a decision-making process, societal actors possessed very little ability to influence policy direction. In terms of trade policy-making, MOFTEC enjoyed a higher degree of control over the policy-making process than other bureaucratic actors, as trade and economic relations were considered to be less sensitive politically than most other policy areas.

China's Communist system has had to expend extra efforts to adapt to the changing international economic environment. In addition to the more subtle changes in China's policy-making process that would make China's policy-making process similar to that of a "normal" trading state, a series of formal institutional changes have taken place to make China's trade policy-making more transparent, streamlined and professional. Importantly, two waves of government restructuring have substantially streamlined the process of trade policy-making in China.

First, in 2001, in anticipation of China's entry into the WTO, the Department of WTO Affairs was established, the specific mission of which was to handle issues related to China's WTO membership. In subsequent years more new departments were created. For example, the Bureau of Fair Trade for Imports and Exports, the Industry Injury Investigation Bureau, and the Department of Information Technology and E-Commerce were created to deal with new trade issues such as antidumping, countervailing duties and subsidies, and so on. Second, in 2003, China's state agencies underwent significant reorganization and a number of new institutions were created. In this government restructuring, the State Economic and Trade Commission (SETC), which used to have control over China's internal trade, was dismantled. The SETC's former functions of industrial injury investigation in the trade remedy process and domestic trade policy-making were shifted to the Ministry of Commerce headed first by Lu Fuyuan and then by Bo Xilai, a former governor of Liaoning Province. The government restructuring described above has substantially strengthened the institutional capacity of China's trade policy-making apparatus.

What do these institutional changes suggest with regard to China's commitment to WTO rules and norms more generally? China's concern about reputation also emerges as a theme from the discussions of China's trade policy. Scott Kennedy, for example, notes that China's adoption of the regime is motivated by a desire to acquire a trade policy instrument available to most major trading states.[3] Like most other developing countries, which perceive that they have been unfairly targeted by the antidumping (AD) actions of their counterparts in the industrialized countries, China started to view AD as "an equal opportunity weapon" and a legitimate right under the WTO system. Prompted by a desire to acquire a policy instrument to defend against unfair trade practices, Chinese business actors have not only started to challenge foreign AD actions against Chinese firms, but have also more actively developed China's own AD regime. In this sense, concerns about reputation and the legitimate rights of China have influenced the evolution of China's AD regime.

Similarly, in her study of China's response to the WTO dispute initiated by the United States against China's value-added tax (VAT) rebate policy for the semiconductor industry, Wei Liang finds that China's WTO commitments, especially the WTO-plus rules designed for transition economies, place a significant constraint on Beijing. Concerns that reneging on China's international legal commitments may be reputation costly in part help to explain why China chose to make concessions to the United States during the bilateral consultations, without escalating to the point of establishing a WTO dispute panel. Hence the norms embedded in the international trade regime have had a constraining effect on Chinese behavior.

A China "threat"?

Are we justified in painting China as a threat?[4] This answer depends on a number of dimensions by which we define the notion of a "threat" as well as what the potential targets of such a threat actually are. The more "hawkish" interpretation is that China can be seen as being frustrated with the status quo. The PRC was not a founding member of the WTO, and, as Liang argues, this led to Beijing's temporary suspension of its willingness to join after 1995. This, coupled with China's traditional suspicion of the international order – by which it was seen as being victimized during its "century of humiliation" – suggests that China is less invested in the status quo than its US, European or Japanese trading partners. One conclusion is that once China is able to leverage the size of its economy and "seduce" its trading partners by holding out the potential of its vast, untapped market, it will engage in rewriting the rules and altering the very norms of the WTO and of international liberal trade more generally.

The more benign view is that China is attempting to update its economic and (to a lesser degree) its political institutions in order to provide a more seamless interface with WTO rules and norms. Once it has done so, according to this view, China will emerge as a formidable competitor. If we invoke neoclassical assumptions to argue that each member of the WTO trade regime is acting in its own self-interest, then the outcome will be a more efficient international trade regime. According to this more "dovish" interpretation, China's increasing ability to compete will strengthen the existing international trading regime, although it will inevitably force other WTO members to undertake structural change in order to successfully compete in this new liberal trading order.

Obviously, these are ideal types, and it is still early in a process that will take decades to unfold. The evidence presented in this book suggests that a dichotomous account of China's behavior in the international trading system may not be terribly illuminating. Predictions of Chinese behavior based on a unitary actor assumption without considering domestic politics may be problematic. For those embracing the view that China is by and large a cooperative actor, the non-unitary aspect of China should sound a cautionary note to China's future role in the world trading system. For those viewing China as a revisionist power seeking to challenge the rules of the organization, the complication of domestic politics may paint an even more bleak picture of Chinese behavior. In either case, the chapters collectively suggest that a simple dichotomous view of China as either a benign or a malignant actor is overly facile. Instead, one has to grapple with the importance of domestic political forces in shaping the future trajectory of China in the world trading system. This section outlines several areas in which domestic politics may complicate the notion that China will be a cooperative player in the world trading system, which, in turn, may provide fodder for both interpretations.

Local government behavior

Andrew Mertha's study suggests that optimism about China's cooperative behavior in the international system should be tempered somewhat. As the priority that local governments place on economic development often diverges from the goal of protecting the intellectual property rights (IPR) of foreign actors, local governments could engage in ambiguous and untargeted threats against foreign firms invested in China so as to prevent the latter from raising their concerns about China's lax IPR enforcement in the US trade policy agenda-setting process. Such threats have in turn prevented US actors from raising their legitimate concerns through trade policy. As local governments pursue economic interests and engage in behavior that contradicts central injunctions, one could witness mercantilist and potentially predatory behavior on the part of local governments in China.

Compliance

In examining the turf battles between the MII and other related bureaucracies, Yuka Kobayashi suggests the competition among bureaucratic agencies has dimmed the prospect of China's trouble-free compliance with its WTO commitments. The MOFTEC (now MOFCOM) has come into increasing conflict with the Ministry of Information Industry (MII), which has an interest in protecting the domestic industries. The conflicts between MOFTEC (now MOFCOM) and the MII have therefore substantially reduced the prospect of China complying with its obligations in the rules-based system. Indeed, the possibility that China's lack of sufficient institutional capacity may complicate its compliance with international agreements has not been ignored by China scholars (e.g., Mertha and Zeng, 2005). China's recent compliance records also raise cause for concern. The United States Trade Representative (USTR) publishes an annual report on China's compliance with its WTO commitments and while the 2005 USTR report notes China's progress towards compliance, it nevertheless raises serious concerns about China's lack of protection for intellectual property rights, regulatory measures that favor domestic enterprises and the continued use of industrial policy in sectors such as auto-parts, steel, high-tech sectors, and so on. To the extent that bureaucratic turf battles are exacerbated by China's entry into the WTO, this bodes ill for China's ability to comply with its WTO commitments.

Market surges and the potential for a protectionist backlash

Findings from this project about the influence of sectoral interests in China suggest that business associations and industries in China are increasingly important actors in shaping China's foreign trade policy. In particular, sectors that face strong competition and declining profitability are likely to become more vocal in pushing for their interests. These cases indicate that such sectors have pushed for the use of AD duties and other legal trade remedies. Industry pressure for protection could heighten in the event that Chinese industries experience a loss of competitiveness in their products. As Robert Lawrence (2006) pointed out, while China's competitiveness in the traded goods sector has facilitated its adjustments to the requirements of WTO membership, trade liberalization has nevertheless led to substantial dislocation. If the current political pressure over the appreciation of the Chinese currency, the RMB, were to force Chinese leaders to undertake more drastic measures to revalue the currency, this could potentially result in China's loss of competitiveness in the international market, which could in turn heighten pressure from industries adversely affected by the market trends. The increasing transparency of the trade policy-making process could potentially make it more difficult for the Chinese leadership to contain such a fallout.

Alternatively, in the event that Chinese products become more competitive, with the potential of increasing China's exports and its bilateral trade surplus with the United States even further, this may prompt China's trading partners to adopt temporary trade restrictions against Chinese products through such measures as safeguards. In such a scenario, Chinese export-oriented producers may potentially lobby for trade protection measures that would advance the entry of export-oriented Chinese producers into the world market, with the possibility of provoking a costly tit-for-tat trade war. This is in part illustrated by Chinese producers' reactions to the safeguard measure that Japan imposes on Chinese agricultural and textile products.

In either of the above scenarios, business interests that are already more vocal in China's trade policy process may react to the erection of trade barriers abroad by calling for comparable measures at home. The growing participation of domestic players in the policy process may therefore render China's trade policy more conflictual than in the scenarios suggested by proponents of either the cooperative or the confrontational view of China.

In sum, the above discussion suggests that a dichotomous view of China as either a benign or a non-status quo power in the international economic system may be oversimplified. The reality is more complex and can only be understood if we invoke the third broad theme of this volume: China's weaknesses as strengths.

China's weaknesses as strengths

The preceding discussion notes that China's political and economic institutions remain fragmented and that decision-making, particularly about compliance, is often decentralized. Again, this can be interpreted in a number of ways, often focusing on the idea of intentionality. On the one hand, does China's "misbehavior" (noncompliance) stem from strategic decisions, or is it a result of structural conditions owing to China's weak institutions? The answer is that it is due to some degree to both. Moreover, one is tempted to use the former as a default interpretation because intentionality is so difficult for outsiders to identify accurately and convincingly.

Perhaps another way of looking at this dichotomy is to recast this as (starting with the status quo as a baseline) China's movement in one direction having the potential to undermine its advantage in another. How can Beijing convince other Chinese actors to give up short-term gain in order to maximize economic efficiencies and social welfare? One way of getting at the answer is by identifying instances where China is – or individual actors within China are – being strategic versus simply being opportunistic. For example, even though Mertha's chapter paints local Chinese governments as perhaps being somewhat devious in their manipulation of the US trade agenda, it is by no means certain that this is a strategic choice on the part of Beijing. Of course, Beijing may be aware of what is going on and it may certainly strengthen its bargaining position vis-à-vis the United States, but it is not policy. Rather, he argues, this is merely a strategic response to opportunities afforded local governments by the fragmentation of the Chinese political and economic system. However, to rein in these same actors robs Beijing of a potentially useful bargaining tool.

Further complicating the picture is the fact that formal institutional changes have been accompanied by concrete changes in the substance of trade policy-making in China. The various chapters in this volume assess the role of business actors, regional powers, sectoral interests and transnational groups in shaping China's foreign trade policy through a series of case studies, including US–China negotiations over China's accession into the WTO, US–China negotiations over intellectual property rights, Sino-Japanese trade disputes between 1970 and 2003, China's antidumping actions and its use of legal trade remedies as well as China's activities in Geneva.

As the chapters in this volume make clear, China's foreign trade policy formulation is becoming increasingly pluralized, interest-based and more transparent.

Instead of being confined to the government bureaucracy, the decision-making process has become more open to the lobbying of business leaders, sectoral and regional interests, and to some extent transnational business groups. As trade policy-making in that country becomes more open, porous and reflective of business realities, one may argue that the trade policy-making process in China has been transformed to such an extent that it is increasingly reflective of business realities. Indeed, domestic political actors have become more heavily involved in China's external trade relations than in the past. However, institutional drag, path dependency and political imperatives nonaligned with trade underscore how fragile some of these changes actually are.

The findings from several episodes of trade policy-making in China, summarized in the following section, suggest that domestic political forces not only drive the outcome of China's bilateral trade negotiations, but they are also increasingly important in shaping China's approach toward the WTO's rules-based international trading system.

Interests

The various chapters in this volume emphasize the growing influence of both sectoral and regional interests on China's foreign trade policy. For example, the chapter on China's use of legal trade remedies assesses the influence of sectoral interests on China's utilization of legal trade remedies. The legal trade remedies analyzed in that chapter include not only the rules of the WTO, but also China's domestic legal trade rules such as antidumping and safeguards. Zeng's chapter shows that even though the Chinese state has actively promoted the use of legal trade remedies, domestic industries have largely shaped the pattern in which such remedies were employed. On the basis of analyses of China's antidumping regime and the China–Japan safeguard disputes over agricultural and textile products, Zeng argues that the Chinese government is increasingly resorting to legal trade remedies both as a sword to open foreign markets and as a shield to protect China's import-competing industries from the forces of foreign competition. Industries such as chemicals and steel have driven the use of China's antidumping and safeguard measures and the use of such trade instruments will likely be more frequent in the future. Moreover, legal trade remedies have been employed to constrain the unilateral exercise of power by the United States. China's subtle shift from a diplomacy-power-oriented negotiation approach to "aggressive multilateralism" therefore has its roots in domestic considerations. Her chapter also assesses the extent to which China's emerging legal trade strategy has succeeded in advancing Chinese interests. In contrast to that of Mertha, Zeng's chapter therefore paints a picture of the new openness in China's foreign trade policy.

At the same time, these positive changes also underscore the rift between China's ability to utilize the international legal infrastructure for trade dispute resolution and its own weak and tenuous legal apparatus. That is, China has the trappings of a mature legal system on paper, but its actual institutions for enforcing these laws and mediating disputes within its domestic jurisdictions remain weak and largely ineffective. Of course, the Chinese – and increasingly, foreign actors – are able to use the back door and rely on informal personal and institutional arrangements to address their claims. And, indeed, one can argue that this provides the requisite degree of "maneuverable space" that allows for such dramatic economic development without having to be burdened by bureaucratic and other institutional checks and balances. However, as this rift continues to grow, the contradictions between China's utilization of international legal remedies and its own supine legal infrastructure will only continue to expand and potentially keep China from progressing to the next stage of economic development.

Similarly, in examining US–China semiconductor trade disputes, Liang finds that China's semiconductor industry has worked closely with the Chinese government in the formulation of policy. The semiconductor trade dispute represents the first WTO case filed by any member of the World Trade Organization against China. In March 2004 the Bush administration filed a complaint with the WTO against China's controversial value-added tax on semiconductors. The dispute was resolved in July 2004 through bilateral negotiations, in the absence of the formation of a panel. This chapter examines the origins, bilateral negotiation and the final resolution of China's first WTO dispute, focusing in particular on the process of policy formation in this case. Specifically, Liang attempts to draw out the role of Chinese industries along with that of trade and industrial bureaucracies in China's dispute activities. In the past, the private sector has largely been excluded from the policy-making process. However, in this case, Chinese semiconductor manufacturers were not the proponents of the VAT rebate policy as the proposed VAT policy did not confer substantial benefits to Chinese producers. Not only are many smaller enterprises not even eligible for tax rebates, the benefits that the larger companies would stand to accrue from the tax rebate were minimal compared to their total revenue. Moreover, the Chinese enterprises were hoping to substitute "the VAT rebate policy with other WTO-compliant government policies that can benefit the semiconductor as a whole" (Liang: p. 111). The lack of resistance by the domestic semiconductor industry helped to facilitate the conclusion of the negotiation. The main role of the semiconductor manufacturers in this case was to provide policy suggestions and policy alternatives. However, this relationship, as Kennedy makes clear, is anything but institutionalized, and, thus, remains fragile. Moreover the ability of these associations to influence policy when they are not allied with the government against an external opponent remains unclear.

Additionally, contributing authors have noted the growing influence of regional interests on China's foreign trade policy. The deepening of economic reform has been accompanied by the progressive delegation of power to local authorities so that over time, localities have become increasingly important agents in China's economic policy-making. This is not only increasingly evident in China's domestic economic policy-making, but also in trade policy-making. Megumi Naoi's chapter on China–Japan trade disputes assesses how ongoing processes of decentralization in a developing country such as China affect trade negotiation outcomes. She argues that the devolution of power from the center to the localities in China has increased local governments' stake in foreign economic policy and made certain trade policy instruments unfeasible for the central government. Through case studies of Sino-Japanese negotiations over specific commodities between the 1970s and 2003, Naoi advances the novel hypothesis that the combination of the degree of government centralization and that of industries' geographical concentration is an important factor explaining why some of the trade disputes between Japan and China were settled via the use of bilateral voluntary export restraint (VER) negotiations, while others have resulted in the use of legal trade remedies such as antidumping and safeguard measures. She argues that China is more likely to resort to safeguard measures when export administration is decentralized and industry is geographically dispersed.

This is because decentralization of export administration, which devolves greater responsibilities to local foreign trade corporations (FTC) and empowers local authorities in export regulation, has enhanced the incentives of local actors in export promotion. Naoi further argues that the effect of export decentralization is compounded by the degree of geographical concentration of industries. Industry-level VER negotiation is difficult to achieve and often requires a government's intervention, as the more dispersed the production and export activities across a few different provinces, the more likely it is that local FTCs and producers will compete to promote export and secure higher market shares abroad. It is also more difficult for local governments to engage in collective action and cooperate to achieve effective enforcement of VERs when the industry is geographically dispersed. Conversely, a high degree of geographical concentration of the industry, combined with government decentralization, ought to more likely result in attempts to resort to bilateral VERs. The contrasting outcomes of the seaweed and *tatami* cases best illustrate these dynamics. Thus, overall, this chapter suggests that fiscal decentralization in China has lengthened the duration of disputes, decreased the use of voluntary export restraints and increased the two countries' reliance on the General Agreement on Tariffs and Trade (GATT)/WTO instruments. In sum, this chapter finds that the combination of geographical concentration and industry concentration is a key factor in an industry's choice of the use of safeguards versus voluntary export restraints (VERs).

Another example of local governments' influence over trade policy can be found in Liang's chapter on China's WTO accession negotiations. Waves of decentralization have increased the stakes of local governments in economic policy and increased their incentives for promoting local economic interests. Liang suggests that rather than playing an important role in influencing the actual negotiations, local governments have constrained the central government's negotiation authority through the implementation of policy. On a few occasions the central negotiation authority's position was undermined by moves by local governments for more policy autonomy. In contrast to the study by Pearson (2001), Liang's chapter suggests that with the exception of Shanghai, most local governments were not actively involved in the negotiations, nor were they aware of the negotiation details. More research could be done on this topic to systematically assess the relative role of the local governments in the trade policy decision-making process.

The strategic benefits provided by decentralization also point to the more general contradiction between the costs and benefits to Beijing of economic and political decentralization over the course of the reform era. In recent years, Beijing has attempted to rein in the degree of such decentralization but is finding it difficult to put the decentralization genie (or elements of it) back into the bottle. This is further complicated by the notion that insofar as those more domestically problematic elements of decentralization actually help strengthen Beijing's hand at the negotiating table, they create conflicting incentives for Beijing to move away from the status quo. For example, Andrew Mertha examines how local governments' retaliatory threats against foreign firms have had the effect of deterring these firms operating within their borders from voicing their dissatisfaction with their home governments. Using intellectual property rights as an example, he shows that in investment disputes foreign companies with operations in China are often constrained from raising the issue with their governments by the Chinese government's explicit or implicit threat to inflict damage on their local operations. As this chapter explains, local governments not only possess the capability, and hence credibility, to inflict pain on foreign firms, they are also able to "strategically manipulate information and maximize ambiguity to minimize accurate knowledge about their retaliatory capabilities" (Mertha: p.64). While the transnational deterrence threat does not necessarily stem from intentional behavior of local governments, it does reflect local governments' increasing ability to deviate from central policy and the inability of the center to discipline such behavior.

Institutions

In addition to the growing influence of regional interests on China's trade policy, contributing authors also note how bureaucratic agencies can influence China's trade negotiations and its implementation of trade agreements. In her chapter on the process of negotiations leading to China's entry into the WTO, Wei Liang illustrates how local industries, bureaucratic agencies and provincial interests concerned with the potential impact of WTO entry on their interests have asserted themselves in the process of China's negotiations with the United States over China's WTO accession. During the negotiations, the Ministry of Commerce had to coordinate and reconcile the divergent interests of various governmental and societal organizations to a much greater extent than it had in the past. This has in turn accentuated the need for both ministerial and supraministerial coordination. Moreover, lobbying by governmental and societal interests significantly influences the ebb and flow of the negotiation process. It explains not only why negotiations sometimes broke down in the way they did, but also the specific design of the deal that negotiators eventually signed on to. The process of trade policy-making depicted in this chapter is therefore one that is considerably more plural, fluid and vulnerable to the jockeying for power by various bureaucratic actors.

Specifically, in terms of the impact of bureaucratic actors on the policy-making process, Liang suggests that compared to the past, bureaucratic interests have more often intruded in the decision-making process and that such bureaucratic involvement has at times slowed down the process of negotiation. Protectionist ministerial interests, including not only those that have traditionally enjoyed support from the Chinese state but also those charged with supervising China's emerging and infant industries, have voiced their opposition to China's market liberalization offers. Opposition from a wide range of bureaucratic actors has therefore resulted in significant deadlock in the negotiation process. For example, while Beijing was able to make reasonable progress liberalizing its goods market and trade-related laws and regulations, it could neither break the policy logjam in the sensitive telecommunications sector nor make market access offers in services negotiations in 1997 due to strong resistance from the Ministry of Post and Telecommunications and ministries charged with the services sector such as the People's Bank of China, China Insurance Regulatory Commission and China Securities Regulatory Commission.

The ability of status quo oriented agencies to penetrate the decision-making process could in turn be explained by the institutional weaknesses of the GATT/WTO Division under the Department of International Trade and Economic Affairs, the agency within MOFTEC which oversaw China's GATT/WTO negotiations. While the GATT/WTO Division was the strongest advocate of liberal trade policy, its influence was nevertheless limited as it lacked final negotiation authority and frequently had to seek approval from a higher level government unit. The insufficient negotiation authority of the WTO Affairs Division thus provided room for protectionist bureaus to flex their muscles.

The increasing involvement of bureaucratic actors in China's decision-making process also elevated the importance of interministerial coordination in the policy outcomes. Liang shows, for instance, that the difficulty in achieving coordinated bureaucratic positions and action has substantially slowed down the progress of negotiations. In 1986, the State Council Interministerial Coordination Group was established to engage in interministerial coordination on issues related to China's GATT/WTO accession negotiation. However, this Interministerial Coordination Committee did not function smoothly both because it only served as a temporary platform for consultation and also because all of its members were vice-ministers of different ministries enjoying an equal standing with MOFERT and, as a result, each ministry had spoken out for its own interests. The difficulty of policy coordination was compounded by the inclusion of more ministries and sectors into the negotiations in the mid-1990s. It was not until 1998 when one of the most comprehensive government restructurings was undertaken that the difficulty of interministerial coordination was eased. By weakening the authority of some previously powerful agencies and downgrading some ministries into bureaus, this restructuring significantly eased the burden of interministerial coordination, making it possible for Beijing to make relatively more concessions in the final negotiation protocol. The government restructuring implemented in 1998 thus provides an example of how the difficulties involved in interministerial coordination could complicate the negotiation process.

The chapter by Yuka Kobayashi reinforces the finding about the increasing involvement of bureaucratic actors in the decision-making process. She demonstrates that bureaucratic actors were more heavily involved in the pre-WTO negotiation process and have continued to be during the post-implementation and compliance stage. Before China's entry into the WTO, bureaucratic actors were barely involved in China's trade policy-making. But this has been undergoing transformation since China became a member of that organization. In particular, the information ministry which used to be in charge of telecommunications policy-making in China has become more heavily involved in the trade decision-making process as telecommunications policy has come to embody telecommunications trade. While the ministries in charge of the telecommunications industry and other non-state entities were largely irrelevant to trade policy-making prior to China's entry into the WTO, their increasing involvement and diverging preferences have bred turf battles that led to near breaches of China's WTO commitments. This chapter thus highlights how growing bureaucratic tussles may present a major impediment to China's compliance with its WTO commitments.

Additionally, these chapters point to the fact that institutional remedies for coordinating this growing universe of interests remain unable to keep up with the pace of change. As Mertha (2005) has argued elsewhere, coordination mechanisms suffer from low administrative rank and from insufficient staffing and budgetary funds. The more successful coordinating mechanisms have relied on personal and other information power dynamics rather than on any recognized institutional mandate, and thus remain institutionally weak.

Cross-border linkages

Standard accounts of trade policy typically focus on the influence of the domestic lobby instead of the foreign lobby. But as Scott Kennedy's chapter shows, transnational actors have been influential even in the case of China. Through an examination of China's antidumping actions, Kennedy shows that transnational alliances can act as a counterweight to protectionist interests and hence constitute a source of openness in economic policy. For example, even though antidumping duties have been imposed on most of the cases in which antidumping petitions were filed, there nevertheless existed substantial variation in the extent to which foreign actors were able to achieve a policy outcome in their favor. More specifically, foreigners have managed to gain victory in a surprising number of cases. This chapter explains the unexpected success of foreign firms in terms of the joint lobbying by the foreign respondents accused of dumping and their Chinese customers. Lobbying by Chinese downstream users of those foreign products accused of dumping benefited from substantially lower dumping margins and in the more speedy removal of the duties imposed. This case study of China's antidumping regime therefore highlights the growing ability of transnational business actors to influence the policy outcomes. This study utilizes original data from in-depth interviews with company executives, association representatives, lawyers and government officials directly involved in these cases. Its findings suggest that analyses focusing solely on the domestic sources of trade policy may no longer be sufficient. Instead, it may also be necessary for us to take into consideration the transnational alliance between Chinese downstream users and their foreign counterparts.

The subtext of this argument, however, is that foreign actors are able to take advantage of institutional weaknesses in China to influence the outcomes of antidumping negotiations. On the other hand these institutional weaknesses – such as those wrought by decentralization – provide the opportunity for domestic political actors to pursue their own interests in ways that flaunt the laws of the land. The case study of US-China IPR negotiations, for instance, suggests that physical investment by foreign producers increases their vulnerability to local Chinese governments' threats to inflict pain on their operations if they engage in activities that contradict the goals of local authorities. Such cross-border linkages therefore alter the dynamics of bargaining between foreign investors and their local hosts.

This finding is not entirely synchronous with the findings from the chapters on China's antidumping actions, which suggest that foreign producers with substantial investment in the Chinese market may have greater influence over China's AD decisions. In the AD cases, foreign investors that are significant to the Chinese economy possess more bargaining power with Chinese authorities. While they do not directly influence the case outcomes, they do affect the timing of the AD decisions.

Finally, Zeng's chapter on Beijing's AD decisions suggests that enterprises engaging in export processing, and thereby exempt from the AD duties, tend to be agnostic about the AD decisions and therefore have AD duties that have minimal effect on market conditions. All of these findings suggest that one must take into account the linkages created by China's integration into the world market in analyzing China's trade policy.

Each of these dimensions underscores a profound irony in our understanding of China: those same dimensions that have been the most effective handmaidens to China's spectacular economic growth can also potentially prevent China from moving to the next stage of establishing its economic infrastructure and, thus, its ability to maintain its trajectory as a mature global trading partner.

Methods and rationale for case selection

Most chapters in this project utilize the single case study method to support their arguments. While these chapters each focus on a distinctive issue area, collectively they are aimed at illuminating the forces shaping China's foreign policy and the changing pattern of trade policy lobbying in China. In other words, even though these chapters may differ from one another in their substantive and analytic focus, they are all organized around the central theme that China's foreign trade policy-making is undergoing a fundamental transformation to become more open to the influence of bureaucratic, sectoral and regional interests in a way that more closely resembles the pattern observed for advanced industrial states. As such, these case studies should not be viewed as disparate analyses of China's foreign trade policy;

they all aim to shed light on the key research questions that drive this project: what are the forces driving China's foreign trade policy-making? Is China's foreign trade policy-making changing? If so, how do we best characterize China's foreign trade policy-making process?

Contributions

As the above analysis makes clear, China's foreign economic policy has undergone a transformation to become more pluralized and more transparent. Lobbying patterns in China are becoming increasingly similar to those observed for advanced industrialized states, with ranked agencies, ministries, sectoral interests, and even transnational actors becoming increasingly able to influence both the possibility that China will reach a trade agreement with its trading partner *and* the terms of such agreements.

In addition to influencing the outcomes of China's bilateral and multilateral trade disputes, domestic political considerations increasingly drive China's behavior within multilateral trade institutions. Just like other countries in East Asia, such as Japan, which has more recently started to embrace the WTO and legal trade remedies in a more aggressive manner, China seems to be actively engaging with the rules of the WTO in an attempt to advance its key trade interests. These findings ought to have important implications for China's trading partners such as the United States in dealing with growing trade challenges from China.

This project makes several important contributions to existing literature on China and international political economy. Above all, it makes up for our lack of understanding of China's foreign policy-making process. As mentioned earlier, in spite of the proliferation of recent studies dealing with China's foreign policy, our understanding of the forces shaping China's foreign trade and economic policy unfortunately remains rudimentary and incomplete. This book provides a detailed account of the motivation behind China's foreign trade policy and systematically teases out the role of sectoral interest, bureaucratic actors, and regional interests in China's bilateral and multilateral trade activities. The findings of this research suggest that just as in other areas of decision-making in China, trade policy-making has indeed become more open, decentralized and pluralistic. Consequently, China has increasingly come to resemble a "normal" trading state, with various societal interests asserting greater influence in the decision-making process.

Second, the findings of this book also contribute to the broader literature on international political economy and on trade policy. Recent scholarly works on the nexus between domestic politics and international behavior (e.g. Evans, *et. al.*, 1993) have sought to develop more systematic analyses of the domestic politics behind international trade policy outcomes. Yet attempts to develop such systematic analyses also hinge on our understanding of the internal political dynamics in individual countries and on evidence from primary research. The findings yielded by this research therefore ought to broaden our understanding of the process of trade policy-making in non-Western, authoritarian states such as China and promise to enrich the literature on comparative trade policy.

Finally, this study should be of interest to the policy community in its efforts to integrate China into the world community. The changes taking place in China's foreign trade policy described above should provide Western policy and business communities with a roadmap for dealing with that country over economic issues. In addition to allowing for a more sophisticated understanding of the successes and failures of the West's bilateral or multilateral negotiations with China, they should help to illuminate choices over future negotiation approaches with that country.

Notes

1   For an exception, see, for example, Zeng (2004).
2   See the concluding chapter for a more detailed survey of this literature.
3   See the Kennedy chapter in this volume.
4   For studies that address the question of whether Beijing is genuinely "learning" global norms and values or simply engaging in tactical "adaptation" of global norms out of narrow self-interest, see, for example, Christensen, 1996; Johnston, 2003.

References

Abbott, F. (1998) *China in the World Trading System: Defining the Principles of Engagement*, Boston, MA: Kluwer Law International.

Alexandroff, A. S., Ostry, S. and Gomez, R. (2003) *China and the Long March to Global Trade*, New York: Routledge.

Cass, D. Z., Williams, B. and Barker, G. R. (2003) *China and the World Trading System: Entering the Millennium*, New York: Cambridge University Press.

Christensen, T. J. (1996) "Chinese realpolitik", *Foreign Affairs*, 75 (5): 37–52.

Drysdale, P. and Song, L. (2003) *China's Entry to the WTO: Strategic Issues and Quantitative Assessments*, New York: Routledge.

Economy, E. and Oksenberg, M. (eds) (1999) *China Joins the World: Progress and Prospects*, Washington, DC: Brookings Institution Press.

Evans, P.B., Jacobson, H.B. and Putnam, R.D. (eds) (1993) *Double-Edged Diplomacy: International Bargaining and Domestic Politics*, Berkeley, CA: University of California Press.

Hamrin, C. L. and Zhao, S. (1995) *Decision-making in Deng's China: Perspectives from Insiders*, Armonk, NY: M.E. Sharpe.

Jacobson, H. K. and Oksenberg, M. (1990) *China's Participation in the IMF, the World Bank, and GATT*, Ann Arbor: University of Michigan Press.

Johnston, A. I. (2003) "Is China a status quo power?" *International Security*, 27 (4): 5–56.

Johnston, A. I. and Ross, R. (eds) (1999) *Engaging China: The Management of An Emerging Power*, New York: Routledge.

Lampton, D. M. (ed.) (2001) *The Making of Chinese Foreign and Security Policy in the Era of Reform: 1978–2000*, Stanford, CA: Stanford University Press.

Lardy, N. R. (2002) *Integrating China into the World Economy*, Washington, DC: Brookings Institution Press.

Lawrence, R. Z. (2006) "China and the multilateral trading system", paper prepared for a conference on "China and Emerging Asia: Reorganizing the Global Economy?" organized by the Korea Institute for Economic Policy (KIEP) at Seoul National University.

Lieberthal, K. (2004) *Governing China: From Revolution through Reform*, New York: W. W. Norton.

Lu, N. (1997) *The Dynamics of Foreign-Policy Decisionmaking in China*, Boulder, CO: Westview Press.

Mallon, G. and Whalley, J. (2004) "China's post accession WTO stance", NBER Working Paper No. 10649.

Mertha, A. (2005) *The Politics of Piracy: Intellectual Property in Contemporary China*, Ithaca, NY: Cornell University Press, 2005.

Mertha, A. and Zeng, K. (2005) "Political institutions, resistance and China's harmonization with international law", *China Quarterly*, 182, 319–37.

Panitchpakdi, S. and Clifford, M.L. (2002) *China and the WTO: Changing China, Changing World Trade*, Singapore: J. Wiley & Sons.

Pearson, M. (2001) "The case of China's accession to GATT/WTO", in David M. Lampton (ed.), *The Making of Chinese Foreign and Security Policy in the Era of Reform, 1978-2000*, Stanford, CA: Stanford University Press, 337–70.

—— (2006) "China in Geneva: lessons from China's early years in the World Trade Organization", in Johnston, A. I. and Ross, R. (eds.), *New Directions in the Study of China's Foreign Policy*, Stanford, CA: Stanford University Press, 587–644.

United States Trade Representative, *2005 Report to Congress on China's WTO Compliance*, Washington, DC: GOP.

Zeng, K. (2004) *Trade Threats, Trade Wars: Bargaining, Retaliation, and American Coercive Diplomacy*, Ann Arbor: University of Michigan Press.

2 Bureaucratic politics, interministerial coordination and China's GATT/WTO accession negotiations

Wei Liang

Introduction

China's accession into the General Agreement on Tariffs and Trade (GATT)/ World Trade Organization (WTO) is arguably the most important and comprehensive foreign economic decision Beijing has made during the reform era. China's WTO membership signifies China's full integration into the global economy from the position of a previously isolated and planned economy. The extended negotiation process reflects the difficulties of achieving this transition in China, economically as well as politically. Thus, a close examination of China's GATT/WTO decision-making sheds light on foreign economic policy-making in China in the current era. The findings from this chapter illustrate that domestic ministries' protectionist preferences and poor internal coordination problems were direct obstacles to the central government's GATT/WTO policy formulation. The close linkage between bureaucratic politics and foreign policy-making characterizes China's fifteen-year GATT/WTO negotiation process.

A case study of China's GATT/WTO accession negotiation contributes to the overall objective of this volume in several ways. First, it centers on the Chinese government's new policy priority: economic development. Second, China's GATT/WTO accession negotiation took the longest time on record: while the average length of GATT/WTO accession negotiation is less than two years,[1] China's accession negotiation took over fifteen years. The negotiations spanned both the Cold War and the post-Cold War eras and covered most of the period of China's economic reform and political transition since 1978. The policy-making process behind the decision to join this important international economic organization thus mirrored the transformation of China's foreign trade policy-making process. Third, the complex nature of these negotiations meant that they touched upon many of the most important and sensitive aspects of China's foreign policy goals, including Sino-American relations, the Taiwan issue, China's grand strategy on economic development, and so on. In this sense, the case of China's GATT/WTO accession negotiations goes beyond the trade arena and paints a broad picture of China's foreign affairs.

China's GATT/WTO accession process has been extremely dynamic and complex, affected by political and economic factors at both the international and domestic levels. To illustrate the impact of domestic politics on China's trade policy, this chapter will only focus on the dynamics at the domestic level. This chapter considers not only the preferences and choices of Chinese domestic actors and the institutional context within which they operate, but also the evolution of preferences and institutional changes in the process of foreign economic policy-making, highlighting how these factors at the domestic level affect the process of GATT/WTO negotiations. Specifically, this chapter addresses the following theoretical and empirical questions:

- How do we explain the protracted and difficult negotiation process?
- Under what circumstances will central leaders override bureaucratic politics and play an arbitrary role?
- What are the organizational structure and administrative processes underlying the interplay between elites (i.e. central leaders) and subelites (i.e. ministerial level government officials)?
- How does bureaucratic structure influence policy-making behavior?
- Why do some domestic ministries carry more weight than others in the making of foreign trade policy?

In the last two decades, the domestic context of Chinese foreign policy has attracted increasing scholarly attention as we are clearly faced with a system in transition. Scholars such as Lampton (2001) suggest that compared to the highly controlled process of policy-making during the Maoist era, China's foreign policy-making process has gone through dramatic changes characterized by four general trends: professionalization, decentralization, pluralization and globalization. In other words, top leaders have become more constrained and have had to consult more broadly with other domestic actors. This view is echoed by other China specialists (e.g. Lu, 1997; Hamrin and Zhao, 1995; Lieberthal, 1995), who pointed out that the decision-making process in China has come to be based on extensive consultation and bargaining. Moreover, while senior political elites continue to play a decisive role in those issues that affected the fundamental interests of the regime during the 1980s and 1990s, the process of noncrisis, recurrent decision-making is more encompassing and has come to involve a broader range of domestic actors (e.g. Lieberthal and Lampton, 1992). Traditionally scholars of Chinese foreign policy-making were more interested in understanding China's military and security policy-making, its arms sale activities (e.g. Swaine, 1998; Nathan and Ross, 1997; Lewis, Hua and Xue, 1991; Lewis and Xue, 1994; Mulvenon, 1997), or the formulation of its Taiwan policy (e.g. Sutter and Johnson, 1994). Starting in the 1990s, the new foreign policy dynamics involving China's participation in global economic affairs and international organizations attracted growing scholarly attention (e.g. Jacobson and Oksenberg, 1990; Lardy, 1994; Economy and Oksenberg, 1999). These works provide us with a useful theoretical framework for understanding the broad domestic context of China's foreign economic policy. However, they inadequately analyze the interministerial and supraministerial levels of decision-making in

China, which have undergone significant transformation and have become increasingly important in recent years. This chapter fills this gap in the literature by identifying and highlighting the vital role of ministerial-level actors in foreign economic policy-making.

The approach of this chapter differs from that of the existing literature, especially the empirical study by Margaret Pearson (2001) on China's WTO accession negotiations, in three aspects. First, instead of providing a comprehensive study of domestic and global variables affecting China's GATT/WTO negotiations,[2] this chapter focuses on the preference formation of ministries and bureaus under the central government. Second, this study explicitly links changes in domestic institutional arrangements (i.e. restructuring) to the preference transformation of the domestic ministries. Third, while a growing number of studies of Chinese foreign economic policy-making look at the pluralization of the policy-making process and the decentralization of organizations, they often do not explicitly link these factors to policy outcomes. This chapter argues that the proliferation of government agencies in the decision-making process slowed down the negotiations; the subsequent institutional changes instead resulted in a smaller number of government agencies with less direct interests at stake, thus facilitating the negotiation process. In particular, the promotion of the Ministry of Foreign Trade and Economic Cooperation (MOFTEC) to the position of the lead agency in international economic negotiation eased the coordination difficulty among ministries. These institutional changes thus removed the structural obstacles to negotiations and allowed Beijing to form coherent and proactive negotiation positions vis-à-vis the United States. In sum, this chapter proposes that a series of changes that have taken place in preferences and institutions during China's GATT/WTO negotiations have resulted in an improved domestic bureaucratic landscape and that these changes have significant implications for the making of foreign economic policy in China in the future.

The remainder of this chapter proceeds as follows. The next section briefly examines the ebb and flow of the fifteen-year negotiation process, namely the events leading up to the final accession protocol. The third section discusses vested ministerial interests and how they affect China's GATT/WTO negotiation. This section relies heavily on field research and interviews. The fourth section further examines the institutional context of China's GATT/WTO decision-making and illustrates the interaction between China's domestic administrative reorganization and its international behavior. The fifth section addresses the question as to when and how policy intervention by top leaders would take place. Finally, the chapter concludes by discussing the broader implications of the analysis for the study of bureaucratic politics and for China's foreign economic policy.

A brief review of the 15-year negotiation

China formally applied to rejoin the GATT on 10 July 1986 when the Chinese Ambassador to Geneva, Qian Jiadong, submitted an application to the GATT to resume China's contracting membership. The initial stage of China's GATT accession negotiations ran smoothly but became paralyzed by the Tiananmen Square Incident in June 1989. The negotiation impasse lasted until 1992. Subsequently the negotiations encountered more bottlenecks, with the Western countries declaring that China's offer on market access and tariff reduction was inadequate. Domestic opposition against a deal that involved wide-ranging concessions on substantive issues also turned out to be too great to overcome. Though the top leaders decided to make a final push, China missed its self-determined deadline in late 1994 and consequently failed to become a founding member of the WTO, which superseded the GATT on 1 January 1995. This pushed the negotiation into stalemate again.

Serious bilateral negotiations between China and major WTO member countries were not resumed until 1997–1998. Compared to the first half of the 1990s, China's bilateral relations with the United States gained a more stable footing. It was in such an improved political environment that the second Clinton administration finally decided to close the WTO deal with China. On its side Beijing also showed a greater willingness to make concessions. China submitted another list of tariff reductions on nearly 6,000 products. At the following fourth session of the China working party held in May 1997, China agreed on the principles of judicial review and nondiscrimination. In October 1997 China agreed to abolish agricultural export subsidies. In March 1998, China submitted another package of tariff reductions, which would have cut back tariffs on 5,600 industrial goods on a line-by-line basis and reduced the average tariff level from 15 percent to 10.8 percent by 2005. Chinese negotiators hoped to achieve a breakthrough on the eve of Jiang Zemin's summit visit to Washington in October 1997 and President Bill Clinton's visit to China in June 1998 respectively. Despite frequent negotiations, Beijing failed to make key concessions in services sectors, as required by the US and the European Union (EU). In fact, Chinese negotiators were even unable to provide a package of market access in services sectors to the China Working Party meetings throughout 1997–1998 and had to submit more tariff reduction packages instead. These strains largely resulted from the resistance of domestic ministries to the further opening of their sectors to foreign competition. Beginning in 1999, top leaders committed themselves to WTO accession. In April 1999 Premier Zhu Rongji arrived in Washington with a long-awaited package for access of China's services sectors, a package which was approved at the Politburo meeting shortly before his departure. The package was so appealing, containing favorable terms on nearly all contentious issues that were unresolved in the previous bilateral talks, that President Clinton reportedly regretted it immediately after his denial of the final deal.[3] Within this context, the bilateral agreement reached between the US and China in November 1999 cleared the biggest obstacle to China joining the WTO. China formally became a member of the WTO in 2001.[4]

Domestic ministries' preferences

With the expansion of the negotiation agenda over time, more and more government constituencies became involved in the GATT/WTO decision-making process in the

1990s. The proliferation of ministerial-level domestic actors thus made distinctive bureaucratic preferences more visible and internal coordination less feasible. As the ministry in charge of China's GATT/WTO negotiations, MOFTEC had its hands tied because of the lack of authority to negotiate internally *and* externally. Unable to prepare a satisfactory package addressing the main concerns of China's major trading partners, MOFTEC had little room to maneuver at the international negotiation table. Progress was made slowly and no major breakthrough was foreseeable by the parties concerned. Consequently China's GATT/WTO decision-making fell into deadlock during most of the 1990s.

The question that merits further investigation, then, is which ministries were involved in the negotiations and how their policy preferences came into being and evolved within the context of China's administrative reorganization. Before we address this question, it is useful to review briefly the administrative structure of the Chinese government. At the apex of the governing regime of the PRC is the Political Bureau (Politburo) of the Chinese Communist Party (CCP). There are two organizational lines. One is the horizontal line operating within the central government: Politburo – State Council – leading small group (LSG) – Ministries and Bureaus; and the other one is the vertical line representing center–local relations: Center (Beijing) – province – prefecture – county – township. Once strategic decisions were made by the Standing Committee of the Politburo (the core or elite), the center relies on the relevant ministries and bureaus (subelite) to carry out the policy. In the meantime, decisions made by the elite also rely on the information, analysis and policy suggestions made by the relevant ministries and bureaus. Members of the State Council include the Premier, a variable number of vice-premiers (currently four), five state councilors (equivalent in protocol terms to vice-premiers but with narrower portfolios) and 29 ministers and heads of State Council commissions.[5] LSGs have become the organ for coordinating the work of several agencies and for ensuring party supervision over government activities. The organizational structure for China's GATT/WTO decision-making is a miniature of the bureaucratic process for decision-making in China.

Identified as a "crucial foreign policy" area in the mid-1980s[6], China's GATT application was initially led by the Ministry of Foreign Affairs (MOFA). The Ministry of Foreign Economic Relations and Trade (MOFERT) and the General Administration of Custom (GAC) took a complementary and secondary role. This stage of China's negotiations focused mainly on examining China's trade regime and tariff reduction package. MOFERT was responsible for preparing answers for the hundreds of questions raised by the China Working Party regarding China's trade regime. Internationally, the Uruguay Round multilateral trade negotiations had just begun and China's accession obligation was only limited to tariff reduction and the elimination of non-tariff barriers (NTBs) for industrial goods. China still claimed itself to be a "planned commodity economy" at that time and did not intend to move toward a "market economy". Since many GATT contracting parties believed that the conventional obligations of GATT membership, such as reducing tariffs and eliminating NTBs to imports, did not have much relevance to a planned economy whose import levels and import prices were determined by state directives,[7] the tariff reduction package prepared by the GAC was not the focal point of the negotiations. In sum, the involvement of these two government ministries was marginal and was restricted to the level of technical support. Under the old planned economy, the fundamental authority and economic interests of the GAC and the MOFERT remained largely untouched in the course of bargaining. Thus there was no obvious clash of interests or divergence of preferences between the two agencies.

However, during the second stage of China's accession negotiations, the international environment of China's GATT accession negotiations changed and was no longer in favor of Beijing. After the end of the Cold War and the collapse of the former Soviet bloc, China became the last major communist regime. Not surprisingly, Washington no longer endorsed Beijing's membership unconditionally for ideological reasons and economic considerations instead prevailed. Ironically, Beijing was more motivated to accede into the GATT. GATT membership would not only bring China long-term economic benefits, it would also help Chinese leaders consolidate power domestically and maintain constructive relationships with the rest of the world. Practically, Beijing preferred to be admitted into the organization before the end of 1994 as the WTO was to formally replace the GATT in January 1995 as the new international organization governing global trade.

As Beijing made great effort to increase the pace of its accession negotiations, it faced enormous resistance from domestic industrial ministries and regulatory agencies. During the second phase more ministerial-level actors joined China's GATT/WTO accession decision-making process, including the Ministry of Finance, the Ministry of Machine Building Industry, the People's Bank of China, the Ministry of Post and Telecommunications and the Ministry of Textile Industry. Vested ministerial interests began to play a key role in influencing the bargaining process. The head of the China delegation in Geneva Gu Yongjiang recalled:

> At the end of 1994, negotiation in Geneva was tough. However, I faced more internal pressure. One influential newspaper in Beijing had a series on how our delegation betrayed China's national interests. It was extremely difficult because I was the head of the delegation and I was responsible for the negotiation outcome.[8]

Ministerial interests reflected the economic benefits and administrative authority that the ministries gained through the legacy of China's 40-year planned economy, benefits that would nevertheless be weakened or taken away in the process of economic liberalization. Economic benefits mainly referred to the revenues gained from the affiliated enterprises or networking (satellite) firms. For instance, the Ministry of Post and Telecommunications was the regulator and at the same time the owner of the national monopoly China Telecom. Another example is that every industrial ministry had its own state trading enterprise (STE) which monopolized the import of goods. For example, the Ministry of Chemical Industry owned China Chemical Imports and Exports General Company (CCIEGC) and its numerous local subsidiaries. Administrative authority refers to their capacity to extract "rent" for their required approvals, especially the authority to issue trading rights licenses, to approve foreign investment over certain limits and to set import quotas.[9] In light of the economic benefits and administrative authorities these ministries had enjoyed under the planned economy, it was not surprising that many of them were inclined to oppose trade liberalization in the name of infant industry protection, economic independence or national security. More importantly, to some agencies such as the State Planning Commission, the decision to adopt GATT/WTO rules and principles would weaken the legitimacy of the agencies themselves.

China's GATT/WTO negotiations in the 1990s were characterized by ministries and agencies defending their narrow economic and administrative interests. Some scholars emphasize the new change toward professionalism in Chinese bureaucracies, and, in particular, the role played by subelites who have either a foreign degree or work experience in foreign countries or international organizations in promoting trade liberalization in China.[10] It is true that the increasing professionalism of the subelite helps the top leaders to make more informed decisions. However, having a foreign background does not necessarily imply that these elites were liberal or that they would support China's GATT/WTO membership. Within the context of China's bureaucratic politics, it appears that ministerial interests largely blur this distinction. Interviews with technocrats in various ministries and agencies confirm that many of them were also advocates of protectionist policies. MOFTEC (formerly MOFERT and now the Ministry of Commerce) officials have earned a reputation as sponsors within the government for China's adoption of international practices.[11] However, different departments within the MOFTEC often held contradictory views toward the bold offers on trade liberalization. For example, when Beijing finally decided to grant trading rights to all foreign firms and individuals, the department in charge of issuing trading licenses to the state-owned enterprises strongly opposed this concession.[12]

Protectionist interests ranged across a broad spectrum of Chinese industry, from old, established industries such as machinery and agriculture to growing industries such as automobiles, telecommunications and chemicals and infant industries such as financial services, insurance, retailing and information.[13] However, these ministries did not enjoy equal power and influence within the central government. The degree of protection accorded to each ministry was thus correlated with the importance of that ministry as perceived by the central government.[14] Generally speaking, information industries and infant industries bore more strategic importance to China's economic supremacy and as a result, their protectionist interests were better voiced to the top leaders than those of the labor-intensive industries. For this reason, Beijing promulgated industrial policies for the automobile industry in June 1994, when its GATT accession negotiations in Geneva were most intense and when the major GATT contracting parties pressed hard to make China's domestic industrial market, particularly the automobile sector, more accessible to foreign competition.

The level of ministerial involvement and resistance grew hand in hand with the expansion of the negotiating agenda. When the WTO was founded in January 1995, WTO members immediately began a new round of multilateral negotiations and, as a result, several important agreements on trade in services were reached during this period. Consequently in the final stage of the negotiations (1995–2001) Beijing was confronted with a much higher bar of entry. At the end of 1994, Beijing mainly struggled with the liberalization of its trade regime, which called for the provision of national treatment and trading rights to foreign firms and the lowering or elimination of tariff and non-tariff barriers for industrial products. However, after 1997 more key issues were added to the negotiation table, including market access offers for agricultural products and services sectors (such as banking, insurance, telecommunications, distribution and transportation), elimination of export subsidies across the board and the enforcement of protection for intellectual property rights. As a result, accession negotiations began to encounter greater domestic resistance than had been the case previously.

For example, negotiations over market access in telecommunications services became extremely difficult between 1997 and 1999. Liberalization of the telecom sector is inherently challenging both because telecommunications is a distinct sector of economic activity and because it provides a means of supporting other economic activities (such as electronic money transfers). More importantly, it would touch upon Beijing's deep concerns about national security if foreign telecommunications companies were allowed to become basic telecommunications services operators or internet services providers in China. Minister Wu Jichuan of the Ministry of Post and Telecommunications (MPT) was a vocal lobbyist for protectionism. While Beijing refused to touch the telecommunications sector in 1994, when the negotiations resumed in 1996 Beijing had no choice but to consider offering concessions on market access in services sectors. However, due to vehement resistance from the MPT and other services ministries including the People's Bank of China, the China Insurance Regulatory Commission and the China Securities Regulatory Commission, Chinese negotiators were unable to bring to the table its services offer as promised in January 1997. Whereas Beijing made progress liberalizing its goods market and trade-related laws and regulations, it could not break the domestic impasse over services sectors. Unable to submit the services liberalization package again in the following third and fourth session of the China WTO Working Party held in March and July respectively, Beijing failed to achieve a major breakthrough as planned during the summit between Chinese President Jiang Zemin and US President Bill Clinton on 28 October 1997. For the same reason, Geneva put off the next round of the China Working Party scheduled for early October. Finally, China circulated its long-awaited offer for access to its services sectors in December 1997 which covered almost all services sectors except for telecommunications. Even at this point Beijing continued to insist on preventing foreign telecommunications companies from owning or operating networks in the region.[15] Whereas the US–China bilateral negotiation gained new momentum between April and June before President Clinton made his first official visit to China on 25 June 1998, Beijing's first offer on basic telecommunications services fell short of the demand of the US[16] and consequently Beijing again missed a good opportunity to wrap up the bilateral agreement. After the direct involvement of top leaders at Politburo meetings, Premier Zhu Rongji brought a comprehensive package including basic tele-communications services with him to Washington in April 1999. Beijing committed to ending its ban on foreign direct investment in telecommunica-tions services, phasing in 50 percent foreign equity in all services in six years and allowing 51 percent foreign ownership for value-added and paging services in four years. While this incredible offer was agreed to by top leaders based on their strategic decision to wrap up a bilateral agreement with the United States, the Ministry of Information Industry (MII) strongly opposed it. As Nicholas Lardy at the Brookings Institution observed, "it is no secret that many of the Chinese concessions have been fiercely resisted by vested domestic interests. It will take all of Mr. Zhu's political skills to keep the offer intact".[17] His worry soon proved to be correct. Unhappy about the offer of 50 percent foreign ownership and claiming that the offer "betrayed China's fundamental national interest", Minister Wu Jichuan tendered his resignation even before Zhu returned to Beijing from his US-Canada visit. Facing President Clinton's refusal and tremendous domestic resis-tance, Zhu put his political life at risk. When Clinton immediately realized it was a mistake to walk away from such a lucrative deal and called Zhu to revisit Wash-ington after his subsequent Canada trip, Zhu said "No". In addition, Chinese nego-tiators stepped back from the offer they made in Washington and claimed that "since the US did not accept the package as a whole, then the individual issues in that package had to be renegotiated one by one".[18] The most visible withdrawal of concessions was the reduction of the percentage of maximum foreign ownership from 50 percent to 49 percent, the latter of which was maintained in the final bilat-eral agreement between the US and China. During the final days of EU–China negotiations, the EU demanded 51 percent foreign ownership for telephone net-works. Premier Zhu Rongji frankly told EU Trade Commissioner Mr Pascal Lamy "I can't do that." In the end, the EU accepted compensation from China that included tariff reductions on 150 EU-concerned export goods.[19] This clearly shows how strong domestic resistance was at the ministerial level toward acces-sion negotiations.

MOFTEC, in particular its GATT/WTO Division, represented an exception to this ministerial preference for protectionism. The GATT/WTO Division under the Department of International Trade and Economic Affairs within MOFTEC was responsible for the daily work on China's GATT/WTO bid. It was respon-sible for conducting bilateral trade negotiations with WTO members and multi-lateral negotiations with China's GATT/WTO working party in Geneva. It also had the duty to consult other relevant domestic bureaus and industries about China's negotiation positions. The division therefore became the sponsor of many interministerial meetings. MOFTEC has long been seen as a strong advo-cate of China's accession within the Chinese bureaucracy during the 1980s and 1990s.[20] Indeed, through its involvement in bilateral and multilateral negotia-tions and in the process of handling international trade affairs, most departments and divisions within the ministry have come to an understanding that globalization is an inescapable trend and that China needs to make a transition toward a market economy in order to meet the challenge. For example, the former chief negotiator and vice-minister of MOFTEC Long Yongtu recently made an argument about China's auto industry which had provoked extensive discussions on the internet. Specifically, Long stated that "government promotion of an independent national auto industry is unnecessary. China is a winner as long as it can successfully attract foreign automakers to invest and manufacture parts in China".[21] As the pro-liberal and pro-globalization unit, the GATT/WTO Affairs Division was the constant target of criticism within the Chinese bureaucracy, sometimes even by other agencies within MOFTEC, as discussed earlier. In the eyes of other ministries, MOFTEC, and the WTO division in particular, was too pro-Western and was a "traitor of China's national interest".[22] In particular, Long Yongtu, the chief negotiator, was fiercely criticized by representatives from other ministries and agencies.[23] For its part, the GATT/WTO Affairs Division had its own complaints about other ministries, such as "some representatives brought to the negotiation table our domestic debate and diffused the priorities" and "they were backseat drivers".[24] These emotional notes quoted from interviews demonstrate the degree of preference divergence between officials from MOFTEC and some other ministries on China's GATT/WTO negotiation.

MOFTEC not only faced intensive domestic bargaining, its role was further weakened by its limited authority in negotiations. First, the ministry did not have final authority to wrap up a negotiation package. The ministry was only responsible for "coordinating ministerial preferences" and reporting them to the relevant LSG and the State Council. Second, it was not a negotiating organ of the government. Unlike the United States Trade Representative (USTR) in the US, the GATT/WTO Division was mainly designed as a unit to study and interpret the norms, principles, agreements and legal issues of the GATT/WTO. Whereas officials from the GATT/WTO Division served as negotiators in the related GATT/WTO bilateral and multilateral negotiations, on many occasions representatives from other departments of MOFTEC and from other ministries and bureaus also participated in the negotiations depending on the issues being discussed. For example, when the subject was currency convertibility, the People's Bank of China would attend the negotiation. This was also true of the Ministry of Agriculture on market access for agricultural products, the Ministry of Internal Trade for distribution, the MPT for telecommunications and the Insurance Regulatory Commission for insurance licenses.[25] Third, officials at the GATT/WTO Division did not have enough authority in the negotiations. Negotiators from MOFTEC were not sanctioned to move beyond the negotiation package they had prepared at home. Even for minor modification of the position they had to take the issue back home and seek approval.

The GATT/WTO Division and MOFTEC several times asked for greater authority over their fellow ministries and for more flexibility at the negotiation table. By the end of 1994, Long Yongtu was said to have asked for the authority to negotiate freely with GATT contracting members and to report back to the State

Council only after the negotiation team had reached a bilateral agreement with a member. But such requests by MOFTEC officials were denied; instead they had to follow exactly the package that was prepared by the affected ministries and approved by the State Council and the Politburo. When asked why China had failed to join the GATT by the end of 1994, Long Yongtu recalled in 2001 on the eve of China's formal admission, "I was trying my best to wrap up a final package. Actually it was not totally impossible to conclude negotiations at that time. Unfortunately we did not win enough support from other ministries. I failed to make concessions I should have made because I did not have the authority to do so. To a large extent this was why we failed to conclude the negotiations as planned."[26]

During 1998–1999 when the negotiations reached a bottleneck, MOFTEC again asked to bypass the procedure of interministerial coordination and report directly to the State Council. This time MOFTEC was granted new authority to coordinate and prioritize the concerns raised by other ministries.[27] After that, MOFTEC enjoyed greater authority in internal coordination and greater independence in selecting external negotiation strategies. Consequently, the pro-liberal preference of MOFTEC gradually outweighed the protectionist preferences held by many industrial ministries. The idea that making sufficient concessions was necessary for China's WTO membership had gradually come to be recognized. However, the tough job was to decide which industry or sector should pay a higher price and which ministry or agency could largely have their fundamental interests untouched.

Apparently many ministries had their own preferences and negotiation positions based on their narrow interest considerations throughout the negotiation process. The resistance from some important industrial ministries and government agencies notably impeded Beijing's GATT/WTO accession negotiations. The pro-liberal MOFTEC did not enjoy more latitude by being in charge of the accession negotiations. That MOFTEC officials lacked enough authority in domestic coordination and international negotiations left the ministry in an awkward position. In the absence of a lead agency in decision-making, it was inevitable that there existed considerable structural obstacles to the creation of a coherent negotiation strategy. Thus the divergent and often conflicting interests of the ministries significantly contributed to the negotiation impasse in the earlier phases of China's GATT/WTO negotiations.

Interministerial and supraministerial coordination

Closely related to domestic actors' preferences are coordination mechanisms. The failure to effectively harmonize conflicting interests and adopt a coherent negotiation strategy was reflected at both the interministerial and supraministerial levels. To understand the functioning of the administrative organizations which oversaw China's GATT/WTO decision-making, we need to look into the relevant interministerial and superministerial organs.

A member of the Politburo Standing Committee conducts direct sectoral supervision through an institutionalized body (such as a committee) or a nonstanding organ (such as a leading small group, LSG). Among the most important of such organs are the CCP Central Military Commission (CMC) which oversees military affairs, the CCP Central Political and Legal Affairs Committee with supervisory duties for legal affairs, the Central Finance and Economic Affairs LSG and the Central Foreign Affairs LSG. This system of sectoral division of management does not appear on any formal organizational chart of the party or the government. However, as an internal mechanism, it allows the CCP Politburo Standing Committee to exercise centralized control over the policy-making process.[28] The Central Financial and Economic Affairs LSG has always been the most important organ in economic decision-making. It has become an important locus for making, coordinating and implementing foreign economic policy, including the responsibility to supervise China's GATT/WTO decision-making. However, it was the State Council that was charged with the day-to-day policy coordination of ministerial interests.

In 1986, China established a GATT policy coordination body, namely the State Council Interministerial Coordination Group on GATT Negotiations (*Guowuyuan GuanShui Ji Maoyi Zong Xieding Tanpan Buji Xietiao Xiaozu*). State Councilor Zhang Jingfu was the first director of this group. The vice-directors included the minister of MOFERT, the minister of foreign affairs and the general director of the GAC. The job division was clear. MOFERT was responsible for preparing the memorandum on China's trade regime and the Tariff Commission under GAC was charged with preparing a list of tariff reductions for industrial goods. Importantly, at this stage the issues under negotiation concerned the limited reform of China's foreign trade regime to make it more explicable and transparent to foreign firms.[29] The involvement of only three units at this stage helped to smooth the process of harmonization.

In 1988 the GATT policy coordination body was renamed the State Council Committee on Interministerial Coordination on GATT, with Vice-Premier Tian Jiyun as chairman. This policy coordination organ also encompassed several vice-chairman-level agencies such as the State Development Planning Commission and the State Economic and Trade Commission. The member agencies of this committee included the Ministry of Finance, the Ministry of Machine Building Industry, the Ministry of Post and Telecommunications, the Ministry of Textile Industry and the State Council Office of Imports and Exports of Mechanical and Electronic Products, among others. According to its mandate, the mission of this interministerial coordination committee was to coordinate policy on issues related to GATT accession negotiations. However, many negotiators the author interviewed, not only those from MOFTEC but also those from other ministries, complained that the committee malfunctioned. The reasons were multiple. First, it was not a standing agency. It only served as a temporary platform for consultation and had no permanent staff. Second, all members were vice-ministers from different ministries and MOFERT was in an equal position. The meetings often turned out to be unproductive as every member would only speak for his or her own ministry. Thus, while the relevant ministry would engage in a sound analysis of whether or not to make a particular concession and how the move would affect the competitiveness and future development of that sector, policy coordination turned out to be rather difficult. As each Vice-Premier supervises several ministries, each ministry had its own channel to report its views to the Politburo members who were supervising that ministry. If there existed conflicting interests on one contentious issue, then the central leaders would step in and interfere. But that happened rarely. In most cases the issue would be put away for further consensus building and policy coordination at the ministerial level. Each new package of concessions was the result of prolonged discussion and bargaining at the ministerial level and the State Council level before it was submitted for approval at the Politburo meetings. In this way, Beijing's negotiating team lost not only efficiency but also flexibility since with limited authority the negotiation team members could not be responsive to the plan their counterparts suggested if it differed from what they were advised at home.[30]

The proliferation of organizations in policy-making increased the difficulty of interagency coordination to a great extent. As a result, efforts at consensus building have become prolonged and, in many cases, futile. This had been the case especially after 1995 when agriculture and services sectors were formally added to the negotiation agenda and more ministries started to participate in China's WTO decision-making. The new services sectors included banking, insurance, telecommunications, distribution, education, tourism, film industry, transportation, retailing and wholesales, and so on. The interministerial coordination started to encounter considerable difficulty at this stage. Some ministries always bypassed this interministerial process and reported directly to the vice-premier or Politburo member who supervised them. In 1998 the State Council Committee on Interministerial Coordination on WTO was dissolved. A new WTO negotiation LSG was established and State Councilor Wu Yi became the head of this new interministerial coordination agency. In other words, this time the new WTO negotiation LSG was upgraded in terms of administrative line and importance. The fundamental change was that MOFTEC was granted more authority to coordinate and directly report to the State Council. In this way MOFTEC gained more influence relative to other ministries on WTO negotiation issues. As one trade official commented: "after this new arrangement, MOFTEC was in a more advantageous position to coordinate different ministerial interests domestically and negotiate with more flexible strategies externally".[31]

The subsequent government restructuring that took place in 1998 also played a positive role in boosting China's WTO accession negotiations by easing the pressure emanating from ministerial interests. In March 1998, the Ninth National People's Congress approved an ambitious government restructuring proposed by Premier Zhu Rongji. The plan would eliminate fifteen government ministries and commissions and cut the jobs of up to four million bureaucrats. This move stood to clear the way for China's WTO negotiations in the sense that it promised to weaken the authority of some previously powerful regulatory agencies that were the cornerstone of the planned economy and downgrade some ministries into bureaus. For example, the State Planning Commission, which once controlled the overall economic planning of the country, was expected to lose most of its power.

In the new government structure, the State Planning Commission's 1,200 member staff would be cut to 300. The Commission would no longer set production quotas for large- and medium-sized state-owned enterprises, and some of its functions and staff would be transferred to an expanded State Economic and Trade Commission. Nor would its approval have to be sought by foreign investors pushing for large projects. Instead the Commission was renamed the National Development Planning Commission which would primarily serve as a think tank and draw up macroeconomic policy proposals. Another example was that the Ministry of Machinery Industry (MMI), the government's organ in charge of the automobile industry, was dissolved. It was replaced by the State Administration of Machinery Industry (SAMI), which had only 95 staff instead of the 400 under the old MMI. The Ministry of Post and Telecommunications was replaced by the Ministry of Information Industry and the near monopoly China Telecom was divided into three companies: China Telecom, China Mobile and China Satellite. The Ministry of Electromechanical Products was replaced by the Department of Import and Export of Electromechanical Products under MOFTEC. The restructuring provided a more flexible environment for WTO decision-making, especially with regard to issues that concerned industrial sectors. Consequently, in the final accession protocol Beijing made relatively more concessions, noticeably in the areas of agriculture, textiles, chemical products, electromechanical products and automobiles.[32]

In an effort to better integrate itself into the international community, Beijing also created new organizations or granted new authority to existing organizations. For example, within the new government structure, the State Economic and Trade Commission was further empowered to formulate long-term strategic plans. It would also take up responsibility for drawing up policies for the metallurgy, chemicals, textiles, domestic trade, coal, machine-building and light-industry sectors as the respective ministries were to be downgraded into bureaus. Within MOFTEC, the WTO Division was separated from the Department of International Trade and Economic Affairs and upgraded to the Department of WTO Affairs. A new office fashioned after the United States Trade Representative (USTR), the Office of the Representative for International Trade Negotiation, was created to specialize in trade negotiations.

As the dynamics of China's domestic and foreign policy change, some domestic constituencies have assumed new roles in foreign economic policy whereas others have been abolished, and additional agencies have been created to accommodate the changed circumstances. This 1998 government restructuring was mainly driven by internal reform, but the reduction of domestic actors at the ministerial level in the form of "lean government" facilitated the domestic bargaining process for China's WTO decision-making and empowered the pro-liberal constituencies with more authority in both domestic policy coordination and in international negotiations.

Top leaders' policy intervention

What were the attitudes and policy preferences of Chinese leaders toward China's GATT/WTO accession, a move that would inevitably shape China's future development path and alter its position in the global economy? Existing studies of Chinese foreign policy unanimously agree that the role of top leaders has always been foremost in Chinese foreign policy-making, even under the current trends of decentralization and pluralization. The question that merits further investigation then is under what condition(s) would the top leaders insert themselves into the GATT/WTO decision-making process and override the discordant opinions at the ministerial level, and under what condition(s) would they rather take a back seat and let a consensus be formed among the industrial ministries and regulatory agencies before taking any actions? In other words, throughout the negotiation process which approach proved more prevalent or effective, the top-down or the bottom-up approach?

Beijing's decision to re-enter the GATT in the mid-1980s was a voluntary decision based in part on political considerations. China did not face strong international pressure to accede into the GATT/WTO. However, Chinese leaders seemed to believe that applying for GATT membership represented a gesture to show Beijing's willingness to become a "responsible stakeholder" in the international community, a follow-up move after Beijing gained its membership in the United Nations, the World Bank and the International Monetary Fund (IMF).[33] As Swaine (1998: 28) correctly points out, within China's decision-making structure, actors at any level but the highest have very little influence over decisions involving grand strategy. China's GATT application was no exception. On 10 January 1986, then Premier Zhao Ziyang invited Director-General Arthur Dunkel (1980–1993) to visit China and expressed in person China's intention to rejoin the GATT.[34]

After the 1989 Tiananmen Square incident, China's GATT accession had come to be linked with many sensitive economic and political issues such as Taiwan, human rights and the US trade deficit with China. Domestically China's GATT accession decision-making had come to be affected by the overall bureaucratic tussle between the conservative and the liberal camps and the ebb and flow of China's economic reform. Between 1990 and 1993, the priority of Beijing's new leader Jiang Zemin was to consolidate his power domestically. Thus China's GATT accession was not on the top of his agenda. This changed in 1994 when Beijing became determined to gain admission before the WTO superceded the GATT. Besides the practical considerations of the lower entry requirements under the GATT framework and the pride attached to becoming a founding member of the WTO, Beijing also hoped to utilize China's commitment to trade liberalization to break the economic sanctions and political isolation following the Tiananmen Square incident.[35] However, Beijing's futile effort to join the GATT by its internally determined deadline caused a backlash at home. The pro-liberal leaders became the target of attack by the conservative camp. There arose domestic debates among elites about the pros and cons of China's WTO membership. Many began to question how much practical benefit this membership would bring to China and some even went so far as to argue that China should stay outside this global trade organization as long as possible in order not to be bound by the requirements of the trade regime. The guiding principle of China's accession underwent a subtle change too as Chinese leaders announced that "China needs the

WTO and the WTO needs China as well to be qualified as a 'world' trading organization".[36] Apparently Beijing was no longer eager to join the WTO after it had missed the 1994 deadline. This policy change suggested that with China's growing market size and trade volume, Beijing was banking on its growing leverage in its GATT/WTO accession negotiations. After 1996 US–China bilateral political relations improved and several summits were held between the presidents of the two countries. With the improvement in US–China relations and the foreign policy goal of maintaining good relations with the US, China's WTO accession negotiations regained momentum. This renewed interest was well reflected in the change of the general principles put forward by the central leaders to guide Beijing's negotiation strategy. In early 1999 Jiang Zemin brought up a specific 16-word principle at one of the Central Finance and Economic Affairs LSG meetings: have a positive attitude, use flexible methods, be skillful at negotiation, and don't be naïve (*Taidu Jiji, Fangfa Linghuo, Shanyu Cuoshang, Buke Tianzhen*).[37] After that, President Jiang and Premier Zhu personally got involved in China's WTO decision-making. Accession negotiations became the central issue in the Politburo and Central Finance and Economic Affairs LSG meetings.

In line with the old practices, the preferences and sometimes the personal involvement of the central leaders were vital to the outcome of China's international trade negotiations. However, confronted with a growing range of ministerial interests, top leaders were forced to consult more broadly. This raises the question as to under what circumstances the central leadership would override bureaucratic politics and under what circumstances they would not?

As the above discussion suggests, state interests would override ministerial interests at decisive times of the negotiation. China's foreign and domestic policy-making processes had become intertwined as China's diplomacy was meant to serve the nation's foremost interests in maintaining a more favorable international environment for its economic development. Top leaders not only had to calculate the narrow economic interests of China's GATT/WTO membership, they also had to take into consideration the political implications of membership for the Chinese economy and society as well as for Sino-American relations. For example, in 1997, determined to sustain the momentum of improved Sino-American relations, President Jiang announced Beijing's decision to join the newly created Information Technology Agreement (ITA) under the WTO, an agreement that was not binding to all WTO member countries and was not even a requirement for China's WTO entry. Chinese leaders' commitment at the APEC summit to eliminate tariffs for all information technology products by the year 2000 was similarly an unexpected shock back home. Obviously this was not an offer made through general consultation as few people at the ministerial level knew about this decision, let alone those in the industrial sector.[38] But it served as a nice surprise to China's trading partners and effectively helped accelerate the pace of China's WTO accession negotiation. In April 1999 President Jiang Zemin reportedly told Zhu Rongji right before his departure to Washington: "the WTO may become a bright spot. The objective of signing this agreement is by no means limited to economic considerations. We are all quite clear on this matter."[39] Similarly, in an interview with the *Wall Street Journal*, Zhu Rongji remarked that "the reason we have made such big concessions is that we have given due consideration to the overall situation of friendly cooperation between China and the US, including China's long-term development strategy and China's international strategy".[40] During the final days of the US–China and EU–China bilateral negotiations, Zhu stepped into the negotiation room, talked directly to the US and EU chief negotiators, and made the final concessions on the few most contentious issues so as to bring about the agreements.

In the second half of the 1990s, the number of agencies participating in the negotiation process increased, as did the number of domestic constituencies with a perceived stake in decisions. This new development required the central leadership to expend a great amount of energy to reconcile divergent interests and to bring into line (*xietiao*) various government organizations. At the same time, as the decisions became more complex and technical, central leaders relied on the respective ministries for objective analysis and reliable policy recommendations in order to evaluate and formulate policy. This was the supraministerial coordination dilemma the central leaders in China confronted in the second half of the 1990s. However, to the extent that trade has come to occupy a central place in China's economic development strategy, top leaders have been and are expected to continue their personal involvement in China's trade negotiations and trade dispute settlement.

Conclusion

China's GATT/WTO decision-making was undoubtedly important and complex. This chapter highlights the active involvement of vested ministerial interests in the decision-making process. That current Chinese foreign policy-making has increasingly incorporated multiple voices has been captured by China watchers, but the expansion of domestic actors should not be exaggerated. In a strategic decision like China's GATT/WTO accession, the involved actors were restricted to those at the ministerial level. Local governments were largely excluded from the process. The role of public opinion was even more marginal. In fact, the general public as well as most affected companies had no clue about the content of the negotiations until the USTR posted Zhu's package on their website in April 1999. However, it is also true that top leaders increasingly had to share power with high-level central organs and government ministries, even for a strategic decision such as China's GATT/WTO entry. This is a mixed blessing. On the one hand, top leaders have received more input from various industries and sectors and were in a position to make more informed decisions. On the other hand, this resulted in prolonged negotiation time, unproductive negotiation processes and frequent negotiation stalemates. The whole process was characterized by extensive domestic bargaining and coordination. Efforts to gain consensus dominated but in most cases were futile. Top leaders had to step into the negotiations at key moments to ensure that the negotiations were moving in the desired direction.

The government restructuring in 1998 successfully reduced the number of government ministries and other agencies. While many industrial ministries and regulatory agencies continued to defend their strong protectionist positions, the organizational consolidation significantly diminished the policy influences of a number of ministries and agencies. During this process, the role of the pro-liberal MOFTEC in China's GATT/WTO decision-making was elevated vis-à-vis other ministries. Though this administrative reorganization was mainly driven by internal processes, it was also a product of China's ongoing interaction with the outside world. In the meantime, the establishment of new regulatory agencies and the division of authority between existing ministries and bureaus have served to create a new institutional setting for China's trade policy-making. The changes in the preferences of government ministries and agencies that took place as a result of this government restructuring have affected the outcome of China's behavior in international economic relations.

In concluding, this chapter examines the dynamics of decision-making underlying China's GATT/WTO accession negotiation and explores the institutional changes that will inevitably affect the development of China's foreign economic policy in the future. Studying how domestic institutional changes may drive China's behavior in the world economy could be a promising direction for future research. This chapter not only contributes to our understanding of China's trade policy-making process, its approach can also be extended to other issue areas in China's foreign economic policy-making such as China's compliance with its WTO commitments, currency reform and trade dispute settlement.

Notes

1   See the section on accession negotiation at WTO's official website, www.wto.org.
2   Pearson (2001) examines four variables affecting China's decision-making on GATT/WTO, including the role of top leaders, the pluralization of domestic actors, external influences and public opinion.
3   For a detailed analysis of the politics behind Zhu's visit, see Fewsmith, 2000.
4   For a detailed chronology of China's GATT/WTO accession negotiation, see Liang (2002).
5   For an official introduction to the Chinese government's organizational structure, see www.state.gov.cn.
6   Author's interview with MOFA officials, December 2000.
7   Feng (1987).
8   Yang (2001).
9   Liang (2002: 703).
10   Lampton (2001).
11   Pearson (2001: 355).
12   Author's interview, November 2000.
13   Pearson (2001: 361).
14   Liang (2002: 703).
15   Zarocostas (1997:1A).
16   Testimony of USTR Charlene Barshefsky on the Renewal of Normal Trade Relations with China, Senate Committee on Finance, 9 July 1998.
17   Lardy (1999).
18   Interview, Summer 2000.

19   O'Clery (2000: 18).
20   Pearson (2001: 347).
21   Xin (2005).
22   Interviews, November 2000.
23   Interviews, January 2001.
24   Ibid.
25   Interview, December 2000.
26   Yang (2001: 1).
27   Interview, August 2000.
28   Lu (2001: 40).
29   Interview with MOFTEC official, January 2001.
30   Liang (2002: 704).
31   Liang (2002: 717).
32   Interview, Spring 2001.
33   Interview, November 2000.
34   Liang (2002: 686).
35   Interview, August 2000.
36   "News Briefing by Chinese Foreign Ministry", 1995: 14.
37   Interview, Winter 2000.
38   Interview, August 2000.
39   Zong (2002).
40   Zong (2002: 42).

References

Economy, E. and Oksenberg, M. (eds) (1999) *China Joins the World: Progress and Prospects*, New York: Council on Foreign Relations Press.
Feng, Y. (1987) "China's tango with GATT", *Journal of Commerce*, 13 August, 8A.
Fewsmith, J. (2000) "The politics of China's accession to the WTO", *Current History*, 99: 268–73.
Hamrin, C. L. and Zhao, S. (eds) (1995) *Decision-Making in Deng's China: Perspectives from Insiders,* Armonk, NY: Sharpe.
Jacobson, H. K. and Oksenberg, M. (1990) *China's Participation in the IMF, the World Bank, and GATT,* Ann Arbor: University of Michigan Press.
Lampton, D. M. (ed.) (2001) *The Making of Chinese Foreign and Security Policy in the Era of Reform, 1978–2000*, Stanford, CA: Stanford University Press.
Lardy, N. (1994) *China in the World Economy*, Washington, DC: Institute for International Economics.
Lardy, N. (1999) "China's WTO deal faces significant challenges", *Asian Wall Street Journal*, 18 April, 1999. Also available www.brook.edu/views/op-ed/lardy/19990418.
Lewis, J. W. and Xue L. (1994) *China's Strategic Seapower: The Politics of Force Modernization in the Nuclear Age,* Stanford, CA: Stanford University Press.
Lewis, J. W., Hua, D. and Xue, L. (1991) "Beijing's defense establishment: solving the arms-export enigma", *International Security*, 15 (4): 87–109.
Liang, W. (2002) "China's WTO negotiation process and its implications", *Journal of Contemporary China,* 11 (33): 683–719.
Lieberthal, K. (1995) *Governing China: From Revolution through Reform,* New York: Norton.
Lieberthal, K. and Lampton, D. M. (eds) (1992) *Bureaucracy, Politics and Decision Making in Post-Mao China,* Berkeley, CA: University of California Press.

Lu, N. (1997) *The Dynamics of Foreign-Policy Decision-Making in China,* Boulder, CO: Westview Press.

—— (2001) "The central leadership, supraministry coordinating bodies, State Council ministries and party departments", in Lampton, D. M. (ed.) *The Making of Chinese Foreign and Security Policy in the Era of Reform, 1978–2000,* Stanford, CA: Stanford University Press: 39–60.

Mulvenon, J. (1997) *Chinese Military Commerce and U.S National Security,* Santa Monica, CA.: Rand Center for Asia-Pacific Policy.

Nathan, A. J. and Ross R. S. (1997) *The Great Wall and the Empty Fortress,* New York: Norton.

O'Clery, C. (2000) "China poised for membership of WTO, China and the EU finally bridge gap on contentious trade issues", *Irish Times,* 20 May.

Pearson, M. (2001) "The case of China's accession to GATT/WTO", in Lampton, D. M. (ed.) *The Making of Chinese Foreign and Security Policy n the Era of Reform, 1978–2000,* Stanford, CA: Stanford University Press: 337–70.

Sutter, R. G. and Johnson, W. R. (eds) (1994) *Taiwan in World Affairs,* Boulder, CO.: Westview Press.

Swaine, M. (1998) *The Role of the Chinese Military in National Security Policymaking,* rev. edn, Santa Monica, CA: Rand Center for Asia-Pacific Policy.

Xin, R. "Long Yongtu's comments on China's auto industry", 31 August 2005. Available online: http:finance.people.com.cn/GB/1045/365564l.

Yang, J. (2001) "*Shiwunian de rushi zhilu*" (a fifteen-year journey to join the WTO), *Beijing Youth Daily,* 10 November.

Zarocostas, J. (1997) "To revive WTO bid, China reworks offer on service sectors", *Journal of Commerce,* 25 November.

Zong, H. (2002) "Visit to the United States", *Chinese Law and Government,* 35 (1): 36–52.

3 Decentralization, industrial geography and the politics of export regulation

The case of Sino-Japanese trade disputes

Megumi Naoi

Introduction

Developing countries today face various external pressures to regulate exports. China is the most targeted emerging economy in this sense. Since its economic opening in 1979, thirty-four countries and regions have launched a total of 665 antidumping duty, countervailing duty and safeguard investigations against Chinese products at the GATT and WTO.[1] More than 4,000 commodities have been involved. Outside of multilateral arenas, moreover, China was involved in numerous bilateral negotiations for voluntary export restraints with countries such as the United States, Europe, Japan and South Korea, to name but a few.

The ways in which these disputes were settled, however, substantially differ across commodity cases and over time. In some cases, disputes were settled via bilateral voluntary export restraints (VER) negotiations, while in other cases they escalated into the use of multilateral rules such as the adoption of safeguard and antidumping measures by China's trading partners. Bilateral VER negotiations have been declining over time and, instead, an increasing number of disputes have been settled using multilateral rules. While there exists a large body of literature on the political economy of trade conflicts, how states choose between different dispute settlement mechanisms is still poorly understood. Nevertheless this question is important because it raises questions about the efficacy of international institutions in shaping states' behavior. While scholars (e.g. Prusa, 1999; Rodrik, 1997; Goldstein and Martin, 2000; Kahler, 2000; Mattli, 2001; Busch and Reinhardt, 2003) argue that international trade has become multilateralized and legalized, states use these rules selectively and strategically.

This chapter explores states' dispute settlement choice by analyzing Sino-Japanese trade conflicts since 1976. The Sino-Japanese case provides several advantages to exploring why some disputes are settled bilaterally while others are solved using multilateral rules. First, Japan had consistently sought to negotiate bilateral VERs with China and fiercely avoided the use of multilateral rules until the year 2001.[2] Thus, the choice between bilateral and multilateral dispute resolution was largely a function of what the Chinese side desired. This allows us to analyze the preferences of the Chinese government and industries for dispute settlement venues while holding the Japanese side's preferences relatively constant. Second, since the late 1980s, the Japanese government and industries have increasingly struggled to induce VERs from China. As discussed in detail later, the Chinese government has rejected Japan's requests to restrain exports on numerous occasions. Even when China agreed to voluntarily restrain its exports, such agreements did not lead to the reduction of exports in an increasing number of cases. The question that merits further investigation, therefore, is what explains the shift from bilateralism to multilateralism in Sino–Japanese trade disputes and why have bilateral VER negotiations become ineffective?

This chapter argues that the Chinese government's dispute settlement choice is a response to two types of costs that arise during export regulation: the cost of nego-tiating the export restraints with domestic firms and foreign countries *and* the cost of enforcing the export quotas on Chinese exporting firms. I further demonstrate that these negotiation and enforcement costs are sensitive to two "decentraliza-tion" factors: the degree of decentralization in a government's export administra-tion and the degree of geographical concentration of industries. As discussed in detail below, bilateralism has declined since the mid-1980s due to the rise of the costs of enforcing the export quotas on provincial and municipal governments and foreign trade corporations (FTCs) under the highly decentralized export adminis-tration system. The rise of multilateralism to solve disputes, that is, the use of WTO rules such as safeguard and antidumping measures by trading partners, is due to the Chinese government's attempt to transfer the negotiation and enforce-ment costs to industries and foreign governments. By replacing informal negotia-tion and enforcement processes with WTO legal rules, the Chinese government shifts the liability of enforcing the export regulation onto exporting firms, local governments and foreign governments.

The approach of this chapter differs from the existing literature in four respects. First, instead of looking at China as a unitary actor, this chapter demonstrates that the central government, sub-national governments and exporting industries in China have different policy preferences for various forms of export regulation.[3] Second, this study explicitly links changes in domestic institutions, specifically decentralization, to the government's choice across different venues of export regulation. I examine how decentralization of export administration has given rise to sub-national actors in foreign trade and has therefore changed the relative effec-tiveness of bilateral vs. multilateral forms of export regulation. Third, while the emerging "forum-shopping" literature (e.g. Mattli, 2001; Busch and Reinhardt, 2003; Davis, 2003) looks at expected *negotiation outcomes* as an important deter-minant of states' choices across different dispute settlement venues, I argue that the expected level of *enforcement* also plays an important role in choosing a venue for export regulation. Finally, studies of Sino-Japanese trade disputes so far focus primarily on economic and political conditions of the Japanese side as major deter-minants of the choice. By identifying the sources of the preferences of the Chinese government and industries, this chapter will show that the dispute settlement choice has also been a reflection of what the Chinese side wanted.

The remainder of this chapter proceeds as follows. The next section discusses the puzzle: cross-commodity and temporal variation in Sino-Japanese dispute settlements during the past three decades. The second section develops my argument that the decentralization of export regulation and industrial geography interact to affect a government's choice between bilateral and multilateral venues of export regulation. The third section provides a study of two polar cases from the 2001 Sino-Japanese disputes: rush and rush-woven products (*tatami*) and seaweed. In the *tatami* industry case, the Chinese government rejected Japan's proposal to bilaterally negotiate VERs and instead let the Japanese government adopt a temporary safeguard measure for the first time in Japan's history. In contrast, seaweed industries successfully negotiated VERs without much government intervention. I show how a high degree of geographic concentration within the seaweed industry led to successful industry-level VER negotiations without major government involvement, while the low degree of geographic concentration within the *tatami* industry led to the failure of industry-level negotiations and the Japanese government's use of a safeguard measure. Finally, I conclude by discussing the broader implications of the analysis for the study of domestic politics and international institutions.

The puzzle

Since the first major Sino-Japanese trade dispute regarding silk yarn between 1976 and 1980, Japan has consistently sought bilateral VER negotiations to deal with the rise of Chinese exports. Japan fiercely avoided the use of multilateral rules, such as antidumping, countervailing and safeguard measures, which are legal under GATT/WTO, for several reasons. First, historically, Japanese export industries have been a target of these measures adopted by the United States and Europe. The government has officially taken a position at GATT/WTO negotiation rounds to support the more restrictive use of these measures. Second, Japan feared that the use of multilateral rules to regulate imports would invoke retaliation by trading countries which would harm its exporting sector. Finally, China was not a member of the GATT/WTO until 2001 and hence was not obligated to comply with Japan's use of multilateral rules.

Since the late 1980s, however, Japan has increasingly struggled to induce VERs from China. The Ministry of International Trade and Industry (MITI) attempted numerous times, in vain, to negotiate VERs with China with respect to textiles (1988), alloys (1991), textiles (1994, 1995), cotton and cotton fabrics (1996), ginger and garlic (1996), and so on.[4] In all of these cases, MITI proceeded to investigate potential antidumping and safeguard measures and the investigations eventually led China to agree to restrain its exports. In other words, Japan used the shadow of multilateral rules to induce bilateral VERs from China throughout the late 1980s and 1990s.

The Chinese government's unwillingness to adopt VERs is puzzling given that VERs create rents through the allocation of export quotas and licenses to exporting firms. The government's unwillingness is also puzzling because Chinese exporters should prefer VERs to tariffs or other non-tariff barriers (such as the adoption of safeguards, antidumping and counterveiling measures by trading countries) for two reasons. First, VERs represent a more temporal form of regulation than tariffs. Second, VERs give exporters an opportunity to collude with Japanese importers by setting the price higher than before the VERs. Given these benefits, why would the Chinese government not agree to voluntarily restrain its exports?

After a series of failed bilateral attempts, Japan adopted a temporary safeguard measure for the first time in its history with respect to *tatami* products, scallions and *shiitake* mushrooms in 2001. Scholars (e.g. Pekkanen, 2001; Hiroomi, 2001) point to several factors in an attempt to explain why Japan ultimately resorted to the use of WTO safeguard measures: special interest politics, electoral cycles and the bureaucracy's shift from bilateral to multilateral diplomacy. These studies, however, tend to suffer from a case selection bias: they look only at the three commodity cases that were granted safeguard protection in the year 2001 and infer their causes. What these studies fail to notice is that there were industries, such as the eel and seaweed industries, that successfully negotiated VERs with China during the same time period. These industries negotiated VERs without much government involvement, which was also puzzling. Why were these private-level VER negotiations successful and credibly committed to by Chinese exporters without legal obligations or government involvement? Two points are worth highlighting from the above discussion.

First, we need to ask not just when Japan and China resort to multilateral rules to resolve disputes, but how they choose across different venues of export regulation. In particular, cases where industries successfully negotiated VERs without government intervention (the so-called "private ordering"[5]), such as seaweed and eel, are intriguing. Second, the Sino-Japanese dispute settlement outcomes have been largely a function of what the Chinese side wanted. When China agreed to VERs, bilateralism was chosen; when China disagreed, its trading partners proceeded to use multilateral rules. It is important, therefore, to explore the sources of Chinese preferences for different venues of export regulation.

Argument and hypotheses

Why were some Sino-Japanese dispute cases settled with bilateral VER agreements while others escalated to the use of multilateral rules? I argue that two "decentralization" factors – decentralization of the government's export administration and geographical concentration of industries – interact to affect the government's choice. The two factors are important because they affect two types of costs that arise during the negotiation and enforcement stages of VERs. First, the degree of centralization in a government's export regulation affects the costs of negotiating VERs. The smaller the number of actors involved in the negotiation (that is, the higher the degree of centralization in export regulation), the lower the costs of negotiations. Second, whether an industry is geographically concentrated or not affects the costs of negotiating VERs as well as the costs of enforcing the export quota. I will explain the logic behind each factor in detail below.

Centralized vs. decentralized export regulation

The process leading to the adoption of VERs can be considered as a three-stage decision:

(a) domestic decision-making as to whether to negotiate VERs;
(b) negotiation with importing countries or firms; and
(c) enforcement of the agreement.

These processes can be centralized (the central government agency decides, negotiates and enforces the arrangement) or decentralized (where many government agencies, firms or lower-level governments are involved). The degree of centralization in a government's export administration affects the government's choice between bilateral and multilateral venues of export regulation both by shaping the number of actors involved in the process and by influencing who bears the costs of enforcing and monitoring the agreement, that is, who bears the "liability".

Under the centralized export regulation system, negotiating VERs is easier for two reasons. First, the costs of negotiation are lower because fewer actors are involved.[6] Second, once an agreement is reached, the costs of enforcing the quota restrictions are also lower under a centralized export administration system because collecting information and monitoring the enforcement is easier when fewer actors are involved.

Finally, not only do the total costs involved in the process of negotiation and enforcement matter, one would also need to take into consideration distributional issues, that is, who bears the costs of the negotiation and enforcement. Here, bilateral and multilateral instruments of export regulation differ fundamentally in terms of who bears the costs. With bilateral VER agreements, the Chinese government and/or exporting firms are responsible for enforcing the quota restrictions. With multilateral rules, tariffs are imposed on commodities and therefore the Chinese government does not bear the costs of allocating and enforcing the quota. Instead, importing countries need to allocate import quotas to firms and monitor their enforcement.[7] Thus, when the costs of enforcing the quota are low (that is, with centralized export administration and geographically concentrated industry), the Chinese government is more likely to use bilateral VERs over multilateral rules to regulate exports.

Concentrated vs. diffused industrial geography

Under the decentralized export administration system, industry geography affects the government's dispute settlement choice by changing the number of actors involved in the process, the geographical proximity of firms and regulatory agencies and the level of competition among sub-national governments. First, under a decentralized system in which sub-national governments promote and regulate exports, the geographic diffusion of industry is a proxy for the number of actors involved in the VER process, including the decision-making, negotiation and enforcement stages. The more geographically diffused an industry is across provinces, the more actors are involved in the VER process.

Second, the geographic concentration of an industry may affect the costs of enforcement because the geographic proximity of firms and regulatory agencies allows easier monitoring and enforcement of the export regulation. The higher an industry's geographic concentration, the easier it is to enforce VERs.

Finally, under a decentralized export regulation system, the degree of geographic concentration is a reflection of the level of competition needed to obtain higher shares of the export market among sub-national governments and local firms. The higher the level of competition among sub-national actors (i.e., the more diffused an industry is across different provinces), the stronger the actors' incentives to defect from the assigned quota restrictions by exporting more products. Multilateral legal forms of export regulation, such as GATT/WTO legal safeguard and antidumping measures, are more likely to be chosen by diffused industries because imposing and monitoring tariffs are the responsibility of an importing country. Thus, the multilateral form of export regulation can significantly reduce the costs of enforcing the export regulation for the Chinese government. On the other hand, when an industry is geographically concentrated, it is easier to achieve VERs because fewer exporters are involved.

Figure 3.1 presents my hypotheses discussed above. The X axis shows whether the Chinese government's export administration is centralized or decentralized and the Y axis shows whether an industry is geographically concentrated or diffused. Each of the Sino-Japanese dispute cases since 1976 is placed into an appropriate quadrant of Figure 3.1. As discussed in detail below, China's export administration has been decentralized over time since the 1980s (which represents a shift from the left to the right row in Figure 3.1). The level of geographic concentration of industries varies across commodities and over time. The next section will provide an overview of the decentralization reform in export administration and explain why decentralization interacts with industrial geography to shape a government's choice between bilateral and multilateral forms of export regulation.

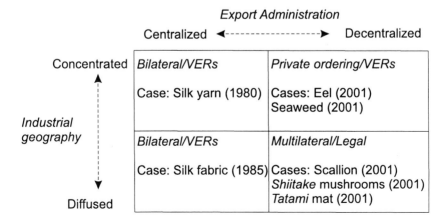

Figure 3.1 Hypotheses and possible cases

Overview: decentralization of export regulation

China's export administration has undergone a series of decentralization reforms. These reforms granted provinces and municipalities the power to promote and regulate exports in three respects:

- the ownership and management structure of foreign trade corporations (FTCs);
- the fiscal system in which localities and central government share gains from foreign trade; and
- the decision-making and enforcement process of export quota and licensing.

First, the ownership structure of foreign trade corporations (FTCs) has become decentralized and internationalized.[8] Before China's open policy was adopted in 1978, only a dozen nationally-owned FTCs monopolized foreign trade.[9] Within a decade, the number of local FTCs increased dramatically to approximately six thousand. Yet the central government's agency, the Ministry of Foreign Economic Relations and Trade (MOFERT), regulated trade composition and flows by issuing FTC export licenses and subsidizing their activities.

Under centralized control by MOFERT, FTCs had a strong incentive to comply with quotas because MOFERT was the source of subsidies and its permission to engage in foreign trade was needed.[10] In 1985, local FTCs were granted autonomy to engage in foreign trade and came under the control of provincial and municipal governments.[11] An increasing number of local FTCs also entered into joint ventures with foreign companies (see Table 3.1). Under the decentralized ownership structure, local and international FTCs competed with each other to win export contracts with producers.

Second, a decentralized fiscal contracting system was adopted between 1980 and 1994 under which provincial governments could retain tax revenues from local enterprises (Wang, 1997: 2001). The foreign exchange contract system (*waihui baogan*) also gave an incentive to local governments to promote exports because they could retain up to 80 percent of such earnings under the assigned quota system.[12] As a result, local governments play a dual role. In addition to being agents of the central government that enforce the export regulation, they are independent actors that seek to maximize gains from foreign trade. Local FTCs owned by provincial and municipal governments also face the same dilemma. They are encouraged to compete against one another to win contracts with producers, but once the government agrees to VERs they need to restrict their exports under the quota.

Finally, a decentralization reform was adopted at the implementation and enforcement stages of export regulation as well. This is so for two major policy instruments for export regulation: export licensing and export quotas.[13] The authority to issue export licenses to FTCs was extended from MOFTEC to the Foreign Economic Relations and Trade Commissions of various provinces, autonomous regions and municipalities in 1996.[14] In 2001, the central office of the Ministry of Commerce (MOFCOM) issued approximately 15 percent of the newly-licensed export commodities, while local authorities (that is, local branches of the Ministry of

Table 3.1 Provincial exports by FTC ownership (10,000 USD)

Province/city	SOEs	Foreign	Others	Foreign (%)
Total	16,881,321	44,420,928	14,897,665	58.30
Guangdong	4,456,248	15,467,100	3,892,911	64.94
Shenzhen	2,014,711	6,758,494	1,378,980	66.57
Jiangsu	1,437,164	9,422,830	1,438,221	76.62
Shanghai	2,068,186	6,157,921	845,861	67.88
Zhejiang	1,629,366	2,726,244	3,324,687	35.50
Ninbo	554,559	748,138	919,036	33.67
Shandong	1,015,562	2,377,119	1,220,138	51.53
Qingdao	442,981	1,070,963	422,863	55.30
Fujian	552,794	2,175,419	756,243	62.43
Xiamen	252,042	1,072,006	402,623	62.09
Beijing	1,751,313	1,191,406	144,342	38.59
Tianjin	337,768	2,199,307	201,401	80.31
Liaoning	597,721	1,332,795	413,398	56.86
Dalian	247,100	945,457	189,013	68.43
Hebei	369,651	345,288	377,746	31.60
Heilongjiang	147,444	47,491	412,136	7.82
Anhui	221,897	150,275	146,757	28.96
Henan	270,176	84,137	154,695	16.53
Xinjiang	161,813	13,677	328,535	2.71
Sichuan	231,846	68,302	169,942	14.53
Hubei	213,517	129,212	100,142	29.18
Hunan	181,817	64,381	128,587	17.18
Shanxi	181,035	51,959	119,878	14.72
Shaanxi	185,709	32,022	89,960	10.41

Source: *China Statistical Yearbook* (2005)

Commerce and municipal and provincial-level Foreign Economic Relations and Trade Commissions) issued approximately 85 percent.[15]

Another instrument of export regulation, the export quota system, has been the subject of decentralization reforms as well. Before 1994, the decision-making process for setting and allocating quotas to FTCs was centralized and controlled by MOFERT, which decided quota allocations in consultation with provincial officials.[16] The quota allocation system became more open and institutionalized during the 1990s. The most notable reform came in 1994 when MOFERT introduced an export quota bidding system.[17]

The quota bidding system is an open process in which MOFCOM (the successor to MOFERT) announces a minimum bidding price and the quantity of exports which should be subject to bidding. FTCs participating in the bid need to submit their past record of export revenues and quantity. The bidding process is decentralized in that locally-owned FTCs submit applications to the Foreign Economic Relations and Trade Commission at the local level, while centrally-managed corporations apply directly to the same commission at the level of the central government.[18] Information regarding when and how the bidding is done, its participants, minimum bidding prices and who wins how much of the bid is made available to the public at provincial or central government offices and on the official website of MOFCOM.[19] The open bidding system has encouraged competition and lobbying by local governments and FTCs to win a larger share of the quota.[20] The export bidding system was internationalized in 1995. Joint ventures with foreign firms and foreign-owned companies are now allowed to participate in the bidding.[21]

These reforms of the open bidding system strengthened the position of local governments vis-à-vis both the central government and FTCs by giving them jurisdiction over export quota allocations. They also provided greater room for locally-owned FTCs to lobby and influence the decision-making process at the level of local governments. Once export quotas are granted to FTCs, enforcement of the quota is largely delegated to provincial and municipal-level governments, which have a strong incentive to allow the FTCs to export more than their permitted quota in order to raise higher revenues and foreign exchange earnings and to promote export-led economic growth.

Case study: the rush and rush-woven products (*tatami*) and seaweed industries

Both the *tatami*-mat[22] and the seaweed industries have been severely hit by Chinese exports since the 1990s. These Japanese industries lobbied their ministries and politicians to regulate Chinese exports. Both industries initially sought to negotiate VERs with China. In the case of *tatami*, the Chinese government rejected Japan's VER proposal knowing that it would then adopt WTO legal safeguard measures, while in the seaweed case, industry-level VERs were successfully and credibly committed to.

The tatami industry

Table 3.2 shows the rapid increase of *tatami* exports to Japan from China in the 1990s. From 1996 to 2000, the quantity of *tatami* imports, as well as its import penetration ratio, doubled. The domestic sales price of *tatami* products fell sharply during this period to just 25 percent of the price in 1996. Responding to the rise of *tatami* imports from China, Japanese *tatami* industry associations organized demonstrations and lobbied members of parliament and prefectural-level representatives to regulate imports.

Table 3.2 Changing domestic production and imports of *tatami* mats in Japan, 1996–2000

	1996	1997	1998	1999	2000
Domestic production (1,000 mats)	26,937	25,088	21,302	15,923	13,872
Imports (1,000 mats)	11,369	8,628	10,344	13,569	20,300
Imports as a percentage of total domestic sales	29.7	25.6	32.7	46	59.4

Source: Survey by the Japanese Government and the Ministry of Agriculture, Forestry, and Fisheries of Japan (2001)

Fearing that the Japanese government would impose safeguard tariffs on *tatami* imports, MOFTEC issued an annual open export quota bidding for *tatami* products to restrain exports in 1999. The quota restriction, however, was ineffective as FTCs competed to export more products.[23] Between 2000 and 2001, the Japanese *tatami* industry attempted, in vain, to negotiate VERs and make the existing export regulations by the Ministry of Foreign Trade and Economic Cooperation (MOFTEC) effective. Long Yongtu, a Vice-Minister of MOFTEC, proposed that "guidelines between private actors, not voluntary export restraints between the states, should be considered" (Yoshimatsu, 2001: 401). The Japanese government requested that the Chinese government participate in bilateral negotiations because the government believed that industry-level agreements would not be enforced.

In the end, the Japanese government resorted to the use of temporary safeguard measures in 2001 for the first time in history. The adoption of safeguard measures provoked retaliation from China in the form of 100 percent tariffs on Japan's exports of automobiles, mobile phones and air conditioners. The estimated economic loss to the Japanese economy was 25 billion yen, seven times more than the benefits enjoyed by the three commodities that were granted the safeguard protection.[24]

Why did China insist on having an industry-level VER negotiation in the face of repeated Japanese requests that the Chinese government formally commit itself to regulating exports? The Vice-Minister of MOFERT argued that China needed to comply with new WTO rules which prohibited a government's involvement in the VER process (see Yoshimatsu, 2001).[25] However, the argument does not hold up under close scrutiny because the Chinese government did negotiate VERs in other cases such as the textile dispute with the United States in 2005. The government also committed to VERs in negotiations with the US over honey and with South Korea over garlic by using the open quota bidding system. I argue that the decentralization and export administration reforms during the past decades have decreased the effectiveness of bilateral VER agreements, and instead, have given rise to the use of multilateral rules in Sino-Japanese disputes.

The effect of decentralization reforms on export regulation, moreover, differs across industries depending on their degree of geographical concentration. While Chinese *tatami* production and exports are characterized by low geographical concentration, the seaweed industry is highly concentrated geographically. I will explain below how the decentralization of export regulation interacts with the degree of geographical concentration of an industry to shape China's choice to use bilateral vs. multilateral instruments for export regulation.

The rush industry in China

Figure 3.2 shows the allocation of export quotas of rush and rush-woven products by province in 2002.[26] It suggests a low degree of geographical concentration of rush and rush-woven production and exports in China. Ningbo city won the highest proportion of quotas while retaining a modest 27 percent of total export volume. The rest of the quotas were distributed broadly to FTCs in other coastal provinces such as Zhejiang, Jiangsu and Shanghai.[27]

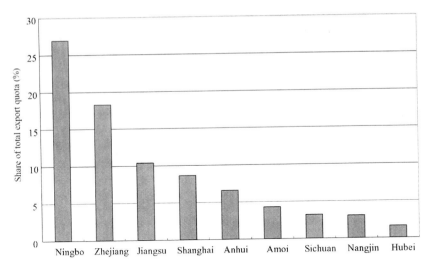

Figure 3.2 Export quota allocation of rush and rush-woven products to Chinese provinces after the open quota bidding

Industry-level VER negotiations are more difficult to achieve and require a government's intervention when an industry is geographically dispersed. First, the number of sub-national actors involved in VER negotiations will be larger, making it more difficult to reach a collective decision. Second, the more dispersed the production and export activities across different provinces, the more local FTCs and producers will compete to promote exports and secure higher market shares abroad. Finally, when a large number of local enforcement agencies (that is, local governments) are involved, it becomes harder for them to cooperate and enforce the export quota collectively. Thus, in the case of the *tatami* industry, China did not agree to voluntarily restrain its exports. Without an attempt to negotiate industry-level VERs, China let Japan adopt temporary safeguard measures with respect to *tatami*. After the temporary safeguard measure expired, the Chinese government instituted an open export quota bidding system to regulate *tatami* exports to Japan. In sum, while Japan sought to negotiate VERs with China on a bilateral basis, China chose to regulate exports multilaterally. Even after the safeguard protection expired, the Chinese government instituted a legal and more transparent method of regulating exports, an open export quota bidding system.

Seaweed: successful VER negotiation

Japan's seaweed industry also suffered a deluge of exports from China. During the 1990s, dried seaweed exports increased by 50 percent and fresh seaweed exports increased by 30 percent.[28] In 2000, Chinese exports comprised 80 percent of domestic seaweed sales. The Japan Fishery Cooperative (JF) and Iwate and Miyagi prefectures' Fishery Cooperatives requested that the government use

safeguard measures to regulate Chinese exports in 2000. Yet the dispute was ultimately settled by industry-level VER negotiation and the agreement was successfully committed to without major government involvement.

The Japanese side initiated the bilateral VER negotiation with China in 2000.
The JF sent a letter to Dalian Seaweed Association in Dalian City requesting bilateral negotiations.[29] In March 2001, the first Japan–China seaweed export–import
negotiation was held in Beijing. The number of participants at the meeting was
quite small. It included the Seaweed Association in Dalian, the China Chamber of
Commerce for Import and Export of Foodstuffs, Native Produce and Animal By-
Products (CCCFNP), officials from Japan Fishery Cooperatives and the Miyagi
and Iwate seaweed producers. The fact that there were so few participants supports
the hypothesis that when an industry is geographically concentrated, the number
of actors involved in VER negotiations will be smaller.

One month after the producer-level negotiations, Chinese export companies and
Japanese import companies met in Tokyo and discussed the details of VERs. At
the third industry-level negotiations in June 2001, executives of industry associations from Japan and China met in Beijing and agreed on final export restraints.
China agreed to voluntarily restrain its seaweed exports to Japan and to "do its best
to balance the demand and supply of seaweed for sustainable seaweed farming".[30]
The Japanese side agreed to "make the best effort to commit to the agreement
while keeping an eye on future efforts made by China".[31] The number of participants at the meeting was quite minimal. The participants included, on the Japanese
side, Iwate and Miyagi prefectures' JF presidents and national-level JF executives
and, on the Chinese side, the CCCFNP's president and Dalian Seaweed Association's president. The participants also agreed to establish bi-annual meetings to
regulate the supply and demand of seaweed and to jointly promote domestic
consumption of seaweed in China and Chinese seaweed exports to other foreign
markets besides Japan.

While negotiating VERs with China, Japanese domestic seaweed producers
also lobbied the Japanese government to seek safeguard protection.[32] Both the
Japanese and the Chinese industries, however, had strong incentives to avoid the
use of multilateral rules. From the Chinese perspective, VERs were preferred not
only because they are a more temporal form of export regulation, but also because
they provide exporters with an opportunity to collude with Japanese importers by
setting the price higher than before the VERs.[33] From the Japanese perspective,
there was a split between domestic seaweed producers and producers that began
outsourcing seaweed farming to China in the 1990s.[34] While the former preferred
the government adopt safeguard measures, the latter pursued bilateral VERs. The
domestic seaweed companies also lobbied the government to enact a law that
would force seaweed producers to disclose a product's country of origin in order to
differentiate their products from those imported from China.

In sum, the Chinese government's intervention in export regulation was minimal
in the seaweed case. Japanese and Chinese seaweed industries successfully negotiated industry-level VERs and no export quota order on seaweed exports was issued
by the Chinese government. Why was such private ordering possible under the

highly decentralized export administration system? As I have argued above, the high geographical concentration of an industry is the key to understanding why private-level negotiations were successful and credibly committed to.

The seaweed industry in China

The seaweed case differs from other dispute cases that have required multilateral rules and government intervention in two major respects. First, the geographical concentration of seaweed production and export activities in China is very high as Dalian city alone accounted for around 90 percent of China's total production and export of seaweed to Japan. Second, seaweed production in Dalian is highly multinational. Japanese seaweed production companies have established factories and joint ventures in Dalian since the early 1990s. Under these two conditions, industry-level negotiation of VERs is easier as producers, exporters and importers share common interests in avoiding an escalation of the dispute to the use of multilateral rules. The negotiations were also less costly because the number of actors involved was smaller. Most importantly, the costs of monitoring and enforcing the VER agreement were much smaller as the industry's exports were concentrated in one region.

What lies ahead? Geographic concentration of export-oriented industries in China

The two cases discussed above show that the geographic concentration of exporting industries has substantial effects on a government's choice between bilateral and multilateral solutions to trade disputes in China. This finding begs another question: why are some industries geographically more concentrated than others? The degree of geographical concentration is not exogenous to China's position in the international economy. Exporting industries in general and agricultural products in particular tend to be geographically concentrated in coastal areas because they require geographic proximity to ports and foreign markets. As a result, Chinese agricultural producers often differentiate production sites depending on whether the commodities are intended for domestic or foreign markets. In addition, more than half of China's export values are generated by joint ventures with foreign firms and foreign-owned companies. Foreign investment tends to be located in coastal provinces because of proximity to ports and favorable investment and tax privileges granted by the government during the 1980s. Finally, both foreign and domestic producers recognize the economies of scale and tend to invest in clusters.

These geographical characteristics of exporting industries in China offer several predictions about the future of China' export regulation. First, the new WTO rule prohibiting government involvement in VERs will not deter China's use of VERs for geographically concentrated industries. As shown in the seaweed case study, industry-level VERs can be credibly committed to and enforced without a government's involvement when an industry is geographically concentrated.

Second, a dispute is more likely to be resolved by multilateral, legal rules for geographically diffused industries. As an increasing number of local FTCs and sub-national governments enter export competition in the future, it will be even more difficult for the Chinese government to negotiate and enforce informal VERs. We expect to see a more legal, open and transparent export regulation process institutionalized in China similar to the introduction of the open quota bidding system.

Finally, China's entry into the WTO in December 2001 is expected to constrain China's retaliation against Japan's future adoption of WTO legal safeguard protection. Under the WTO's Agreements of Safeguard (Article 8),[35] targeted states are not allowed to retaliate against a safeguard measure for a period of three years. If China complies with this rule, then Japan is more likely to pursue multilateral rules to protect industries that suffer from a deluge of Chinese exports.

Conclusion

This chapter has explored the reasons why some trade disputes are settled via bilateral VER negotiations while others are settled using multilateral rules. Contrary to what has been argued elsewhere, it has been shown that two "decentralization" factors – the decentralization of export administration and geographical concentration of industries – account for Sino-Japanese dispute settlement choices. The two dispute cases discussed above, the *tatami* and seaweed industries, reached multilateral and bilateral solutions, respectively, due to their different degree of geographical concentration. The degree of geographical concentration of an industry is a key to understanding dispute outcomes because it affects the costs of negotiation and enforcement in export regulation.

The broader implications of these findings are threefold. First, we need to reconsider a unitary actor assumption often employed in the existing "forum-shopping" literature. Even in an authoritarian and state-controlled economy like China, domestic actors – the central government, local governments and exporting industries – have various preferences for different venues of export regulation due to the differential distribution of negotiation and enforcement costs of VERs. The process of export regulation has also become more decentralized, open and transparent.

Second, domestic institutional changes, such as the decentralization of export administration, may significantly affect a government's incentive to use bilateral as opposed to multilateral venues of export regulation. One must analyze how industry-level characteristics interact with domestic institutional changes to shape the government's choice across different dispute settlement fora.

Finally, it is not simply expected negotiation outcomes that influence a government's choice among different venues. Rather, negotiation and enforcement costs as well as the issue of who bears these costs have a substantial effect on how a government will choose among different venues of export regulation.

In concluding, I suggest a few promising directions for future research. First, comparative analysis of how the Chinese government chooses between bilateral and multilateral venues of export regulation *vis-à-vis* other major trading partners such as the United States and South Korea will be a promising line of research.

Second, the open export quota bidding system introduced by China in 1994 offers interesting data over time to test various political economy hypotheses. For example, why were some industries subject to the open bidding while others were not? Why did some firms and localities obtain more favorable quota allocations than others? Finally, research on how provincial élites choose between compliance with the center and promotion of exports will be another promising line of future research.

Acknowledgements

Part of this research was supported by the Japan Society for the Promotion of Science and Princeton University's Center for Globalization and Governance. I would like to thank Ka Zeng, Barry Naughton, Judy Goldstein and participants at the Conference on Chinese Trade Policy at the University of California, San Diego (UCSD) for their comments on an earlier draft and Christina Chen, Derek Taiwei Liu, Naoko Takenaka and Yu Zheng for their excellent research assistance. The Institute for International, Comparative, and Area Studies (IICAS) and the Institute on Global Conflict and Cooperation (IGCC) provided generous support to hold the Conference.

Notes

1 See People's Daily (2004).
2 On this, see Naoi (2006).
3 In this sense, I follow Stigler (1971) and Peltzman's view (1976) that "the primary determinant of the form of regulation is the way in which it transfers wealth among members of society". See also Viscusi, Vernon and Harrington (1995: 800). On the literature on endogenous regulation, see Stigler (1971); Peltzman (1976); Fiorina (1982); Campos (1989).
4 See commodity-level dataset on Sino-Japanese trade disputes and outcomes (1976–2005) collected by the author using newspaper articles in Japanese, Chinese and English.
5 On the various mechanisms through which private actors are able to credibly commit to and enforce the agreement without government intervention, see Harold (1967); Ostrom (1990).
6 Olson (1965); Axelrod (1984).
7 Existing literature on rent-seeking in trade suggests that a rent-seeking government prefers VERs to tariffs precisely because the former creates rents through quota allocations. VERs also offer an opportunity for exporters to collude with importers by setting the price higher than the world price as seen by the Japanese auto industry's adoption of VERs with the United States in the 1980s. See Krueger (1974: 291–303).
8 On this, see Lardy (1992: Chapter 3); Zweig (2002: Chapter 3).
9 Lardy (1992: Chapter 2).
10 Ross (1988: 34).
11 Zweig (2002: 111).
12 Fukasaku, Ma and Yang (1999: 25).
13 On the early development of the export license system, see Lardy (1992: 45–46). China restored its export licensing system in 1980 and expanded the number of commodities covered by the system (Lardy, 1992: Chapter 3). The share of trade values regulated by export and import licensing has risen sharply since 1980. Export licenses were extended from 12 nationally-owned FTCs to FTCs owned by provincial and municipal governments throughout the 1980s and 1990s. See Lardy (1992); Zweig (2002).

14 MOFERT (1996).

15 Ministry of Commerce (2001a). In 2001, 66 commodities were subject to export licenses. The central office of MOFCOM issued licenses to nine of the 66 commodities, the provincial and municipal branches of MOFCOM issued licenses to 46 commodities, and the remaining 11 commodities were subject to export licensing by local-level government organizations such as the Foreign Economic Relations and Trade Commission at municipal- and provincial-levels.

16 An example of this is a news report about a meeting to set quotas for the tin industry in 1995. Participants at the meeting included officials from MOFTEC, the China National Nonferrous Metals Import and Export Corporation (CNIEC) and the China National Metals and Minerals Import and Export Corporation, as well as provincial trade officials from Xiamen in Fujian Province. See Metals Week (1995).

17 There are two types of export quotas: active and passive quotas. Active quotas are controlled by the Chinese government while passive quotas are controlled by foreign governments. For instance, in the year 2000, 32 commodities were subject to open quota bids. Among these, 11 were subject to active quotas the quantity of which were controlled by China, while the remaining 21 commodities were subject to passive quotas whereby foreign governments set the limits.

18 Ministry of Commerce (2001b).

19 One of the rationales of the quota reform was to balance the power between MOFERT and producers and between FTCs and commodities producers. On this see Zweig (2003: 115).

20 Zweig (2002).

21 Ministry of Commerce (2001c).

22 *Tatami*-mats are a form of Japanese flooring made from rush woven together in a knit-like pattern. Japanese people started using *tatami*-mats during the *Nara* period in the eighth century. Traditional Japanese houses usually have rooms with *tatami*-mats and even modern apartments often have one room with *tatami*-mat flooring. However, during the past fifteen years hardwood floors have become more popular among younger generations and, as a result, the use of *tatami*-mats has been declining.

23 Testimony by a Chief of the Tariff Section of the Ministry of Finance at the Special Tariff Sectional Meeting of Tariff/Foreign Exchange Council, 25 December 2001.

24 Author's interview with a mid-level official at MAFF, 10 January 2002; interview with *Nominren* official, March 2002, Tokyo; and interview with a member of parliament who lobbied for the adoption of safeguards, 28 July 2006.

25 WTO (1994a).

26 Ministry of Commerce (2001d).

27 It is important to distinguish geographical concentration of production from export activities. Ningbo port, for instance, exports around 80 percent of total rush and rush-woven products due to its proximity to neighboring rush production sites. See, for example, Chinaningbo (2004).

28 Internal document submitted by the Japan Fishery Cooperative to the Upper House Research Room on Accounts, 19 March 2001.

29 Japan Fisheries Cooperatives (JF), "Chronology of Safeguard Investigation on Seaweed", an internal document obtained at headquarters of the JF.

30 Mainichi Daily News (2001).

31 Japan Fisheries Cooperatives (2001).

32 Petition letter sent from Miyagi and Iwate prefecture's Fishery Corporative to Fishery Agency, 13 December 2000 and January 2001.

33 As Harris (1985: 800) aptly put it: "VERs serves as a device through which partial collusion on price is achieved leading to higher profits for [exporting and importing] firms."

34 Phone interview with Miyagi prefecture's member of prefectural parliament, Tokyo, March 2002.

35 WTO (1994b), *Agreement on Safeguards*, Article 8: Level of Concessions and Other Obligations.

References

Axelrod, R. (1984) *The Evolution of Cooperation*, New York: Basic Books.

Baldwin, R. E. (1985) *The Political Economy of U.S. Import Policy,* Cambridge, MA: MIT Press.

—— (1989) *The Political Economy of Trade Policy: Integrating the Perspectives of Economists and Political Scientists*, Cambridge, MA and London: MIT Press.

Becker, G. (1976) "Toward a more general theory of regulation", *Journal of Law and Economics*, 19 (2, Conference on the Economics of Politics and Regulation): 245–8.

Busch, M. L. and Reinhardt, L. (1999) "Industrial location and protection: the political and economic geography of U.S. nontariff barriers", *American Journal of Political Science,* 43 (4): 1028–50.

—— (2000) "Geography, international trade, and political mobilization in U.S. industries", *American Journal of Political Science,* 44 (4): 703–19.

—— (2003) "Developing countries and General Agreement on Tariffs and Trade/World Trade Organization dispute settlement", *Journal of World Trade,* 37 (4): 719–35.

Campos, J. E. L. (1989) "Legislative institutions, lobbying, and the endogenous choice of regulatory instruments: a political economy approach to instrument choice", *Journal of Law, Economics, and Organization*, 5 (2): 333–53.

China Statistical Yearbook (2005) Beijing: National Bureau of Statistics of China.

Chinaningbo (2004) "Tatami exports to Japan face pressure" (*woguo lincaoxi chukou riben jiang shou chongji*) 12 January, Available online: http://chinaningbo.com/ detail_new.php?newId=17182

Davis, C. L. (2003) *Food Fights Over Free Trade: How International Institutions Promote Agricultural Trade Liberalization*, Princeton, NJ: Princeton University Press.

Fiorina, M. P. (1982) "Legislative choice of regulatory forms: legal process or administrative process?" *Public Choice*, 39 (1): 33–66.

Fukasaku, K., Ma Y. and Yang, Q. (1999) "China's unfinished open-economy reforms: liberalization of services", OECD working paper no. 147.

Goldstein, J. (1986) "The political economy of trade: institutions of protection", *The American Political Science Review,* 80 (1): 161–84.

—— (1988) "Ideas, institutions, and American trade policy", *International Organization,* 42 (1): 179–217.

—— (1996) "International law and domestic institutions: reconciling North American 'unfair' trade laws", *International Organization,* 50 (4): 541–64.

Goldstein, J. and Martin, L. L. (2000) "Legalization, trade liberalization, and domestic politics: a cautionary note", *International Organization* 54 (3): 603–32.

Grossman, G. M. and Helpman, E. (1994) "Protection for sale", *American Economic Review,* 84 (4): 833–50.

Harold, D. (1967) "Toward a theory of property rights", *American Economic Review,* 57 (2): 347–59.

Harris, R. (1985) "Why voluntary export restraints are voluntary", *Canadian Journal of Economics*, 18 (4): 799–809.

Hillman, A. L. and Ursprung H. W. (1988) "Domestic politics, foreign interests, and international trade policy", *American Economic Review,* 78 (4): 729–45.

Hiroomi, T. (2001) "*Korekara Dousuru Safeguard*" ("What to do next with safeguard measures?"), *Ronza*, October.

Japan Fisheries Cooperatives (JF) (2001) "On Japan–China industry-level negotiation on seaweed", an internal document obtained at headquarter of the JF, 15 June.

Kahler, M. (2000) "Legalization as strategy: The Asia-Pacific case", *International Organization,* 54 (3): 549–71.

Krueger, A. O. (1974) "The political economy of rent-seeking", *American Economic Review,* 3: 291–303.

Lardy, N. R. (1992) *Foreign Trade and Economic Reform in China: 1978–1990,* Cambridge: Cambridge University Press.

Mainichi Daily News (2001) "Seaweed farming: China decided to VERs — Japan and China reached a broad agreement", *Mainichi Daily News*, 15 June.

Mansfield, E. D. and Busch, Marc L. (1995) "The political economy of nontariff barriers: a cross-national analysis", *International Organization,* 49 (4): 723–49.

Martin, L. L. and Beth S. A. (1998) "Theories of empirical studies of international institutions", *International Organization,* 52 (4): 729–57.

Mattli, W. (2001) "Private justice in a global economy: from litigation to arbitration", *International Organization,* 55 (4): 919–47.

Metals Week (1995) "China setting quotas this week", *Metals Week*, 66: 50 (18 December).

Milner, H. V. (1988) *Resisting Protectionism : Global Industries and the Politics of International Trade,* Princeton, NJ: Princeton University Press.

⎯⎯⎯ (1997) *Interests, Institutions, and Information: Domestic Politics and International Relations,* Princeton, NJ: Princeton University Press.

Ministry of Agriculture, Forestry, and Fisheries of Japan (2001) *"Igusa Tatami Omote no Kouzou Kaikaku Taisaku"* ("A plan for structural reform for *tatami* industry"), unpublished document, 17 September.

Ministry of Commerce (2001a) "Year 2001: List of Commodities That Are Managed by Export License *(chukou xuke zheng guanli shangpin mulu)*."

⎯⎯ (2001b) "Method of Managing Export Commodity Quota Allocation" (*chukou shangpin peie guanli banfa*), Chapter 4, Section 13.

⎯⎯ (2001c) "Method of Managing Export Commodity Quota", 12 Order.

⎯⎯ (2001d) "Announcement of the First Invitation to Bid for Export Quota on Rush and Rush-woven Products for the Year 2002" (*lincao ji qizhipin chukou peie diyici xieyi zhaobiao gonggao),* 3 December.

Ministry of Foreign Economic Relations and Trade (MOFERT) (1996) Article 3 of "Several Provisions on the Administration of Export License", 2 January.

Moore, M. O. and Suranovic, S. M. (1993) "A welfare comparison between VERS and tariffs under the GATT", *Canadian Journal of Economics,* 26 (2): 447–56.

Naoi, M. (2006) "Who is shopping?: GATT/WTO and domestic politics of choosing trade policy instruments in Japan, 1980–2001", manuscript under review.

Olson, M. (1965) *The Logic of Collective Action*, Cambridge: Harvard University Press.

Ostrom, E. (1990) *Governing the Commons,* Cambridge: Cambridge University Press.

Pekkanen, S. M. (2001) "International law, the WTO, and the Japanese state: assessment and implications of the new legalized trade politics", *Journal of Japanese Studies* 27 (1): 41–79.

Peltzman, S. (1976) "Toward a more general theory of regulation", *Journal of Law and Economics,* 19 (2): 211–40.

People's Daily (2004) "China suffers the most in anti-dumping disputes for nine consecutive years", *People's Daily*, 26 October.

Prusa, T. J. (1999) "On the spread and impact of antidumping", NBER Working Paper 7404.

Ray, E. J. (1981) "The determinants of tariff and nontariff trade restrictions in the United States", *Journal of Political Economy,* 89 (1): 105–21.

Rodrik, D. (1997) *Has Globalization Gone Too Far?* Washington, DC: Institute of International Economics.

Rogowski, R. (1987) "Trade and the variety of democratic institutions", *International Organization,* 41 (2): 203–23.

Rosendorff, P. B. (1996) "Voluntary export restraints, antidumping procedure, and domestic politics", *American Economic Review,* 86 (3): 544–61.

Ross, M. C. (1988) "China, the United States, and the world: changing the foreign trade system", *China Business Review,* 15 (3): 34–6.

Simmons, B. A. (2000) "The legalization of international monetary affairs", *International Organization,* 54 (3): 189–218.

Stigler, G. J. (1971) "The theory of economic regulation", *Bell Journal of Economics and Management Science,* 2 (1): 3–21.

Tharakan, P. K. M. (1995) "Political economy of contingent protection", *Economic Journal,* 105 (433): 1550–64.

Viscusi, W. K., Vernon, J. M. and Harrington, J. E. (2000) "Introduction to economic regulation", in W. K. Viscusi, Vernon, J. M. and Harrington, J. E., *Economics of Regulation and Antitrust*, 3rd edn, Cambridge, MA: MIT Press: 297–336.

Wang, S. (1997) "China's 1994 fiscal reform: an initial assessment", *Asian Survey*, 37 (9): 801–17.

World Trade Organization (1994a) *Agreement on Safeguards*, Article 11: Prohibition and Elimination of Certain Measures.

—— (1994b) *Agreement on Safeguards*, Article 8: Level of Concessions and Other Obligations.

Yoshimatsu, H. (2001) "Social demand, state capability and globalization: Japan–China trade friction over safeguards", *Pacific Review*, 15 (3): 381–408.

Zweig, D. (2002) *Internationalizing China: Domestic Interests and Global Linkages*, Ithaca, NY: Cornell University Press.

4 Putting your mouth where your money is

How US companies' fear of Chinese retaliation influences US trade policy

Andrew Mertha

> You have multinational companies in China – I used to work for one, so I know – who are afraid of retaliation against their businesses so they often praise the Chinese government. When President Hu visited Microsoft several weeks ago, Chairman Bill Gates thanked him for the improvements in their protection of intellectual property … these companies are being politically correct in the most politically incorrect country in the world.
>
> Daniel Chow, US China Economic and Security
Review Commission Hearing, 8 June 2006

Introduction

Throughout China's extended negotiations with the United States over intellectual property rights (IPR) from 1991 to 1996, Beijing's strategy during the formal talks relied on consistently defensive posturing, surrendering as little as possible until the last possible moment,[1] as well as demonstrating an apparent unwillingness or inability to exact concessions not directly related to the initial catalog of US demands. This interpretation holds that after sufficient hemming and hawing, the Chinese side accepted most of the US demands – which focused overwhelmingly on copyright issues – even though it did not implement many of them. If we ignore the implementation problem for a moment and concentrate solely on the negotiations, we would conclude that the Chinese "lost" at the negotiating table.

But such a conclusion is wrong. China "lost" what it could afford to lose at the negotiations because it was extremely successful at ensuring that the most troublesome issues facing US IPR holders, and the most embarrassing and intractable issue facing Chinese authorities at the time – trademark counterfeiting at the local level in China – remained off the trade agenda altogether. In other words, China was able to shape US talking points so that they concentrated almost exclusively on copyright, not trademark, protection. China was able to accomplish this by what I call here "transnational trade deterrence", or the explicit or implicit threat of sanctions by local Chinese governments to deter foreign firms operating within their borders from making their dissatisfaction with local government performance widely known.

The term, "transnational trade deterrence" (TTD), although somewhat unwieldy, is deliberate. It exists as a counterpart to the notion of "transnational alliances" derived by John Odell in his work on two-level games. Using the notion of transnational alliances, Odell was able to explain trade outcomes that were in the interests of neither of the negotiating parties (the governments of the US and Brazil), but were very much in the interests of the domestic constituencies of both countries (IBM US and IBM Brazil). These outcomes were possible because of the linkages established between these two domestic (Level 2) constituencies (Odell, 1993).

In the case of transnational trade deterrence (I have inserted the term "trade" because deterrence in the traditional strategic studies context is almost always *transnational*), the relationship between the two domestic constituencies is a conflictual one. Rather than seeing eye to eye on a particular trade issue – in this case, intellectual property protection – these two constituencies have very different goals and priorities. The power and informational asymmetries between these two parties, which I explain later in this chapter, have the effect of influencing the negotiations between their two respective governments in ways that are impossible to explain by focusing solely on the negotiators themselves.

A primer on IPR trade policy: special 301

The Office of the United States Trade Representative (USTR) is the key US Government agency charged with pursuing US trade policy. Section 301 of the *1974 Trade Act* requires the USTR to identify and investigate countries that engage in trade practices deemed unfair to US interests and to impose sanctions where appropriate. Section 301 grants the United States unilateral power to punish countries that were considered a threat to US trading interests and to enforce US rights under existing bilateral and multilateral trade agreements (Puckett and Reynolds, 1996: 676).

The *1988 Omnibus Trade and Competitiveness Act* established statutory mandates for investigations of (and the leveling of trade sanctions against) countries deemed to be violating US intellectual property. It institutionalized government–business intellectual property relations by requiring the USTR to post notices in the *Federal Register*, soliciting comments on the issue of IPR infringement of US products abroad, including specific evidence of IPR violations and recommendations for action.

Because of its small staff size and high turnover rate, the USTR relies on US firms and associations to provide much of the data on unfair trade practices (including IPR violations) abroad to ensure the accuracy and bolster the credibility of the charges leveled by the USTR at the target country. Thus, USTR action depends upon the provision of clear, concise and compelling information by the various business interests hurt by these practices. As one former negotiator put it, "informing, explaining become persuading."[2]

Moreover, Special 301 institutionalizes this informational requirement: it compels the USTR to act in response to the information – and more importantly, to the recommendations – it receives from interested actors within the business community. The establishment of Special 301 was an exceptionally successful strategy by the IPR associations. They were able to institute a set of statutory constraints on the conduct of US trade policy that enhanced the position and the power of the individual firms and the IPR associations vis-à-vis the USTR. Thus, access to the USTR was institutionalized, and the USTR was compelled to respond.[3] Finally, simply having one's intellectual property violated abroad provided the requisite "standing" to participate in the Special 301 process.

Given the ease of entry into the trade agenda setting process, why did (and do) so many companies whose losses were in the millions, even hundreds of millions, of dollars in China owing to poor IPR protection demonstrate an unwillingness to take part in the Special 301 process when they had every incentive to do so? One might argue that trademark-related losses were not that significant. Although the International Intellectual Property Alliance (IIPA) estimates piracy levels in 2000 at 90 percent for motion pictures, 85 percent for sound recordings and musical compositions, 93 percent for business application computer software, and 99 percent for entertainment computer software (IIPA, 2001: 26), these losses are based on potential sales, which assumes that purchases of pirated products substitutes or displaces the purchases of their legitimate counterparts. Given the cost differentials ($1 for the former vs. $200–300 for the latter), this is a dubious assumption. By contrast, the China Quality Brands Inspection Committee estimates that sales of counterfeit products on average account for 15 to 20 percent of total sales[4], that is to say, actual product, or actual sales as opposed to potential sales. This runs into the billions of dollars.

Additionally, it can be argued that trademark enforcement was significantly better than copyright enforcement. Indeed, I have argued this elsewhere (Mertha, 2006). However, this improvement in trademark enforcement actually postdates the Sino-US negotiations over IPR, which culminated in 1996. It was only after these negotiations were concluded that trademark enforcement began to improve.

Finally, one can argue that the trademark trade associations did not engage the USTR. Indeed, the International Trademark Association (INTA) deliberately engaged in a non-confrontational strategy. However, the international Anti-Counterfeiting Coalition (IACC) did not. In fact, the IACC was among the most aggressive of the IPR trade associations, but was hampered and ultimately marginalized because its members refused to go "on the record" to document Chinese malfeasance.

In this chapter, I argue that the answer is to be found within the transnational deterrent threat leveled by local Chinese governments against US trademark-intensive industries, which, unlike their copyright-intensive counterparts, had a substantial physical presence on the ground in China, half a world away from USTR headquarters.

The transnational trade deterrent threat

"Deterrence", stated simply, is the attempt to influence another actor to refrain from engaging in a particular action. Rational deterrence is based upon a cost-benefit calculation: weighing the costs of conflict together with the benefits of cooperation. All things being equal, if the costs of conflict (and/or the benefits of cooperation) are sufficiently low, deterrence will fail; if the costs of conflict (and/ or the benefits of cooperation) are sufficiently high, deterrence is more likely to succeed. The focus of deterrence theory has been primarily, although not exclusively, on the role of the "defender" or the "issuing" country (the defender of the status quo; the country issuing the deterrent threat, in this case, China). The analysis below looks at both the defender and at the "initiator" (the USTR on behalf of US industry).

The actual behavior that the Chinese TTD threat is designed to prevent is foreign firms' bringing unwanted attention to China's shortcomings vis-à-vis implementation and enforcement of trade policy (including, but far from limited to, intellectual property). A representative from a US beverage company summarized the transnational deterrent threat in this way:

> [We do] not get too directly involved with the Chinese government in complaining about the trademark issue. First of all, [we need] to maintain good relations with the Chinese government. The rules are always changing and the government can announce an "audit" if [we rub] them the wrong way. [We] also [have] expansion plans and will certainly need the Chinese government to be on [our] side in undertaking such a plan. There are also tax issues. In short, [we do] not want to put [ourselves] on any Chinese governmental "black list.[5]

And this is by no means a new phenomenon, as Jim Mann (1989: 191–2) wrote almost 20 years ago about the early reform period:

> Why were the foreign companies so unwilling to complain? Each company feared Chinese retaliation. China had successfully created a climate in which favoritism was expected. If Coca-Cola complained that it was being unfairly restricted, Chinese authorities might counter by making life tougher for Coke (or better for Pepsi) ... Foreign correspondents doing stories on business conditions in China regularly found that unhappy local representatives were willing to voice bitter complaints, but only in private. They might talk to the press, but only on background or off the record ... Few news articles were written about difficult business conditions in China, and the ones that appeared had a remote, abstract feel to them. They contained few names or concrete examples.

Moreover, even in the post-China WTO era, this sentiment continues to inform US business strategy:

> In reaction to the explosion of counterfeiting and other theft of intellectual property, [multinational enterprises] doing business in China have adopted a non-confrontational strategy of long term cooperation and informal lobbying. ... MNEs that approach the United States government have been careful in the past not to ask the U.S. government to initiate any formal action

under U.S. federal trade law. Many MNEs have adopted a strategy of publicly praising the PRC government for improving its IP enforcement regime, while privately these same MNEs lament that the piracy problem is worse than ever … MNEs pursue a non-confrontational strategy because MNEs are afraid of doing anything that might offend the Chinese government and that might lead to retaliation against their businesses in China. For this reason, MNEs avoid any actions that might be interpreted as hostile or threatening, but instead take every opportunity to praise the Chinese government for any improvements in IP enforcement.[6]

Where does this fear of retaliation come from? Whether arising from a firm's own actual experience, from that of a competitor or an associate, or because it simply exists "out there" as a thinly-disguised threat, the specter of such retaliation has become an unremitting fact of life that contributes to a chronic sense of insecurity for foreign commercial actors operating in China. This threat of retaliation has become internalized by these foreign actors and shapes their behavior to a great extent. The size of the Chinese market, the substitutability of most foreign firms and their products, and the power asymmetries at the local level between Chinese government officials and foreign company representatives, all underscore the high stakes and the ease of execution that underlie this threat. However, although this threat is taken as a fact of life in doing business in China, its impact beyond China's borders is less well understood.

Much of deterrence theory revolves around "strategic deterrence", which states that " 'if you do x I shall do y to you'. If the opponent expects the costs of y to be greater then the benefits of x, he will refrain from doing x; he is deterred." However, once the application of strategic deterrence theory extends to increasingly complex situations – such as the trade negotiations examined here – it begins to run out of explanatory power (George and Smoke, 1974: 49). It is thus necessary to revisit some of the basic assumptions of traditional deterrence theory, specifically, the degree of anticipated retaliatory damage following a deterrence breakdown, and the specificity of the deterrent threat. By examining these concepts, we are able to explain analytically and theoretically the empirical phenomenon that very few are willing to acknowledge even exists, at least in public.

The degree of retaliatory damage

George and Smoke apply traditional deterrence onto strategic deterrence theory as resulting from the ability of states to inflict greater degrees of pain on the target state's general population without first destroying the state itself. In other words, it is the ability to inflict a substantial degree of "pain" that makes deterrence possible. But as we move from a military context to that of international trade, these concepts need to be revisited and perhaps "weighted" somewhat differently.

The "degree of retaliatory damage" is important for the defender's (China's) deterrent strategy. In order to make his deterrent threat credible, the defender must demonstrate both the capability and the will to carry out the threat. However, this raises questions about how to think about credibility when the deterrent threat may not, in the end, be sufficiently "painful." On the one hand, the fact that the stakes are lower increases the likelihood that the issuing country will carry out the threat. On the other hand, if the stakes are lower than in the case of military action, they are arguably easier to absorb. Insofar as credibility involves both the capability and the will to carry out the threat, if a critical dimension of credibility ("capability") is deemed absorbable, the "will", and, by extension, the defender's overall threat may be seen by the target country as far more credible, but somewhat less threatening than in a military context. As a result, the defender must develop a strategy that compensates for this. In the present context, the most important of these is the manipulation of information to make it ambiguous, or to deliberately render it "incomplete".

What type of reputation is China after?

Traditional deterrence theory stipulates that the deterrent threat must be clearly stated for deterrence to hold (Harvey, 1999: 842). However, transnational trade deterrence is more likely to be successful in situations of incomplete information, in which the defending country's intentions, and to a lesser extent, its capabilities, are sufficiently opaque (Betts, 1985: 154). In other words, the TTD threat is effective even when it is not clearly stated. How do these Chinese actors cultivate the reputation they are after?

First, when the ability to inflict substantive pain is curtailed, it becomes increasingly important for the defender to strategically manipulate information and maximize ambiguity and thus minimize accurate information about its retaliatory capabilities, including the limits of the damage that could be brought about by such retaliation. Limits on the knowledge about an actor's weakness can contribute to, and even drive, other actors' inflated assumptions about its strength. Under conditions of "perfect information", it is easier to gauge an opponent's likely moves, as well as to analyze and break down the threat (and make arrangements to absorb it), thus mitigating its impact. Under conditions of "imperfect information", it is far more difficult, if not impossible, to establish *ex ante* defenses against the transnational deterrent threat.

Second, it should be noted that TTD has never been articulated as national policy in China precisely because it originates within the domain of local political officials, and leaders in Beijing may not support such threats – for domestic political reasons – even as they help Beijing's negotiating posture.[7] TTD represents the degree to which Beijing is unable to rein in local government defection from national policy. In fact, locally articulated threats may actually be more potent the more they depart from national policy: the fact that these threats can be made in the first place implies Beijing's inability to guarantee the "safety" of a foreign firm operating outside Beijing's immediate jurisdiction even if national policy pledges to do so.[8] The diffuseness of these threats also contributes to the effectiveness of their strategic ambiguity. The threats cannot be isolated or systematically identified and aggregated; this feeds foreign firms' perception that they are omnipresent, and, therefore, it is easy for these firms to exaggerate their range and power.

Third, the decision to bluff, or to refrain from doing so, can have a significant impact on a country's reputation. Such a mixed-strategy equilibrium is captured by Barry Nalebuff (1991: 319):

> If it was thought that a weak country would never attempt to bluff or act tough, then seeing a country act tough would indicate true strength. This would improve its reputation immensely, possibly enough even to motivate a weak country to act tough (which would not be in equilibrium). As bluffing becomes increasingly likely, the enhancement of a reputation following tough behavior is diminished. At some point, the probability of bluffing is sufficiently high (and the improvement of reputation is sufficiently small) that the cost of the weak country acting tough is exactly offset by the gain in reputation.

Nalebuff raises the notion that acting tough (that is, through an explicit demonstration of an actor's ability and/or will to carry out a deterrent threat) reaches a point of diminishing returns. One can similarly argue that the decision not to act tough may actually be an equilibrium strategy. In other words, an optimal strategy for a country to demonstrate its capability and will to exercise retaliation, under certain conditions, may be to simply do nothing.

Fourth, the TTD threat need not pose a direct threat to the US, or to a particular commercial sector, to be capable of inflicting a tremendous amount of damage on a single firm, or even a small group of firms. Therefore, to the individual foreign firm operating in China, the diffusion and the ambiguity of the TTD threat combined with local Chinese governments' ability to inflict pain, creates an environment that provides a substantial disincentive to rock the boat regarding IPR and other trade-related issues.

Credibility of transnational trade deterrence

Successful deterrence must be credible. For a deterrent threat to be credible, the defender must demonstrate the capacity and the will to carry out its threat. The "targets" of such deterrence in the context of this chapter are the actors within the US IPR trade lobby that set the US trade agenda through Special 301. Is an objective TTD threat credible to this set of targets?

The issue of capability is relatively straightforward. "Capability", in this context, means the ability to severely undermine continued or future penetration of the domestic Chinese market, or utilization of its inexpensive labor force. Local Chinese officials have the ability to carry out a deterrent threat. The absence of an effective, autonomous legal system throughout most of China and the lack of transparency within the political process provides few checks and balances on arbitrary local power (Lampton, 1987; Lieberthal, 2003).[9] Moreover, the national government lacks the requisite power to substantially rein in local officials, and therefore is unable to reduce local manifestations of this deterrent threat even if it sought to do so.

Retaliatory action would also inflict a considerable degree of pain on the *individual* foreign firm (as opposed to US interests writ large). The lure of the vast Chinese consumer market as well as China's equally large (and low-cost) manufacturing capacity is sufficiently compelling to inhibit foreign firms from risking their ability to capture such a lucrative consumer market and manufacturing base.

> I think basically companies have decided that it's better to be in China and get your technology stolen than to not be in China. That's basically what people have decided. Companies go into China with their eyes wide open. They're willing to put up with things in China they would never put up with in any other country of [sic] the world. Why? Because the dream, ever since the British started this whole thing several hundred years ago with thinking … if we could only sell a shirt to every person in China … everybody is afraid not to be a part of that dream.[10]

In some cases, this might mean the closure of a foreign firm's operations on some pretext. It may also take a more basic form of "flexing local governmental muscle" to force a foreign firm to go along with the wishes of its Chinese host. Or it may involve both. In either case, the power asymmetries between local governments and foreign firms are pronounced, and although it is impossible to be systematic in presenting such examples, the following instance of this second type is as representative as it is illustrative.

In the latter half of the 1990s, a foreign firm had signed a contract with local authorities in a town in Northwest China to build a high-tech factory (the "interior factory"), capable of producing two "families" of sophisticated industrial generators. This arrangement was undertaken as a joint venture between the foreign company and a local manufacturer, the Zhonghua Motor Factory. While this interior factory was being built, another factory was under construction in a commercial area (the "coastal factory") along China's eastern seaboard. This second factory was literally a "carbon copy" of the interior factory, all the way down to the minute details in the material specifications. Moreover, the coastal factory had actually begun operations while the interior factory was still under construction. Representatives from the coastal factory approached the foreign firm and said that they had established a "similar" facility and that they would like to establish a partnership with the foreign firm. If the latter refused, the coastal factory threatened to "dump" its generators on the domestic market at a third of the projected interior factory price and crowd the interior factory (and its foreign joint-venture partner) out of the market. As a result, the foreign firm had little choice but to abandon its nine million dollar investment in the interior factory, and entered into a forced partnership with the coastal factory.[11]

In addition to illustrating the power asymmetries between foreign firm and local government (both the "coastal" and "interior" factories enjoyed varying degrees of local governmental involvement), this example underscores the financial resources and the coordination abilities across broad geographic areas that some local governments have at their disposal.

It is somewhat more difficult to generalize about the notion of "will". It should be noted that while such "strong arm" tactics, as in the example above, characterized national-level contracting to foreign firms during the 1980s and early 1990s, they are far less the case today.[12] However, at the local level (the provincial level and below), such tactics remain the norm. It is therefore necessary to look at the incentives facing local leaders in China.

At the grassroots level, cadres are generalists, and must often choose from competing (and often conflicting) policy objectives to implement with the limited resources at their disposal. This decision is greatly simplified by the prioritization of these tasks by their administrative superiors. These priorities vary somewhat from region to region, but the most important of these almost invariably include economic development, tax extraction, the "alleviation of poverty", and the implementation of the "one-child policy" birth control program. They are institutionalized within performance indicators under the "cadre responsibility system" (*ganbu gangwei mubiao guanli zerenzhi*) and reinforced by the "one-level down management" supervision system (*xiaguan yiji*) (O'Brien and Li, 1999).[13] At higher levels, performance appraisals are far more complex, although it is ultimately the generalist officials in the government and Party organs that make the final decisions on local priorities and these overall priorities are largely the same as at the grassroots level. Moreover, in the absence of a concerted national campaign (with the corresponding extrabudgetary outlays) to shift these priorities in an alternate direction, they are unlikely to change.

"Intellectual property rights enforcement" is generally far too specific to make it onto local performance indicators. However, several of the most important of these indicators can be in direct *conflict* with intellectual property protection. The first three indicators listed above, generally deemed the most important, and which encompass the "general principles" of the top leadership, are often inconsistent in practice with effective intellectual property protection.[14] Insofar as IPR-infringing activities on the part of local factories, middlemen or retailers contribute to economic development, the alleviation of poverty, and the supply of tax revenue, a disincentive for intellectual property enforcement[15] is institutionalized into the priorities on which local officials' performance is appraised.[16] As one Party Vice-Secretary of Chongqing put it, "I believe that intellectual property and economic development are both important, but I consider economic development to be the more important of the two."[17]

When local priorities dovetail with those of foreign firms operating in those areas, these firms are unlikely to articulate dissatisfaction with local governments. When the goals of a foreign firm do come into conflict with the priorities of local officials, the former (in the absence of a TTD threat) are far more likely to raise the issue with higher-level governmental units in China, or directly through the Special 301 process. Because local governments have a strong preference to stay out of Beijing's crosshairs, and because of the possibility that Beijing could make an example of the local government in question, there is an extremely strong incentive for the latter to prevent such behavior on the part of the foreign firm. Implicit or explicit deterrent threats are almost always far less costly than the alternative.[18] Therefore, it is reasonable to claim that local Chinese leaders do, indeed, have the will – whether overt or latent – to deter foreign firms operating within their jurisdictions.

The transnational trade deterrent effect and impact on US trade policy

If the empirical puzzle of this chapter is to explain why the US copyright lobby was so aggressive (during the early 1990s – far less so now) while the trademark associations were so feeble in bringing their case to the USTR, how can TTD explain such variation? Much of the answer has to do with the fact that during the Sino-US negotiations over intellectual property, which spanned the period from 1991 to 1996, trademark-intensive firms had a physical presence on the ground while copyright-intensive ones did not. As a result, throughout the Special 301 process, trademark demands were muted and vague while copyright-related demands were aggressive and specific. The USTR had no alternative than to move forward on those issues for which it had credible information and to shelve (or at least focus less on) those for which it could not make a credible case. After all, insofar as the USTR relies on US firms to provide information on the basis of which it makes its international case against China (or any other country), its credibility is inextricably linked with the credibility of those firms providing the data to make its case. If the firm fails to provide adequate information because it is deterred from doing so, the USTR has no political choice but to table those demands until such information is available. The result was that the negotiations focused almost completely on the less problematic issue (at the time) of copyright protection than on the rampant counterfeiting that was draining US companies of hundreds of millions of dollars.

This is supported by the fact that that the copyright-intensive firms have become far less confrontational vis-à-vis their Chinese hosts, as evidenced by the quotation that began this chapter. And this has led to a far less confrontational strategy by the US today than that which framed US trade policy throughout the 1990s. Indeed, one can point to the fact that the US has been quite skittish in bringing an IPR case against China under the WTO. Although many in the government (and in business circles) are chomping at the bit to undertake such action, the US has been reluctant to do so for one important reason: it cannot bring a *case* for the WTO mediation if no company wants to go on record as being that case. Remarked former congressman Dave McCurdy, now the head of the Electronics Industry Alliance (EIA):

> It's not the failure of the WTO as an instrument … The question is, do you have evidence to bring a case that's credible so that you don't lose all of your international credibility in using this mechanism? It cannot be a political tool based on anecdotal information or a kind of broad-based sociological and general economic information. There has to be a clear case of failure to

comply with these rules. I will tell you that when we went through the process of building this document, we had a hard time. We had a lot of examples, but there was not one single company prepared to put their [sic] name on that document. Now, we gave this to the Chinese government, we're distributing this. Because there is the real potential for retaliation or retribution. It may not be direct; it may not be today. It may not be six months from now, but there is this long term fear.[19]

And the impact on the US negotiating position is no less dramatic:

When I worked for a multinational company, we also went to the US govern-ment and we said we would like you to bring this issue up with China, but please don't use our name. And that's what is going on here. Because the companies are screaming at the US government, but there's only so much in my opinion that can be done if the companies are not willing to take this, are not willing to do anything to offend the Chinese government. If the US government tries to negotiate with China and says to China you cannot retal-iate against these companies, nothing is going to happen. China is not going to agree to that.[20]

In other words, the US is not going to have a tenable bargaining position vis-à-vis Beijing without such credibility. Rather than show its empty hand under the spot-light of international scrutiny, the rational choice for the USTR is simply to jettison non-credible demands from its negotiation agenda (as it did throughout the 1991–1996 period) or to refrain from (or at least to demonstrate extreme reluctance in) bringing about a case against China in the first place, as is currently the case regarding the WTO action against China.

Conclusion

I have argued that China has been able to manipulate the substance of the agenda setting process through transnational trade deterrence. Variation within the agenda setting and ratification processes can be explained by the degree to which a given company or member of a trade association was in the direct line of fire of the TTD threat. Companies and trade associations that had credible information – names, places, dates, times, and so on of IPR violations they faced – were able to mobilize the USTR on their behalf as a result of the information they provided under Special 301. Those firms that were unable to provide such credible data were not taken seriously by the USTR and certainly not by Beijing. As a result, they were unable to mobilize the USTR on their behalf.

The irony is that those firms and associations that were losing the most, and who could make the most credible cases, were precisely those who were sidelined by the process. I have endeavored to account for this anomaly by arguing that these companies were deterred from taking effective action against China as a result of a threat that emanated not from Beijing as a coherent, concrete policy, but rather which arose from the political context of the physical location in which these firms were operating in China. The result was that this transnational trade deterrence was able to shape the US trade policy agenda by preventing those issues that were most troublesome for China from appearing in the first place.

The problem always is, how do you explain a *non*event? How do you explain something that did *not* occur? How do you account for the *lack of* items on a trade negotiating agenda? The off-the-record and rare public expressions of frustration are not enough to explain such an outcome, only to articulate the perception that something is going on behind the scenes. It is the purpose of this chapter to account for this nonevent by making the case that this behind-the-scenes activity is very real, very potent, and can be explained by an analytical framework – transnational trade deterrence – that may be all but invisible, but which keeps many US CEOs and government officials awake at night, and which has shaped and continues to shape US trade policy in ways that are as substantial as they are imperceptible.

Finally, it should be noted that the foregoing is not terribly stable. This is because reputation can also work against these same local governments. If local governments establish a reputation as being hostile to foreign firms under the rubric of TTD, they will lose out on the benefits of foreign investment. In addition, there is variation across local governments in terms of their calculations for attracting foreign investment and/or a foreign manufacturing presence. Arguably, areas in the interior are far more likely to be more accommodating – and less threatening – to foreign firms in their midst because of the relative value of a single or a small group of foreign firms or investors within their jurisdictions. In order to attract these firms and to keep them happy, these local governments seem to be less inclined to engage in TTD-type behavior. Indeed, these governments are likely to bend the laws and regulations in order to attract and accommodate these firms (the willingness of the Sichuan provincial government to do so in order to attract Intel is a case in point).[21] The flip side, however, is that if we make this claim, then it can be argued that it is in the more developed areas of China where TTD is likely to occur. This is because – to simplify greatly – local governments can pick and choose among those firms that can offer them the most benefit. If this is the case, then TTD, from the dimension of local government calculations, is likely to continue, possibly even expand.

Acknowledgements

I would like to thank Judith Goldstein, Barry Naughton and Ka Zeng for their insightful comments on earlier drafts of this chapter. In spite of their contributions, some errors may inevitably remain, for which I take full responsibility.

Notes

1   Interviews with Chinese trade official, Beijing, March and August, 1999.
2   Interview with former USTR official, December 1998.
3   Ibid.

4   CAFEI Quality Brands Protection Committee [QBPC] Pamphlet.
5   Interview with US beverage executive, Shanghai, 5 April 1999. This source mentioned that as far as investigative work is concerned, he outsources to private investigation firms in order to guarantee the safety of his staff, noting that in several instances investigators hired by his company were threatened and even physically assaulted.
6   Chow, written comments, 8 June 2006.
7   In this paper, I am implying that TTD does not stem from national policy. I am also assuming that the national government does not assist local governments in intimidating foreign firms. This does not mean that the national government does not really know what is going on. Rather, because it is easier to claim that the Chinese state acts with one voice, I am arguing that we can explain these trade outcomes by simply looking at the actions of local governments. This is not meant to let Beijing off the hook, but rather to underscore the complexity of the structures and processes that result in China's trade policy behavior. My focus on local governments, and my claim that Beijing is not directly involved, is meant to simplify my argument for the sake of clarity. However, what I am arguing is not at all inconsistent with the notion that Beijing may be fully aware of what is occurring locally.
8   Local officials are often fond of saying "above has its policies, below has its countermeasures" (*shang you zhengce, xia you duice*), much to the chagrin of national-level officials in Beijing. This dimension of state capacity was a frequent lament among national-level government interviewees.
9   Of course, one can argue that by issuing a deterrent threat, local leaders will simply force foreign firms to move their operations to a location in which local officials are less inclined to make such threats. However, this involves significant costs on the part of the foreign firm. Moreover, when combined with the uncertainty regarding the new government hosts' propensity to level such a threat once the relocation is consolidated, the benefits of such a move – when viewed against the associated transaction costs – may not be able to overcome the prohibitive costs. To a considerable degree, the foreign firm is at the mercy of the local host government, and not the other way around.
10 Chow, oral remarks, 8 June 2006.
11 It later came to light that the foreign firm's joint venture partner in building the interior factory, the government-owned Zhonghua Motor Company, was responsible for giving the original (and highly confidential) factory plans to the coastal factory because it was unable to pay for its technology transfer payments at the time, and the coastal factory offered Zhonghua generous partnership terms in return. The foreign firm had very little choice but to go along with the Chinese. Although the foreign firm had been advised that it could take the case to court, by the time any settlement could be reached, they would have already been pushed out of the local markets in both the coast and the interior (interview with IPR lawyer, Shanghai, 27 May 1998; and Interview with US company executive, 17 August 1998). Both sources insisted that, for their own protection, place and company names must be changed; I have honored their requests.
12 Interview with US auto-parts executive, Beijing, 9 July 1998.
13 Interview with Chinese scholar, Shanghai, 15 June 1998; and interview with private investigator, Shanghai, 16 June 1998.
14 Interview with private investigator, Shanghai, 16 June 1998.
15 The Xichang VCD wholesale market in Kunming is an important source of revenue for the Wuhua District Administration for Industry and Commerce (AIC) through the management fees (*guanli fei*). The Wuhua District AIC was, until recently, firmly under the control of the Wuhua District Government, and provided a considerable source of revenue (interview with provincial official, Kunming, 22 June 1999). As a result, it was able to engage in the widespread and open sales of pirated VCDs, with only cursory and largely ritualized raids twice a week (interview with vendors, Kunming, 23 June 1999).
16 As a result, some local authorities choreograph raids to demonstrate that they are doing something, often ensuring that the actual punishments are relatively benign. Another tactic is to delay the investigation until all (or most) of the product is moved out of the factory (interview with Chinese scholar, Shanghai, 15 June 1998).
17 Meeting with Chongqing Municipal Party Vice-Secretary, Chongqing, March 12 1998.

18   Even when foreign and local official interests converge, it may be useful to maintain some sort of deterrent signaling to forestall any potential future change in the status quo.
19   McCury, oral remarks, 8 June 2006.
20   Chow, oral remarks, 8 June 2006.
21   All the more so because included in the package was the offer that the Sichuan government would build the factory and all the physical aspects of the operations, making it easy for Intel to "exit" if they found local conditions to be sufficiently "inhospitable" after the fact (conversations with bankers in Chengdu, March 2003).

References

Betts, R. (1985) "Conventional deterrence: predictive uncertainty and policy confidence", *World Politics* 37: 164–79.

CAFEI Quality Brands Protection Committee [QBPC] Pamphlet.

Chow, D. (2006) Prepared statement for the hearing on China's Enforcement of Intellectual Property Rights and the dangers of the Movement of Counterfeited and Pirated Goods into the United States, US–China Economics and Security Review Commission, Washington, DC, 8 June 2006.

—— (2006) Oral remarks at the hearing on China's Enforcement of Intellectual Property Rights and the dangers of the Movement of Counterfeited and Pirated Goods into the United States, US–China Economics and Security Review Commission, Washington, DC, 8 June.

George, A. and Smoke, R. (1974) *Deterrence in American Foreign Policy: Theory and Practice*, New York: Columbia University Press.

Harvey, F. (1999) "Practicing coercion", *Journal of Conflict Resolution*, 43 (6): 840–71.

International Intellectual Property Alliance (2001) "2001 Special 301 Recommendation to the United States Trade Representative", 16 February.

Lampton, D. (ed.) (1987) *Policy Implementation in Post-Mao China*, Berkeley: University of California Press.

Lieberthal, K. (2003) *Governing China: From Revolution Through Reform*, 2nd edn, New York: Norton.

McCury, D. (2006) Oral remarks at hearing on China's Enforcement of Intellectual Property Rights and the dangers of the Movement of Counterfeited and Pirated Goods into the United States, US–China Economics and Security Review Commission, Washington, DC, 8 June 2006.

Mann, J. (1989) *Beijing Jeep: The Short, Unhappy Romance of American Business in China*, New York: Simon and Schuster.

Mertha, A. (2006) "'Policy enforcement market': how bureaucratic redundancy contributes to effective IPR policy implementation in China", *Comparative Politics*, 38 (3): 295–316.

Nalebuff, B. (1991) "Rational deterrence in an imperfect world", *World Politics* 43: 313–35.

O'Brien, K. and Li, L. (1999) "Selective policy implementation in rural China", *Comparative Politics* 31 (2): 167–86.

Odell, J. (1993) "International threats and internal politics: Brazil, the European Community, and the United States, 1985–1987", in Evans *et al.* (eds) *Double-Edged Diplomacy: International Bargaining and Domestic Politics*, Berkeley: University of California Press, 233–64.

Puckett, L. A. and Reynolds, W. (1996) "Rules, sanctions, and enforcement under Section 301: at odds with the WTO?" *American Journal of International Law* 90 (4): 675–89.

5 China's porous protectionism

The changing political economy of trade policy

Scott Kennedy

As China becomes more integrated into international economic institutions and markets, there is a growing awareness of the importance of external factors in shaping the regulatory structure, laws and policies governing its economy. Moreover, there is a consensus among observers (Moore, 2002: 34–58; Zweig, 2002: 1–22) that greater integration into the world trading and investment systems can be equated with further economic liberalization and that any lack of openness is due to entrenched domestic factors. China's entry into the World Trade Organization (WTO) is thus seen as pivotal in furthering this transformation.[1] Although such a close link between economic openness and participation in international economic institutions is largely accurate, the gap between how these organizations actually operate and a *fully* liberal economic order are increasingly important in explaining some protectionist elements of China's evolving trade regime. Conversely, economic integration has led to growing diversification of interests within China and to the emergence of non-state advocates of openness, tempering efforts at protection. The role of liberal business interests in China suggests a growing need to understand their place in trade policy, even in authoritarian regimes.

The new dynamics of China's trade policy can be best appreciated by considering its recent experience with the rules of the WTO that permit member countries to enact tariffs or other barriers to counter unfair practices of their trading partners. Between March 1997, when China adopted its first antidumping (AD) statute, and the end of 2005, Beijing launched investigations into cases of 42 products involving 136 countries in which foreign companies were accused of injuring Chinese industry by exporting their products to China at prices below normal value (see Table 5.1 and Appendix 5.1). Since 2003, China has been the third most frequent initiator of AD charges, trailing only India and the United States. In May 2002, China also invoked safeguard measures to counter what it claimed were dramatic and unexpected surges in steel imports.

However, such tools have encountered numerous obstacles in China. The foreign respondents have won a partial or complete victory in over 48 percent of all concluded AD cases. Moreover, the average duties leveled against those found guilty of dumping are low compared to such penalties levied in cases carried out by other WTO members, including the United States and the European Union (EU).

Although foreign respondents do not win a majority of the cases, their victories

Table 5.1 China's antidumping targets

Region	Number of cases
South Korea	27
Japan	26
United States	22
EU (or member)	21
Taiwan	10
Russia	9
Others (11 countries)	21

are nevertheless impressive and surprising. Why have the domestic Chinese applicants seeking protection from their own government not won more consistently? Antidumping cases are administrative proceedings adjudicated in the applicant's country, not the respondent's. To borrow a sports analogy, the domestic applicants not only have home court advantage, the referees are on their team. Despite such a favorable setting, applicants occasionally steal defeat from the jaws of victory. How is that possible?

The most common explanations for China's openness focus on officialdom. Numerous scholars stress that China's increasing openness has been due to the stewardship of reformist leaders, who have managed to keep the upper hand over other leaders less committed to openness and local interests who oppose such moves (Jacobson and Oksenberg, 1990; Shirk, 1994; Fewsmith, 2001: 204–217). Another version of the élite-centered perspective could stress that even if China's leaders prefer that Chinese applicants win every case, in order to avoid costly reprisals or trade wars that would harm China's national interest, they occasionally order rulings on behalf of foreign defendants. A second set of explanations would shift attention to how the growing rule of law has made the bureaucracy and courts behave more as neutral arbiters rather than as biased advocates. As such, China's government is seen as increasingly composed of a corps of well-trained, politically protected professionals that decide cases on their merits (Peerenboom, 2001; Yang, 2004). Where dumping exists, duties are appropriately instituted; where the respondents have demonstrated that the charges are baseless, no penalties are exacted from the foreign exporters. A final prominent reason (e.g. Pearson, 1999; 2001) given for China's greater openness – which could translate into rulings on behalf of foreign respondents – is that through extensive participation in the GATT and WTO, China's leaders and trade officials have undergone fundamental "learning" and internalized the free-trade norms of the global trading system. The "learning" explanation does differ from the above rationales by showing that officials' values can be shaped by external forces; however, even those observers who stress the international transmission of beliefs focus on political élites and bureaucrats as the most important recipients of these ideas and concur that China's national policy-making process is dominated by officialdom.[2]

As helpful as these explanations are at highlighting some general trends in China's trade policy, they are less useful when analyzing discrete trade disputes. China's élites may establish general policy parameters, but they rarely become directly involved in individual cases. And although the national bureaucracy is being streamlined and outfitted with better procedures, there is still evidence that the decisions of officials and judges are affected by their location in the bureaucracy and their desire for self-aggrandizement, and not an impartial reading of facts. And finally, although most aspects of the global trade system promote liberalism, as will be detailed below, the antidumping regime does not; the more Chinese officials absorb its norms, the more likely they are to favor domestic over foreign industry.

The puzzling victories by foreign respondents are better explained by China's integration into the global economy. Interviews in China and the United States with the various parties to antidumping cases reveal that uneven participation in international supply chains has divided elements of the government and industry into competing camps, with some favoring protection and others preferring lower barriers.[3] The relative power of both sides in specific cases, filtered through the prisms of China's AD rules, explains why in some cases penalties are instituted, and why in others the foreign respondents (and their domestic Chinese allies) come away unscathed. This explanation is similar in character to the findings that international market structures and complaints by domestic non-state interests have created external and bottom-up pressure, respectively, that has resulted in more liberal Chinese policies (Moore, 2002; Zweig, 2002). However, the argument presented here goes further by stressing the *direct* involvement of industry, Chinese and foreign, in the national economic policy process, a practice that increasingly occurs across many issue areas.[4]

The story of China's antidumping regime strengthens the position found in the broader international political economy literature that industry interests can be crucial in defending liberal trade policies. Some scholars (e.g. Haggard and Kaufman, 1992; Goldstein, 1993; Destler, 1995; Biglaiser, 2002) have held that because interests in favor of protection are better organized and more influential than those favoring openness, liberalization must be explained by the intervention of political élites, well-crafted political institutions that limit the influence of protectionists, and/or the spread of liberal ideology. Others (e.g. Milner, 1988; Rogowski, 1989; Frieden, 1991) though, have deftly shown that those in favor of openness can be equally proactive in defending their interests. This chapter builds on the latter perspective in several ways. First, it highlights the extent to which firms' location in global production networks shapes their policy preferences and leads elements of both domestic and foreign industry, occasionally in concert, to lobby for liberal outcomes. Second, although previous research (Hansen and Prusa, 1997; Tharakan and Waelbroeck, 1994) on the US and EU antidumping regimes only found political influence by protectionist interests, this may be because those studies did not incorporate the potential role of foreign industry and their downstream domestic partners into their models. Hence, this paper draws attention to an under-appreciated dynamic of the antidumping regime itself.

Lobbying may partly explain why those seeking protection win, but it also may explain why they lose. And third, because China is an authoritarian state with a large state-owned sector and where organized policy advocacy is not expressly encouraged, its recent experience demonstrates the need to understand the role that business has in trade policy formation in a wide variety of political settings.

To appreciate the role of competing non-state interests in trade disputes, the chapter begins by explaining the process by which China entered the antidumping game in the first place. This involves articulating the motivations the Chinese had to adopt an AD regime, the steps they took to learn and institute the regime, and the rules and procedures that define the competition. This is a prerequisite to the central focus of the paper, explaining the varying outcomes of cases by pinpointing the relevant economic and political factors at work. The argument is clarified by comparing several cases that had different outcomes. The discussion concludes by considering the implications of this new appreciation of the forces shaping trade policy.

China's move from protectionism to fair trade

Although China's entry into and full compliance with the WTO is consistently portrayed by the Western media and politicians as an abandonment of protectionism, the WTO routinely permits members to protect domestic industry in a limited number of circumstances and by certain methods. The underlying norm, what John Ruggie (1991) has aptly termed, "embedded liberalism", encourages states to liberalize their economies, but it also permits them to adopt countermeasures to soften the blow to domestic labor and business interests. Antidumping is among a group of internationally approved safety valves used to defend against purportedly unfair trade practices, such as dumping and subsidies.

The primary force motivating China to adopt an AD regime is the same one that pushed other developed and developing countries alike along the same path: the reduction of tariffs and other traditional non-tariff barriers.[5] The world's first AD law was adopted by Canada in 1904, but until the late 1960s the AD tool was rarely used. Only after advanced capitalist countries had sharply reduced their own trade barriers and began to feel competitive pressures from each other and Japan, did they begin to regularly employ this long-dormant weapon. In the 1970s, as developing countries liberalized their economies, they too began to use the same fair-trade tool. These countries tired of simply being the targets of what they perceived to be the over-aggressive use of the AD weapon by their industrialized counterparts. AD has gone from a tool monopolized by a few developed countries to an equal opportunity weapon used by countries rich and poor alike.[6] The most significant exception to this trend is Japan. Although the leading object of AD investigations in the 1980s, Japan's government has opted not to employ AD measures itself in order to avoid further criticism of its trade regime by the US and Western Europe and in the hope that the AD code would be reformed or eliminated.[7]

China's route to AD fits the general pattern. The Mao-era policy of autarky gave way to a highly managed trading regime in the 1970s and 1980s. During the 1990s,

Table 5.2   Antidumping investigations initiated against China, by importing country, 1995–2005

Rank	Country	Cases	Percentage of total
1	India	86	18.3
2	United States	61	13.0
3	EU	60	12.8
4	Argentina	47	10.0
5	Turkey	38	8.1
6	South Africa	25	5.3
7	Australia	21	4.5
8	Peru	17	3.6
9	Canada	17	3.6
10	Republic of Korea	16	3.4

Source: WTO Anti-Dumping Database, available online: www.wto.org

as part of the effort to promote growth and gain membership in the GATT/WTO, the old system was gradually dismantled, and it was buried for good upon China's entry into WTO in late 2001.[8] As China discarded its traditional trade barriers, the question became what, if anything, could China do to shelter domestic producers from foreign competition upon accession. Although most have focused on the obligations China must meet to be a WTO member, early in the application process, China began to stress that membership also carried with it certain rights.[9]

A sense of urgency to defend their rights existed because of how often China itself had been an object of AD investigations by other countries. From 1979 to 2005, China's trade partners investigated Chinese firms in over 700 cases. Between 1995 and 2005, Chinese companies were hit with dumping tariffs almost 340 times.[10] Although the United States and the EU were the primary instigators of cases in the 1980s, as Table 5.2 shows, India has leapt to the front.

These cases jarred the Chinese into recognizing that the world trade order was not a purely free one. Chinese officials and enterprise heads were particularly upset that China had been treated as a non-market economy when investigated. The United States, the EU and others argued that the Chinese government set prices and provided subsidies to industry, allowing the Chinese to sell goods abroad at lower prices than otherwise would be possible. In such circumstances, GATT/WTO rules allow investigating countries to ignore the price of the good in the Chinese market and use a surrogate country to determine normal market value against which the actual export price is compared. In short, the US and others were seen as hypocrites who discriminated against China.[11]

This experience also taught China that challenging dumping accusations pays off. Prior to 1994, Chinese firms never responded to investigators' notices and requests for information (Chang, 2003). From 1987 to 2002, Chinese firms escaped penalties in only 25 percent of cases, but beginning in the late 1990s, they achieved some notable victories in cases they proactively challenged.[12] Winning marginally reduced the sense that the trading rules are invariably rigged against China and demonstrated the value of learning the complicated AD system as both a defensive necessity and an offensive tactic. A Chinese trade lawyer spoke for many when he said that because the United States uses AD to protect its producers against the Chinese, "We're going to learn how to use the same weapon."[13]

Adequately motivated, the next step was for the Chinese to become proficient at using what is an extremely complicated regime that requires economic, business and legal expertise that was in short supply in China. Beginning in the late 1980s, a community gradually emerged composed of international trade specialists, lawyers and trade officials, who became committed to the notion that within the context of liberalization, China should use internationally authorized legal means, including AD, to protect domestic industry. Early proponents of this approach emerged at the University of International Business and Economics (UIBE) among professors and graduate students in international trade law. Two of the most influential have been Zhou Shijian and Wang Xuehua. In 1997, Zhou became vice-president of the China Chamber of Commerce of Metals, Minerals and Chemicals Importers and Exporters, where he has spearheaded those industries' responses to AD cases abroad. Wang and a colleague opened their own private law firm in 1993. The two later parted ways, and since then Wang has become the country's most prominent advocate for initiating AD cases against foreign firms exporting to China. As part of his effort to raise legal awareness and, not coincidentally, attract business, Wang has lectured on AD before numerous national and local government agencies, universities, research institutes and companies (Interview D3; Wang and Yong, 2000; Wang and Yiwei, 2002b).

Critical to the domestic community's growth has been its interaction and integration with the AD regime's global legal and bureaucratic leadership.[14] Several international law firms with offices in China have active AD practices, most often representing the foreign companies accused of dumping in China. Because these foreign law firms have not been allowed to participate in hearings (or in court), they work in conjunction with local firms. Foreign firms also have hired and trained Chinese lawyers, many of whom are especially useful because of their contacts with government officials. In addition, since the mid-1990s, just like Wang Xuehua, foreign lawyers have held seminars and given lectures to officials, lawyers and companies across the country (Interviews #D7, #D12). On top of these efforts, the WTO Secretariat has been quite active in teaching developing countries about the global AD regime. Its Rules Division has led dozens of training seminars around the world, including in Beijing and Geneva, and it has provided AD law templates to member countries (Interview #D18). It is through such cooperation that Chinese lawyers have been exposed to international "best practices". Once trained themselves, trade officials have gone on to host training programs for officials in other ministries, local governments, industry associations and enterprises (Interviews #D10, #D27). Such direct communication has been supplemented by a rich assortment of books and articles (Chen, 2002; Han, 2002; He,

2002; Liu, 2001). The result of these efforts has been the emergence of a group of specialists and a growing awareness among local industry of both China's responsibilities and rights as a WTO member.

China's antidumping code: adopting "best practices"

Motivated by the need to compensate for reduced barriers and led by a community of officials, lawyers and industry representatives, China has adopted rules and procedures that are largely consistent with the requirements of the WTO. What makes China's AD regime appear protectionist is not how much it diverges from, but rather how closely it approaches international "best practices." This can be seen by examining the principles and specific rules that define dumping and provide the guidelines for determining if dumping has occurred, and the institutions and procedures by which cases are handled.

Consistent with global practice, China does not define dumping as selling below cost in an effort to eliminate competitors. Although such behavior, known as predatory pricing, embodied the original conception that dumping was part of an effort to gain a monopoly, it is extremely difficult to prove (Mastel, 1998; Krishna, 1997; Finger, 1993). Thus, in the 1910s, dumping was redefined as price discrimination, in which exporters sell a product abroad at a price below what it sells for in the home market, what is known as "normal value." Dumping is deemed unfair because this behavior, it is argued, can only occur when the exporters operate in a sheltered home market in which the government institutes high trade barriers, provides subsidies, or permits cartels. Firms can then sell their products abroad more cheaply than would be the case in a competitive market, and thus, the perpetrators take away customers (and profits) from competitors in the destination market.[15] If competitors in the importing country can demonstrate that they have been injured by dumping, then their government is within its rights to institute a tariff against the exporting firms equal to the "dumping margin", that is, the gap between the product's actual export price and its proper normal value. Thus, the underlying principle of AD law shifted from opposing monopolies to opposing unfair trade practices, and the standard of proof shifted from demonstrating intent (predation) to showing the consequences (injuring domestic producers).

China has inherited not only the global regime's basic principles but also its more detailed rules and procedures. China's first AD statute, adopted in 1997, was partially consistent with GATT/WTO guidelines but was quite vague in many areas (Ross and Ning, 2000). The regulation was substantially revised in November 2001, just prior to China's WTO entry; multiple implementing rules were issued in 2002, and a modestly revised version of the statute was issued in 2004. The revised AD statutes closely follow the WTO's Antidumping Agreement, even verbatim in some instances.[16]

Thus, China's regime has incorporated changes in the global rules adopted over the past thirty years that have eased, not tightened, the standards necessary to prove that foreigners have dumped goods and that such actions significantly injured domestic producers. Proving dumping originally involved making a direct comparison of a good's export price and its home-market price based on detailed information provided by the accused exporters. With the statutory changes, when the home market price is too difficult to determine or unreliable, investigators can estimate it in a variety of ways, such as estimating the cost of production (plus a profit margin) or using actual or estimated prices of the good from a third country. The standard in China for proving injury, like the global AD regime, involves merely showing the dumping is just one of the causes of domestic industry's plight. In practice, investigators the world over have only had to find the coexistence of dumping and poorly performing domestic companies to prove causation between the two (Prusa and Skeath, 2001; Messerlin and Reed, 1995). Moreover, under pressure from import-competing industries, the United States and others made sure that GATT and WTO rules do not require that the damage to other domestic interests (such as downstream users or consumers) of raised tariffs be considered by investigators when determining whether or not to find in favor of the accusers. Such a "public interest" provision, which is not in Chinese law, has only been adopted by a few countries.[17] These rules, in China and elsewhere, tilt the scales strongly in the accusers' favor, leaving many to believe that the antidumping system that purports to stop unfair trade is itself inescapably biased (Lindsey and Ikenson, 2003).

China's antidumping procedures: new roles for state and society

Because of the potential benefits to domestic industry, it is not surprising that China has adopted the principles and rules of the global AD regime. Less expected, though, is the extent to which the government has been willing to modify the process by which trade disputes and policy are handled. These changes are inconsistent with perspectives that stress either a dominant role for élites or an autonomous bureaucracy that strictly follows the law. Non-state actors are central to the entire process.

In the past, foreign economic policy was strictly a government concern. Trade and investment authorities, in consultation with other ministries and the senior political élite, determined which sectors and products to protect and by what means. Those decisions were not open to systematic influence from Chinese enterprises, let alone from foreign industry. In the case of fair trade disputes, by contrast, the government acts in response to complaints lodged by domestic industry. The Chinese government's role has switched from that of advocate to that of arbiter; even if it prefers to play advocate, it must at least maintain the pretense of being even-handed. The division of labor within the government in China also mirrors that of other WTO members. Once the authorities accept a case, they launch investigations into whether there has been dumping and whether the dumping caused the injury claimed by the applicants. China copied the American system in having these two elements of the case investigated by separate agencies. The Ministry of Foreign Trade and Economic Cooperation (MOFTEC) Fair Trade Bureau for Imports and Exports has investigated dumping, while the State Economic and Trade Commission (SETC) Industry Injury Investigation Bureau has examined the injury claim. Although these bureaus were placed under the new Ministry of Commerce in March 2003, their respective responsibilities have remained the same.

As the role of government has shifted, that of the "interested parties" – the accusing domestic applicants and the accused foreign respondents – has grown. Domestic companies threatened by imports are assisted in their claims by legal counsel. While industry often seeks legal aid after feeling the effects of dumping, lawyers also alert industry to such behavior. Following the example of some foreign firms, Wang Xuehua's Huanzhong Law Firm operates as the international trade law equivalent of an "ambulance chaser", tracking industries and initiating contact with potential clients. Wang's firm has represented the domestic applicants in a majority of the AD cases in China.[18] Chinese trade associations have become involved as well. They have helped their members initiate cases, have initiated cases themselves, and have participated in investigations.[19] And like associations elsewhere, several have established monitoring systems to track the prices and market shares of domestic and foreign firms (Han, J., 2001; Han, Q., 2002; Yu, 2002; China Petrochemical News, 2003). On the other side, the foreign firms accused of dumping and their representatives also are institutionally included in the process. And although their direct interests are not required to be considered, the downstream users of the imported goods, who in principle are allies of the foreign companies, are often involved in the cases as well. The last notable aspect regarding the participants is how China has modified its definition of "domestic" and "foreign" industry to be consistent with WTO requirements. Since the law aims to protect firms that produce within China's borders, foreign-invested companies, even wholly foreign-owned enterprises, can apply for relief, a request that has been granted in several cases.

The process by which cases are adjudicated also differs from that of the past. The Fair Trade Bureau uses questionnaires, onsite investigations and formal hearings with the interested parties to determine if dumping has occurred. The Industry Injury Investigation Bureau relies on interested parties' written submissions, hearings and informal meetings to determine whether the dumping has injured domestic industry. If both bureaus find on behalf of the applicants, preliminary dumping tariffs are announced. Further information is collected, allowing applicants and respondents to elaborate their positions before a final determination is issued. Both the preliminary and final rulings are required to spell out the reasoning of the decision.[20]

In its earliest cases, the Fair Trade Bureau and Industry Injury Investigation Bureau cut many corners in their investigations and did not provide sufficient explanations for their determinations. Almost without exception, observers interviewed for this study agree that the various aspects of investigations increasingly conform to WTO rules. Such progress reflects both a process of learning by doing and the approaching requirement to adhere to the WTO Anti-dumping Agreement. The questionnaires are clearer, and hearings, originally not well run, have improved. In an early Fair Trade Bureau hearing on dumping, much of the discussion focused on injury, even though that is an issue only the Industry Injury Investigation Bureau (then under the SETC) is supposed to investigate. At an early SETC hearing, a company not party to the case was allowed to attend and make remarks, despite violating standard international procedures by doing so. Over time, hearings have become better structured, with more opportunity for both sides to present their positions. In the injury hearings, in particular, the official panelists pepper both the applicants and respondents with questions. The Fair Trade Bureau has become more open to using pricing information and arguments from respondents; its dumping determinations have gone from stating only their findings to including detailed justifications of how the dumping margins were calculated. And finally, investigators increasingly abide by time requirements concerning the period between domestic industry's application and their decision of whether to accept the case, and the length of the investigation itself. Despite some continuing problems, China's antidumping system increasingly looks and operates like those in advanced industrialized countries.[21]

Determining winners and losers

Reviewing why the Chinese government adopted antidumping into its trade regime and how the system operates in China provides the necessary foundation for analyzing the factors that determine the outcome of specific cases. Despite the existence of an authoritarian state with a well-deserved reputation for aiding domestic industry at the expense of foreign interests, domestic applicants' success rate (the proportion of cases in which they win relief) is far from 100 percent. As Table 5.3 shows, China has a higher success rate than most countries, but some other long-standing WTO members have even higher rates. In addition, the way the WTO calculates success rates (at the country level) masks instances in which individual foreign companies are not found guilty, even when others from their country are, or when their products have been exempted from AD duties, outcomes which have occurred several times in China. If one tallies outcomes by product (more than one country is typically investigated in any given product case), in only 18 of 35 concluded cases has the decision been entirely in the applicants' favor (see Appendix 5.1). Moreover, the average penalty China invokes against foreign dumpers is much lower than most countries (see Table 5.4).

Previous research on other countries' AD regimes suggests that case outcomes are affected by three factors: the specific AD rules, the nature of the government institutions that adjudicate cases, and pressure from industry interests. From 1955 to 1968, the success rate of cases in the United States was only 3.2 percent. Following the adoption of more lax standards for determining dumping and injury, the success rate jumped to over 50 percent during 1980–1993.[22] Because their expected missions and autonomy from outside pressures vary, which institutions are responsible for adjudicating AD disputes also can affect case outcomes. After responsibility for determining the dumping part of an applicant's claim in the United States shifted from the Treasury Department to the Commerce Department (DOC) in 1979, claims found a more sympathetic ear, with the DOC finding

Table 5.3 Success rate of major initiators of antidumping cases, 1995–2001

Rank	Country*	Success rate (%)
1	India	95.5
2	Egypt	89.3
3	Turkey	79.2
4	Venezuela	75.9
5	China	75.8
6	Mexico	73.9
7	South Africa	73.3
8	United States	66.2
9	Republic of Korea	65.9
10	Canada	64.7
11	EU	61.8
12	Argentina	61.5
13	Colombia	58.8
14	Peru	58.1
15	Brazil	55.3
16	Indonesia	45.2
17	Australia	29.5
18	New Zealand	29.4

* Includes only countries that initiated at least 20 cases during the period

Sources: Compiled from the WTO members' reports of their dumping activity, available in the WTO Anti-Dumping Database, and the Ministry of Trade Remedy Information website: www.cacs.gov.cn

dumping in 95 percent of applications. By contrast, in Australia the government created an independent Anti-Dumping Authority in the late 1980s to act as a check against the more pro-domestic industry slant of the Customs Service. The independent office was eliminated in 1998, and since then, Australia's success rate has almost doubled (Feaver and Wilson, 1995; Whitwell, 1997; Australian Financial Review, 2000; WTO Anti-Dumping Database).

Despite the technical features of AD, industry lobbying has also played a major role in determining case outcomes. In the United States, companies with a large number of employees and with production facilities in districts with a member on the House Ways and Means Subcommittee on Trade have the greatest chance of winning their cases, as do those who give greater campaign contributions to those members. The trade subcommittee members can bring pressure to bear on the DOC and International Trade Commission through the holding of hearings, by adjusting the agencies' funding, and by back-room lobbying (Hansen and Prusa, 1997; Hansen, 1990; Mundo, 1999). In the European Union, industries concentrated in a

Table 5.4 Average antidumping tariffs of major initiators, 1995–99*

Rank	Country	Tariff (%)
1	Argentina	84.8
2	Australia	59.3
3	Mexico	59.1
4	Brazil	53.2
5	United States	47.6
6	South Africa	45.2
7	Canada	44.7
8	China	31.1
9	Reputlic of Korea	28.9
10	EU	27.7
11	Turkey	10.6

*Non-China data are based on cases initiated 1995–99; China data are from cases initiated 1997–2001. Data for India and some others in Table 5.3 are not available.

Source: Non-China data: Arnold (2001:70); China data: Ministry of Commerce, WTO and media reports

certain region or dominated by a few companies win more often than less-concentrated ones. In addition, the members of the EU's Council of Ministers, which makes the final rulings, regularly engage in horse-trading on cases at the behest of business interests from their respective countries (Tharakan and Waelbroeck, 1994; Interview #D19). But not only do protectionist interests pressure governments, the foreign respondents and their domestic allies – importers, downstream users, and consumer groups – make their voices heard as well. In the United States, downstream users of steel, semiconductors and other inputs have successfully lobbied to have trade penalties lowered or shortened (Destler, 1995: 195–6; Mundo, 1999: 266).

Similar pressures exist in China and are more important in determining the outcome of cases than reformist political élites or bureaucrats acting on their own accord to defend their interests or impartially implement the rules. It is unclear how China's AD statutes affect the success rate, because the rules apply across cases and are similar to those in other countries. And since the success rate has not changed appreciably since the Ministry of Commerce took over adjudication of cases, the bureaucratic structure does not appear to independently affect cases.

The impact of competing interest-group pressures in China, on the other hand, is quite visible. Interested parties' ability to influence whether their cases are investigated and the case outcomes are determined by their economic circumstances and their political clout.

The vast majority of cases investigated to date have involved chemical and steel products. Both industries are highly concentrated relative to other sectors in China.

Because the AD rules require that applicants control at least 25 percent of the domestic market, high concentration makes it easier for firms in these industries to meet this threshold and coordinate the submission of a petition. Equally important, these industries are relatively less integrated into international production and sales networks than most industries; they are involved in relatively few joint ventures, and they primarily produce for the domestic market.[23] Thus, chemical and steel firms generally see imports as anathema to their interests. And because they are large and state-owned, the most important firms in these industries have significant political influence at the local, and sometimes national, level. Hence, when they complain, the government is more likely to respond with help. Given the usual applicants, respondents face an uphill fight in defending themselves.

Despite rules which favor domestic producers and the economic and political weight of many of the domestic firms that apply for protection, foreign respondents have achieved partial or complete victories in more cases than one might expect. The key to explaining this puzzle is to recognize that foreign exporters may be economically and politically powerful themselves, and even more important, they have important allies – the Chinese industries that buy and use their products. When the Chinese importers and downstream users of their goods come to their defense, foreign respondents have a strong chance of winning their case. This is despite the fact that China's AD regulations have not officially recognized the interests of these groups as a legitimate concern. In cases where they have pressed their views before the Chinese government, respondents have never been fully defeated.

Three conditions determine whether the natural economic allies of the foreign respondents become involved in a case. The first is how important the imported product is to its domestic users. When there are not very good domestic substitutes for the imported product and quality is critical (for example, when using the imported good as an input for another good that is to be exported), the interest of downstream users in the AD case rises. Second, if downstream users are large, and thus important economically and politically, they are more able to influence the outcome of cases. And third, a downstream user that has a bureaucratic representative who can assert his opinion into a case is more likely to have its interests taken into consideration.

Blowing home court advantage

The integration of Chinese industries into global supply networks has divided Chinese into competing camps, alternatively aligned against and allied with foreign business. The relative strength of each side and their relative access to the deliberation process directly affect the outcome of antidumping disputes. To demonstrate how these dynamics operate, what follows is a description of three cases that had different outcomes due to the varying involvement of the Chinese allies of the foreign respondents.

Newsprint

In China's first antidumping case, launched in November 1997, domestic news-print producers accused Canadian, South Korean and American firms of selling newsprint in China at far below normal value, leading to a surge in imports that left domestic producers in terrible financial difficulty. Although little evidence was presented to demonstrate that the applicants were injured by dumping, they still won a complete victory in the case (Gao, 1999; Almstedt and Norton, 2000). And although they may have been justified in their claims, equally importantly, the foreign respondents were unable to persuade the importers of their products to speak up. That was unlikely because newsprint of similar quality could be provided easily by producers in China. Moreover, even if their costs rose, that did not matter much since the state-owned newspapers that used newsprint had very soft budget constraints. Hence, switching suppliers mattered little, regardless of the cost. In addition, although some of the end-users, such as the *People's Daily*, were big and politically relevant, they were organizations that typically followed orders. And these producers had no obvious bureaucratic ally who would come to their defense. These factors all conclusively worked to the domestic applicants' favor and against the interests of the foreign respondents (Interviews #D9, #D15).

Stainless steel

By contrast, Japanese and South Korean stainless steel producers achieved a partial victory in a case initiated in June 1999. That seemed unlikely at the outset because the applicants were three important steel producers (Taiyuan Steel, Shaanxi Precision Steel, and Pudong Specialty Steel), and Pudong Steel had just been merged into Baoshan Iron & Steel (Baogang), China's most advanced and politically influential steel manufacturer. Despite being the world's largest producer of steel, in the 1990s China became a large importer of high-quality stainless steel that its firms could not produce themselves. It was, therefore, in the domestic applicants' interest to lock foreign firms out of the market while they developed a greater independent capability in this area. Behind the scenes the applicants and Baogang lobbied hard for an affirmative ruling, which they won. Several Japanese respondents paid AD duties, while one Japanese and six South Korean firms agreed to a price undertaking in which they raised the prices of their goods an amount equal to the dumping margin.

Despite the apparent ruling in favor of the applicants, the respondents won a partial victory. Many of their goods were granted exemptions from the penalties, and any of the goods they sold to duty-free zones in China were exempted from having to pay any tariff, standard or AD. The compromise was reached because the respondents persuaded their Chinese customers to submit briefs to MOFTEC and the SETC in their defense. They argued that the domestic stainless steel producers did not produce precisely the same goods as the foreigners (the width and quality of the steel sheets were different) and that the imported goods were critical to the final products, which were to be exported. In addition to the vital role of these products to their businesses, the end-users that complained were famous large home appliance and auto manufacturers that could gain the ear of senior trade officials and could also mobilize local and national officials to carry their banner. Multiple industry and government interview sources report that MOFTEC and the SETC, feeling pressure from both sides, decided to split the difference (Norton and Almstedt, 2000; Interviews ##D7, #D12, #D21, #D48, #D51). Since the ruling, stainless steel imports have risen significantly (Steel Business Briefing, 2003).

Lysine

Three producers of the chemical lysine, an amino acid often added to animal feed, brought a case against American, South Korean and Indonesian producers in June 2001. One of the three applicants was a typical state-owned enterprise seeking import protection; the other two were joint ventures hoping to lock out of the Chinese market their foreign rivals who had not invested in the People's Republic of China.[24] After an eighteen-month investigation, the government determined that the three respondents had dumped their products in China but that the sales did not injure domestic lysine producers. So the case was dismissed.

The foreign respondents benefited from three circumstances. First, the trade association to which the domestic applicants seeking relief belonged, the China Feed Association, had members that both produced lysine and others that used lysine in their products, most importantly, animal feed. At a hearing held in January 2002, the China Feed Association presented evidence on behalf of its downstream members. One such member is the Hope Group, one of China's largest private feed producers, whose president is also a member of the National People's Congress. An interview source suggests that the Hope Group persuaded the Feed Association to take its side, deflating the arguments of the applicants.

Second, the Ministry of Agriculture weighed in on the side of the respondents as well, arguing that a victory for the applicants would result in a rise in the price of animal feed, the brunt of which would be borne by China's farmers. Besides having a vested interest in the stake of farmers, the Ministry of Agriculture was allowed to contribute its opinion because Article 7 of China's AD regulations states that in any case involving agricultural products, the Ministry of Agriculture must be consulted. Hence, while some of the downstream users of the respondents' products (feed producers) were large and influential, the respondents also benefited from a situation in which farmers, fragmented and likely unaware of the case, had a bureaucratic patron that the law specified should defend their interests (Huanzhong Law Firm, 2003; Interviews #D11, #D17, #D27).

Third, the clout of the foreign respondents, while it likely did not affect the case's ultimate ruling, did impact the timing of the verdict. The three foreign companies were some of the largest chemical producers in the world – Germany's BASF, Samsung from South Korea, and the American firm Archer Daniels Midland.[25] They dwarfed the Chinese applicant as well as the foreign-invested companies that were trying to keep them out of the market. Most importantly, BASF is one of the largest foreign investors in China. The decision in June 2002 to delay making a final verdict was made just as BASF was set to announce a new multi-billion-dollar joint venture in Jiangsu province. And the final judgement in favor of the foreign producers was issued in late September 2002, just prior to the thirtieth anniversary of the establishment of German–Chinese diplomatic relations. Although several sources, including government officials who were involved in the decision, agree that the lobbying of the Ministry of Agriculture on behalf of farmers was the determining factor that resulted in the case being dismissed, BASF's importance to the Chinese economy certainly did not hurt its case and provided the opportunity for a quiet diplomatic gesture.[26]

Although the effect of downstream users was felt in earlier cases, according to government and industry sources, the lysine case was a watershed. Despite the lack of an explicit public-interest provision in China's AD statute, trade officials at that point informally decided that they would follow the European Union's example of carefully weighing the interests of downstream users and consumers before making a decision in all future cases. This practice has angered applicants and their lawyers, because it both violated Chinese law and is detrimental to their desire for protection. In defiance of such complaints, considering all sides' preferences has become standard procedure. In fact, to the chagrin of those seeking protection, China's revised AD statute, issued in early 2004, includes a new public interest provision (Article 37), making what was once implicit now explicit.

Conclusions

One of the most ubiquitous phrases spoken by Chinese from all walks of life over the past decade is the admonition for China to *"yu guoji jiegui"*, or "get on the international track". Its invocation is a call for China to adopt global best practices in corporate business behavior, economic regulation, foreign policy, the political process and even personal relationships. And in almost every instance, the implication is that following foreign practice will make Chinese society more efficient, liberal, open, prosperous and safe. Although this is often accurate, many foreign "best practices" do not live up to that image. The global AD code is one such area. Full integration into the global trade system is not equivalent to complete liberalization. Seen in this light, the well-worn popular phrase deserves to be reinterpreted.

The normative bias of the individual Chinese is mirrored in the literature about learning in foreign policy (Levy, 1994). With regard to China, besides economic liberalization, research (Economy and Oksenberg, 1999: Economy, 2001; Johnston, 1996; Guthrie, 1999) has focused on the transfer of Western corporate governance practices, environmentalism, human rights norms and liberal arms control regimes. But just as the Chinese have learned about embedded liberalism and a new style of protectionism rooted in the principle of fairness and dressed in the garb of the rule of law and complicated technical calculations, so too have they been exposed to, internalized, and drawn upon foreign behaviors which contradict "reformist" tendencies in other areas. The Chinese have learned about cartels as a tool to prop up prices, a sustainable development paradigm which stresses protecting the environment only in the broader context of promoting rapid growth, and the legitimacy of possessing and using nuclear weapons in certain contexts (Kennedy, 2003; Jahiel, 2003). The learning of such behaviors may not represent a complete break with their own past, but the education has provided new vocabulary, rationale, tools and procedures that indicate an important evolution in Chinese policies. There is every reason to believe that China's experience of learning both "good" and "bad" norms from the world's dominant powers is commonplace. The spread of antidumping regimes is just one example among many (Lindsey and Ikenson, 2003; Nye, 1987).

Despite such learning, trade disputes are not always resolved to the satisfaction of the protectionist side. Antidumping is not an exception to the rule, but an indicator of the common involvement of business in the policy process that results in maintaining openness. China also has had difficulty utilizing other WTO-authorized protective tactics for the same reasons. To give just one example, in March 2002, the US government adopted "safeguard" duties against a supposed glut of foreign steel it claimed was injuring US producers. At the behest of domestic steel manufacturers, China joined other steel exporters in challenging the US action before the WTO, and it invoked its own safeguard measures (quotas and duties) against foreign steel, claiming that the US tariffs had led others to suddenly sell their steel to China.[27] Before long, though, Chinese steel importers and large downstream users in the automobile, oil and consumer appliance sectors complained loudly about shortages in critical types of steel and rising costs. In a September 2002 public hearing, lawyers for the Chinese oil drilling industry claimed that their clients had to buy imported equipment because the domestic machinery they had previously used led to the deaths of several workers. As a result of public and private complaints, the government drastically reduced the number of products against which the measures applied (Norton and Almstedt, 2003b; Interviews #D17, #D42, #D46, #D51). Although there are undoubtedly some protectionist success stories in China and elsewhere, the existence of counter-liberal domestic interests means such outcomes are far from preordained.

Although political élites and the bureaucracy may be central to the initiation of liberalization policies that may have originally been unpopular or for which there was no obvious domestic constituency, the unfolding of liberal reforms generates the emergence of industrial interests favoring the continuation and expansion of such policies.[28] In antidumping cases, importers of inexpensive or high quality products not easily substituted by domestic producers and their downstream customers compose a critical coalition to keep trade flowing. One might hold that business influence is due to antidumping rules that create an institutionalized path for industries to have voice. Yet in the Chinese case, downstream producers opposing applications, first, overrode the formal rules that guide investigators to ignore their interests, and then, because of their lobbying, forced officials to re-define how they adjudicate cases. Institutions may structure opportunities for influence, but they likewise may be the product of industry influence.

In sum, the more economically important and politically powerful pro-openness interests are, the more porous protectionism becomes. The global antidumping regime offers a valuable opportunity for analysts to measure the influence of competing interests. Although countries' antidumping statutes are increasingly similar, as Tables 5.3 and 5.4 show, applicant success rates and average tariff penalties vary widely. A productive next step in the research agenda would be to engage in a carefully structured comparison of cases involving several countries in order to further explain why protectionist efforts – and the liberal response – are more successful in some contexts than in others. The recent experience of China suggests that even if the comparison involves highly authoritarian regimes, non-state actors favoring liberalism will likely be a central part of the story in countries with diverse political institutions.

Acknowledgements

This chapter is a slightly revised version of my article of the same name published in *Political Science Quarterly*, 2005, vol. 120, 407–32, and reprinted by permission. Earlier versions of it were presented at the 55th Annual Meeting of the Association for Asian Studies, New York City, 27–30 March 2003, the 33rd Sino-American Conference on Contemporary China, "New International Order in East Asia in the 21st Century: Implications for Taiwan–US–China Relations", Institute for International Relations, National Chengchi University, Taipei, Taiwan, 27–28 May 2004, and the 46th Annual International Studies Association Convention, Honolulu, Hawaii, 1–5 March 2005. Appreciation is expressed to interview sources who must remain anonymous, and to Kermit Almstedt, Bruce Arnold, Gary Hufbauer, Ethan Michelson, Thomas Moore, Patrick Norton, Margaret Pearson, Daniel Rosen, Vivienne Shue, Lee Sigelman, Dorothy Solinger and Yifeng Tao for their comments on previous drafts.

Notes

1   Prominent contributions on China's WTO entry that stress the WTO's transforming role are Lardy (2002), Cass, Williams, and Barker (2003), and Panitchpakdi and Clifford (2002).

2   Lieberthal and Oksenberg (1988), Lieberthal and Lampton (1992), Shirk (1993). More recently, the policy community has been extended to include the legislature and some specialists, but policy is still portrayed as government-driven and determined. See Tanner (1999), Fewsmith (2001), and Naughton (2002).

3   This chapter's data is primarily from over 50 interviews conducted mainly in Beijing and Shanghai in 2002 and 2003, with Chinese and other countries' government officials, business executives, association leaders and lawyers directly involved in antidumping cases. Because of the sensitivity of the information obtained, interview sources must remain anonymous.

4   On the growing direct influence of industry, domestic and foreign, on a wide variety of China's national economic policies, see Kennedy (2005).

5   Traditional barriers include: tariffs, subsidies or loans to domestic industry, limited trading rights for foreign firms, bans or quotas on imported products, licensing systems for imports, foreign exchange controls and cartels. Protective steps available under the GATT/WTO include: anti-dumping measures; anti-subsidy (countervailing) measures; safeguard measures; standards for health, safety, the environment, labor and technical standards; and anti-monopoly statutes that discriminate against foreign companies.

6   Boltuck and Litan (1991) correctly predicted that because of the US and EU's frequent use of

antidumping, developing countries would eventually use these same tools against their origina-
tors. Also see Lindsey and Ikenson (2003).

7 Yoshimatsu (2001). Interview sources also suggest that Japan has had adequate alternative non-
tariff barriers, making AD measures unnecessary. Interviews #D33, #D34, #D38, #D39, #D40.
While some sources believe that the Japanese prefer to avoid formal legal disputes, their activism
in the WTO suggests otherwise. See Pekkanen (2003).

8 On the evolution of China's trade regime, see Lall (1994) and Lardy (2002).

9 The other rights include permanent most-favored nation trading status, national treatment, access
to WTO dispute resolution and participation in the revision of WTO rules. Language emphasizing
rights and obligations has been used regularly by Chinese trade negotiators and senior leaders
since at least the early 1990s. See BBC (1993), and Pan, Ban and Shao (2001).

10 For worldwide data since 1995, see the WTO Anti-Dumping Database, available
www.wto.orgenglish/tratop_e/adp_e/adp_e.htm>. For a Chinese report, see Zhang (2004).

11 According to China's WTO accession agreement, WTO members are permitted to treat China as a
non-market economy for the first 15 years of its membership. Chinese firms and officials opposed
this status because they believe China's market economy is well developed and that the cost structure of production in the surrogates chosen, most often India, is higher than in China, making it
easier to find dumping by the Chinese. Said Cho Tak Wong, chairman of a glass company hit with
AD duties in the United States: "Out of the Americans' mouths come speeches about free trade,
but what they do is something else" (King and Wonacott, 2002). Also see Holloway (1996: 61). In
April 2004, China began a campaign to have other WTO members officially declare China a
market economy. As of November 2005, 42 countries had granted China's request. However,
collectively they only consumed 18 percent of China's exports in 2004. For an example, see
Xinhua News Agency (2004).

12 WTO Anti-Dumping Database. Of the metal and chemical product cases Chinese have contested
between 1995 and 2000, 71 percent went in their favor (ChinaOnline, 2001).

13 Smith (2000). Said a Chinese government researcher (Wang, Z., 2002: 168), "We should admit
antidumping is a demand for fair trade in the international market. Antidumping is based on the
WTO Anti-Dumping Agreement. These rules are not aimed at China; they are for use in regard to all
members' imported products. For Chinese products to enter overseas markets, we must use WTO-
related rules, obey and abide by these rules, play cards according to the rules, and only in this way
can effectively protect enterprises' own rights and interests." Also see Wang, Yiwei (2002a).

14 It should be stressed that the norms and behavior of trade lawyers differs substantially from that of
lawyers in other areas (Michelson, 2003).

15 Critics of antidumping identify many legitimate reasons to sell goods below typical prices,
including clearing out inventory when goods are in over-supply and gaining a foothold in a new
market. These practices are common – and legal – when done within a country. See Horlick and
Sugarman (1999).

16 The text of China's current antidumping regulation and implementing rules are available at the US
Department of Commerce's Trade Remedy Compliance Staff website, at HTTP <ia.ita.doc.gov/
trcs/downloads/documents/china/index.html> (accessed 13 June 2006). For analysis, see Norton
and Almstedt (2002), and Norton and Almstedt (2003a).

17 The EU and Canada have explicit public interest provisions. Australia has issued subsidiary legal
interpretations of their laws authorizing investigators to consider the effect of dumping on the
overall national Australian interest. See Feaver and Wilson (1995).

18 Boheng Law Firm, also located in Beijing, has also recently become one of the leading firms to
represent Chinese clients seeking protection from imports.

19 On the evolution of government policy toward trade associations and their role in other economic
policy-making, see Kennedy (2005).

20 Final determinations are formally issued by the State Council Tariff Policy Commission.
Composed of officials from trade and other parts of bureaucracy, it has the authority to adjust
tariff levels but not fully reverse a verdict. Interview #D48.

21 As of 2003, foreign respondents still criticized procedures, rulings and limits on appeals. Authorities have granted more latitude to domestic applicants than to respondents in making their

documents confidential, and domestic applicants appear to have more *ex parte* communications with officials than do foreign respondents (although foreign respondents and their domestic customers also usually have good connections with officials). The justifications for the dumping margins, injury and causation are claimed to be unpersuasive and not as detailed as decisions issued by the EU and the United States. And although judicial review regulations have been issued in accordance with WTO requirements, an appeal has yet to be heard in a Chinese court. Losing respondents could appeal to the WTO for dispute resolution but have yet to do so.

22   (Destler 1995: 141, 154). According to Finger (1993: 26), during the AD regime's first 47 years (1921–1967), the global success rate was just over 10 percent. According to Lindsey (2000), the average AD tariff rate imposed on foreign respondents in US cases has also risen as well.

23   Using Milner's typology (1988: 24–6), such characteristics are indicative of Type 1 firms, which are typically most in favor of protection.

24   Foreign chemical producers with production facilities in Australia have used a similar strategy (Whitwell 1997: 326–54).

25   The accused respondents were a BASF subsidiary in South Korea, a Samsung subsidiary in Indonesia, and Archer Daniels Midland's production facility in the US.

26   Interviews #D43, #D44, #D45, #D48, #D50. BASF, through its German headquarters or overseas subsidiaries, has been a respondent in seven other dumping cases in China. They have either been cleared of the charges or penalized with relatively low tariffs.

27   In response to the US action, China's trade minister, Shi Guangsheng, said that China also "has to learn to protect its own industries". The head of one large state-owned enterprise echoed Shi, saying, "We're studying America. If you do things that way [use safeguards, antidumping and technical standards as barriers to trade], then we can too." Interviews #D2, #D8, #D10, #D24; Dorgan (2002).

28   On how early state-led efforts to promote development in East and Southeast Asia resulted in the growth of firms that subsequently became politically active and advocated policies contrary to original state preferences, see MacIntyre (1994).

References

Almstedt, K. W. and Norton, P. M. (2000) "China's antidumping laws and the WTO antidumping agreement (including comments on China's early enforcement of its antidumping laws)", *Journal of World Trade*, 34: 75–113.

Arnold, B. (2001) "Antidumping action in the United States and around the world: an update", Congressional Budget Office Paper, June.

Australian Financial Review (2000) "Antidumping needs review", *Australian Financial Review*, 19: 68.

BBC (1993) "Li Lanqing Receives GATT Official, Calls for Membership", BBC Monitoring Service, 19 October, available from the Factiva database, www.factiva.com (accessed 30 November 2003).

Biglaiser, G. (2002) *Guardians of the Nation? Economists, Generals, and Economic Reform in Latin America*, Notre Dame: University of Notre Dame Press.

Boltuck, R. and Litan, R. E. (eds) (1991) *Down in the Dumps: Administration of the Unfair Trade Laws*, Washington, DC: Brookings Institution.

Cass, D. Z., Williams, B. G. and Barker, G. (eds) (2003) *China and the World Trading System: Entering the New Millennium*, Cambridge: Cambridge University Press.

Chang T. (2003) "Chinese companies fight for rights", *China Daily*, 21 February.

Chen, J. (2002) *Anyi WTO fanqingxiao xieyi* (Annotations by cases to WTO antidumping agreement), Beijing: University of International Business and Economics Press.

China Petrochemical News (2003) "Huagong fanqingxiao 're' zhong you 'leng'" (Cold spell in petrochemical antidumping fever), *Zhongguo huagong bao* (China Petrochemical News), 7 April.

ChinaOnline (2001) "China is primary target of international anti-dumping campaign, vice minister says", *ChinaOnline*, 22 February, available at www.chinaonline.com> (accessed 1 February 2003).

Destler, I. M. (1995) *American Trade Politics,* 3rd edn, Washington, DC: Institute for International Economics; New York: Twentieth Century Fund.

Dorgan, M. (2002) "China already flexing its muscle in WTO", *Knight-Ridder Tribune Business News*, 13 March, available online from Factiva database, www.factiva.com (accessed 2 February 2003).

Economy, E. (2001) "The impact of international regimes on Chinese foreign policy-making: broadening perspectives and policies ... but only to a point", in Lampton, D. M. (ed.) *The Making of Chinese Foreign and Security Policy*, Stanford, CA: Stanford University Press: 230–53.

Economy, E. and Oksenberg, M. (eds) (1999) *China Joins the World: Progress and Prospects*, New York: Council on Foreign Relations Press.

Feaver, D. and Wilson, K. (1995) "An evaluation of Australia's anti-dumping and countervailing law and policy", *Journal of World Trade*, October, 29: 207–37.

Fewsmith, J. (2001) *China Since Tiananmen: The Politics of Transition*, Cambridge: Cambridge University Press.

Finger, M. J. (1993) "The origins and evolution of antidumping regulation", in Finger, M. J. (ed.) *Antidumping, How It Works and Who Gets Hurt*, Ann Arbor: University of Michigan Press, 13–34.

Frieden, J. A. (1991) "Invested interests: the politics of national economic policies in a world of global finance", *International Organization*, 45: 425–51.

Gao, Wei (1999) "Anti-dumping ruling on newsprint imports", *China Daily*, 4 June.

Goldstein, J. (1993) *Ideas, Interests, and American Trade Policy*, Ithaca, NY: Cornell University Press.

Guthrie, D. (1999) *Dragon in a Three-Piece Suit: The Emergence of Capitalism in China*, Princeton, NJ: Princeton University Press.

Haggard, S. and Kaufman, R. R. (eds) (1992) *The Politics of Economic Adjustment*, Princeton, NJ: Princeton University Press.

Han, J. (2001) "Officials prepare for anti-dumping lawsuits", *South China Morning Post*, 16 April.

Han, Q. (2002) *WTO 100 wen: hangye xiehui zai zhongguo ru shi hou de sikao* (100 questions on WTO: thoughts for industry associations after joining WTO), Shanghai: Shanghai People's Press.

Hansen, W. L. (1990) "The International Trade Commission and the politics of protectionism", *American Political Science Review*, 84: 21–46.

Hansen, W. L. and Prusa, T. J. (1997) "The economics and politics of trade policy: an empirical analysis of ITC decision making", *Review of International Economics*, 5: 230–45.

He, M. (2002) *Zhongguo duiwai jingji maoyi baipishu 2002* (China Foreign Trade and Economy White Paper 2002), Beijing: China Materials Press: 470–527.

Holloway, N. (1996) "Sweet Smell of Excess", *Far Eastern Economic Review*, 5 September: 61.

Horlick, G. N. and Sugarman, S. A. (1999) "Antidumping policy as a system of law", in Mendoza, M. R. (ed.) *Trade Rules in the Making: Challenges in Regional and Multilateral Negotiations*, Washington, DC: Organization of American States and the Brookings Institution: 341–64.

Jacobson, H. K. and Oksenberg, M. (1990) *China's Participation in the IMF, the World Bank, and GATT: Toward a Global Economic Order*, Ann Arbor: University of Michigan Press.

Jahiel, A. R. (2003) "The neo-liberal paradigm and the construction of knowledge: the shaping of the Chinese state's environmental concerns around accession into the WTO", paper presented at the International Studies Association Annual Convention, Portland, Oregon, 1 March.

Johnston, A. I. (1996) "Learning versus adaptation: explaining change in Chinese arms control policy in the 1980s and 1990s", *China Journal*, January, 35: 27–61.

Kennedy, S. (2003) "The price of competition: pricing policies and the struggle to define China's economic system", *China Journal*, January, 49: 1–30.

—— (2005) *The Business of Lobbying in China*, Cambridge, MA: Harvard University Press.

King, N. and Wonacott, P. (2002) "Bush's China-trade dilemma: get-tough or go-easy method?", *Wall Street Journal*, 14 November.

Krishna, R. (1997) "Antidumping in Law and Practice", *World Bank Working Paper Series*, September, No. 1823.

Lall, R. (1994) *China: Foreign Trade Reform*, Washington, DC: World Bank.

Lardy, N. R. (2002) *Integrating China into the Global Economy*, Washington, DC: Brookings Institution Press.

Levy, J. S. (1994) "Learning and Foreign Policy: Sweeping a Conceptual Minefield", *International Organization*, 48: 279–312.

Lieberthal, K. and Oksenberg, M. (1988) *Policymaking in China: Leaders, Structures, and Processes*, Princeton, NJ: Princeton University Press.

Lieberthal, K. and Lampton, D. M. (eds) (1992) *Bureaucracy, Politics and Decision-Making in Post-Mao China*, Berkeley, CA: University of California Press.

Lindsey, B. (2000) "The US antidumping law: rhetoric versus reality", *Journal of World Trade*, February, 34: 1–38.

Lindsey, B. and Ikenson, D. J. (2003) *Antidumping Exposed: The Devilish Details of Unfair Trade Law*, Washington, DC: Cato Institute.

Liu, W. (2001) *Zhimian fanqingxiao* (Facing Antidumping), Guangdong: Guangdong Economics Press.

Huanzhong Law Firm (2003) "Lysine Antidumping Case", Huanzhong Law Firm website, www.huanzhonglaw.com (accessed 1 February).

MacIntyre, A. (ed.) (1994) *Business and Government in Industrialising Asia*, Ithaca, NY: Cornell University Press.

Mastel, G. (1998) *Antidumping Laws and the US Economy*, Armonk, NY: ME Sharpe.

Messerlin, P. A. and Reed, G. (1995) "Antidumping policies in the United States and the European Union", *Economic Journal*, 105: 1565–75.

Michelson, E. (2003) "Unhooking From the State: Chinese Lawyers in Transition", Ph.D. dissertation, University of Chicago Department of Sociology.

Milner, H. V. (1988) *Resisting Protectionism: Global Industries and the Politics of International Trade*, Princeton, NJ: Princeton University Press.

Moore, T. G. (2002) *China in the World Market: Chinese Industry and the International Sources of Reform in the Post-Mao Era*, Cambridge: Cambridge University Press.

Mundo, P. A. (1999) *National Politics in a Global Economy*, Washington, DC: Georgetown University Press.

Naughton, B. (2002) "China's economic think tanks: their changing role in the 1990s", *China Quarterly*, 171: 625–35.

Norton, P. M. and Almstedt, K. W. (2000) "Defending dumping claims: exporters to China beware", *China Law & Practice*, 14: 32–9.

—— (2002) "China's New antidumping Rules: Battleground for a New Protectionism?" *China Law & Practice*, 16: 79–83.

—— (2003a) "China Joins the Trade Wars", *China Business Review*, 30: 22–9.

—— (2003b) "China Invokes the WTO 'Escape Clause'", *O'Melveny & Myers LLP Research Report*, May.

Nye, J. S. (1987) "Nuclear learning and U.S.-Soviet security regimes", *International Organization*, 41: 371–402.

Pan, G., Ban, W. and Shao, J. (2001) "Solemn commitments", Xinhua News Agency, 11 November, available from the Factiva database, www.factiva.com (accessed 30 November 2003).

Panitchpakdi, S. and Clifford, M. L. (2002) *China and the WTO: Changing China, Changing World Trade*, New York: John Wiley & Sons.

Pearson, M. M. (1999) "China's integration into the international trade and investment regime", in Economy, E. and Oksenberg, M. (eds) *China Joins the World: Progress and Prospects*, New York: Council on Foreign Relations Press: 161–205.

—— (2001) "The Case of China's Accession to GATT/WTO", in Lampton, D. M. (ed.) *The Making of Chinese Foreign and Security Policy in the Era of Reform*, Stanford, CA: Stanford University Press: 337–70.

Peerenboom, R. (2001) "Seek truth from fact: an empirical study of enforcement of arbitral awards in the PRC", *American Journal of Comparative Law*, 49: 249–327.

Pekkanen, S. M. (2003) "International law, industry and the state: explaining Japan's complaint activities at the WTO", *Pacific Review*, 16: 285–306.

Prusa, T. J. and Skeath, S. (2001) "The economic and strategic motives for antidumping filings", *NBER Working Paper Series*, August, No. 8424.

Rogowski, R. (1989) *Commerce and Coalitions: How Trade Affects Domestic Political Alignments*, Princeton, NJ: Princeton University Press.

Ross, L. and Ning, S. (2000) "Modern protectionism: China's own antidumping regulations", *China Business Review*, May–June, 27: 30–3.

Ruggie, J. G. (1991) "Embedded liberalism revisited: institutions and progress in international economic relations", in Adler, E. and Crawford, B. (eds) *Progress in Postwar International Relations*, New York: Columbia University Press: 201–34.

Shirk, S. L. (1993) *The Political Logic of Economic Reform in China*, Berkeley: University of California Press.

—— (1994) *How China Opened Its Door: The Political Success of the PRC's Foreign Trade and Investment Reforms*, Washington, DC: Brookings Institution.

Smith, C. S. (2000) "Joining the club: like others, China will try to protect its own industries", *New York Times*, 23 May.

Steel Business Briefing (2003) "China's 2002 imports top those into the USA", *Steel Business Briefing*, 21 February.

Tanner, M. S. (1999) *The Politics of Lawmaking in China: Institutions, Processes, and Democratic Prospects*, Oxford: Clarendon Press.

Tharakan, P. K. M. and Waelbroeck, J. (1994) "Antidumping and counterveiling duty decisions in the E.C. and in the U.S.: an experiment in comparative political economy", *European Economic Review*, 38: 171–93.

Wang, Yiwei (2002a) "Fanqingxiao shang xu jiandun limao" (Antidumping still needs firm shield and sharp spear), *Zhongguo gongshang shibao* (China Business Times), 7 March.

Wang, Yiwei (2002b) "Zhongguo qidong fanqingxiao 5 zhounian – yige haode kaishi – fang beijing huanzhong lushi shiwusuo wang xuehua" (5th anniversary of launching antidumping – a good start – interview with Huanzhong Law Firm's Wang Xuehua), *Zhongguo gongshang shibao* (China Business Times), 25 March.

Wang, Yong (2000) "Dumping allegation trashed", *China Daily Business Weekly*, 5 November.

Wang, Z. (2002) *WTO guize shiwu peixun duben* (Practical training reader on WTO rules), Beijing: CPC Party School Press.

Whitwell, R. (1997) *The Application of antidumping and Countervailing Measures by Australia*, Australia: Central Queensland University Press.

WTO Anti-Dumping Database, available online: www.wto.org/english/tratop_e/adp_adp_e.htm.

Xinhua News Agency (2004) "Armenia recognizes China's full market economy status", Xinhua News Agency, 27 September.

Yang, D. (2004) *Remaking the Chinese Leviathan: Market Transition and the Politics of Governance in China*, Stanford, CA: Stanford University Press.

Yoshimatsu, H. (2001) "The political economy of antidumping in Japan", *Journal of the Asia Pacific Economy*, 6: 22–46.

Yu, H. (2002) *Hangye xiehui ji qi zai zhongguode fazhan* (Industry associations and their development in China), Beijing: Economic Management Press: 88–110.

Zhang, L. (2004) "Learning to use WTO rules for protection", *China Daily*, 6 July.

Zweig, D. (2002) *Internationalizing China: Domestic Interests and Global Linkages*, Ithaca, NY: Cornell University Press.

Appendix 5.1
The state of China's antidumping cases, 1 June 2006

Case no.	Product	Foreign respondents (firms from)	Date case initiated	Preliminary determination (date, tariff rates)	Final determination (date, tariff rates)	Winner
1	Newsprint	Canada, ROK, US	11/10/97	7/9/98, margin n/a	6/3/99, 9–78%	China
2	Silicon steel	Russia	3/12/99	12/30/99, 11–73%	9/11/00, 0–62% 1 firm no margin	Both sides
3	Polyester film	ROK	3/16/99	12/29/99, margin n/a	8/25/00, 13–46%	China
4	Stainless steel	Japan, ROK	6/17/99	4/13/00, 4–75%	12/15/00 7 firms price undertaking; 12/18/00, 17–58% Exemptions given to other firms	Both sides
5	Acrylates	Japan, US, Germany	12/10/99	11/23/00, 24–71%	6/9/01, 31–69% Not on Germany	Both sides
6	Methylene chloride	ROK, UK, US, France, Netherlands, Germany	12/20/00	8/16/01, 7–75%	6/20/02, 4–66% Not on France	Both sides
7	Poly-styrene	ROK, Japan, Thailand	2/9/01	12/6/01, case dismissed (dump, no injury)	–	Foreigners
8	Lysine	US, ROK, Indonesia	6/19/01	9/30/02, case dismissed (dump, no injury)	–	Foreigners
9	Polyester short stable fibers	ROK	8/3/01	10/22/02, 4–48%	2/3/03, 2–48%	China
10	Polyester strips (PET chips)	ROK	8/3/01	10/29/02, 6–52%	2/3/03, 5–52%	China
11	Propenoic acid ester	ROK, Malaysia, Singapore, Indonesia	10/10/01	12/5/02, 11–49%	4/11/03, 2–49%	China
12	Capro-lactam (CPL)	Japan, Belgium, Germany, Netherlands, Russia	12/7/01	1/7/03, 5–28%	6/9/03, 5–28%	China

Case no.	Product	Foreign respondents (firms from)	Date case initiated	Preliminary determination (date, tariff rates)	Final determination (date, tariff rates)	Winner

China joins WTO (11 December 2001)

Case no.	Product	Foreign respondents (firms from)	Date case initiated	Preliminary determination (date, tariff rates)	Final determination (date, tariff rates)	Winner
13	Coated art paper	ROK, Japan, US, Finland	2/6/02	11/26/02, 5.58–71.02%	8/7/03, 4–71% Not on US, Finland	Both sides
14	Catechol	European Union	3/1/02	11/4/02, 50–88%	8/28/03, 20–79%	China
15	Phthalic anhydride	India, Japan, ROK	3/6/02	1/7/03, 14–66%	9/3/03, 0–66%	China
16	Styrene-butadiene rubber	Russia, ROK, Japan	3/15/02	4/16/03, 0–46%	9/11/03, 0–38%	China
17	Cold-rolled steel coil, strips	Russia, ROK, Ukraine, Kazakhstan, Taiwan	3/22/02	5/20/03, 8–55%	9/24/03, 0–55%. Duties began 1/14/04, ended 9/10/04	Both sides
18	Polyvinyl chloride (PVC)	US, ROK, Japan, Russia, Taiwan	3/29/02	5/14/03, 10–115%	9/29/03, 6–84%	China
19	Tuoline diiso-cyanate (TDI)	Japan, ROK, US	5/22/02	6/11/03, 6–49%	11/22/03, 3–49%	China
20	Phenol	Japan, ROK, US, Taiwan	8/1/02	6/9/03, 7–144%	2/1/04, 3–144%	China
21	Polymeric MDI	Japan, ROK	9/20/02	11/28/03, applicant withdrew case	–	Foreigners
22	Ethanol-amine	Japan, Taiwan, Germany, Iran, US, Malaysia, Mexico	5/14/03	3/25/04, 9–137% Not on Germany	11/14/04, 9–74%	Both sides
23	Chloroform	EU, ROK, US, India	5/30/03	4/8/04, 16–96%	11/30/04, 32–96% 6 firms price undertaking	China
24	Optical fiber	US, Japan, ROK	7/1/03	6/16/04, 7–46%	1/1/05, 7–46% Not one US firm	Both sides
25	Nylon	Taiwan	10/31/03	8/27/04, 5–29%	4/28/05 No dumping Case ended	Foreigners

Case no.	Product	Foreign respondents (firms from)	Date case initiated	Preliminary determination (date, tariff rates)	Final determination (date, tariff rates)	Winner
26	Chloro-prene rubber	EU, Japan, US	11/10/03	12/1/04, 151%	5/11/05, 2–151%	Both sides
27	Hydrazine hydrate	Japan, ROK, US, France	12/17/03	8/3/04, 28–184%	6/17/05, 28–184%	China
28	Un-bleached kraft liner, linerboard	ROK, Taiwan, Thailand, US	3/31/04	5/31/05, 11.0–65.2%	9/30/05, 7–65.2% Order repealed 1/9/06	Both sides
29	Trichloro-ethylene (TCE)	Japan, Russia	4/16/04	1/7/05, 5–159%	7/22/05, 3–159%	Both sides
30	Bisphenol-A	Japan, Russia Singapore, ROK, Taiwan	5/12/04	11/7/05 Case withdrawn by applicant	–	Foreigners
31	Dimethyl cyclo-siloxane	US, Japan, UK, Germany	7/16/04	9/29/05, 13–35%	1/16/06, 13–22%	China
32	Ethylene-propylene ethylidene (EPDM rubber)	US, ROK, Netherlands	8/10/04	11/16/05 3–43%	2/9/06, Case withdrawn by applicant	Foreigners
33	Benzo-furanol	Japan, EU, US	8/12/04	6/16/05, 74.6–113.2%	2/12/06, 44–113.2%	China
34	Nucleotide food additives	Japan, ROK	11/12/04	8/14/05, 25–144%	5/12/06, 25–119%	China
35	Epichloro-hydrin	ROK, US, Russia, Japan	12/28/04	9/21/05, 0–71.5%		
36	Urethane elastic fiber	Japan, US, Singapore, ROK, Taiwan	4/13/05	5/24/06, 0–61% Not on ROK		
37	Dihydro-xybenzene (catechol, pyro-catechol)	US, Japan	5/31/05	12/14/05, 6–46.81%	5/22/06, 4–46.81%	China
38	Poly-butylene tereph-thalate resin (PBT)	Japan, Taiwan	6/6/05	3/22/06, 12.78–17.31%		

Case no.	Product	Foreign respondents (firms from)	Date case initiated	Preliminary determination (date, tariff rates)	Final determination (date, tariff rates)	Winner
39	Wear resistant overlay	US, EU	6/13/05			
40	Octanol	ROK, Saudi Arabia, Japan, EU, Indonesia	9/15/05			
41	Butanol	Russia, US, S. Africa, Malaysia, EU, Japan	10/14/05			
42	Nonyl phenol	India, Taiwan	12/29/05			
43	Potato starch	EU	2/6/06			
44	Paper for electrolytic capacitator	Japan	4/18/06			

Sources: Ministry of Commerce, "China Trade Remedy Information", available online: www.cacs.gov.cn; China's "Semi-Annual Report of Anti-Dumping Actions", submitted to the WTO, 11 September 2002, 14 July 2003 and 3 March 2004; WTO Anti-Dumping Database; Huanzhong Law Firm website: www.huangzhonglaw.com; and media reports.

6 China's WTO commitment compliance

A case study of the US–China semiconductor trade dispute

Wei Liang

Introduction

Prior to China becoming a member of the World Trade Organization (WTO), the question had often been raised in Washington and elsewhere as to whether the country would be able to honor its commitments and abide by the rules and norms of the organization. Now that China has been a member of the organization for more than five years, we can engage in a tentative examination of China's behavior in this multilateral economic institution, particularly with regard to its commitment compliance.

States reach agreement when they believe that the agreement is mutually beneficial. But these benefits cannot be achieved without active implementation and oversight. Implementation of international agreements is as important as negotiating these agreements. In some cases, states can receive short-term unilateral benefits by defecting from agreements or by delaying implementation despite the long-term desirability of such agreements. In these instances, the risks of cheating and abrogation loom large. In other words, cooperation requires actors to demonstrate or to convince others that they have both the capability and the willingness to behave as promised. This is directly related to the concept of credibility. This credibility problem can become particularly acute when it comes to new members of an international organization such as China and its membership in the WTO.

This chapter explores China's WTO commitment compliance by analyzing the case involving Beijing's semiconductor Value Added Tax (VAT) rebate policy. In March 2004 the Bush administration filed a WTO complaint against China for its controversial semiconductor VAT rebate policy. This was the first WTO case filed against China by any WTO member country. China is the largest transition economy in the world. Thus this case can serve to shed light on the distinctive pattern of commitment compliance by a non-democratic transition economy such as China.

This chapter argues that international regimes, particularly the WTO-plus rules designed for transition economies, do constrain these governments' compliance choices. International legal commitments raise the penalty for national governments for reneging on their obligations. To shield the system against the potential abuse of the rules and the principle of free trade on the part of participating countries, transition economies and non-market economies have often been required to accept a discriminatory safeguard clause upon accession. This was the case for some East European countries during the Cold War. When China applied for membership in the General Agreeement on Tariffs and Trade (GATT)/WTO, it was asked to accept much more complicated arrangements than simply a general safeguard clause. These strict arrangements designed specifically for China were mainly reflected in three areas: the non-market economy designation, the product-specific safeguard clause and the annual review system. These special arrangements represented the dual threat China posed to the GATT/WTO – both as a non-democratic transition economy and as an export engine of the world. Since the eligibility and credibility of transition economies, and China in particular, were fiercely questioned during the accession negotiation, it is reputational costly for these economies to breach their international commitments. While this chapter argues that international legal rules matter, the preferences of the domestic industry also contribute to explaining the variation in China's willingness to comply with international commitments. Though industry associations played a surprisingly insignificant role in the process of China's accession negotiation, as discussed in Chapter 2, they have been more heavily involved in the trade dispute settlement process since China became a WTO member. This new development is reflected in the semiconductor VAT case. When Washington first raised the issue with China through bilateral negotiations, the Chinese Semiconductor Industry Association (CSIA) was invited to meetings with officials from the Ministry of Commerce (MOFCOM) for "policy consultation". The CSIA did not favor this government subsidy policy via VAT rebate as much as other policy alternatives which would provide more financial support to Chinese enterprises and which would be more WTO-friendly. However, it has been an established national strategy of the Chinese government to promote technological innovation in the semiconductor sector. Therefore, the policy preferences of the CSIA alone could not have changed the government's VAT rebate policy. While the constraints imposed by WTO rules and China's accession protocol directly contributed to China's complete concessions in the negotiations, the preferences of the CSIA also helped to explain the relatively speedy resolution of this trade dispute.

The remainder of this chapter proceeds as follows. The next section discusses the theoretical literature on the relationship between regime type and states' ability to comply with their international commitments. The third section provides a brief overview of the content and implications of the WTO rules that were specifically designed for China's accession. The fourth section provides a background to the semiconductor VAT refund case. This section emphasizes the strategic importance of China's semiconductor industry and explains why, among a number of bilateral trade disputes between the United States and China, the dispute over China's semiconductor VAT rebate policy was elevated to the WTO dispute settlement mechanism. The fifth section reviews the process of negotiations over this issue, taking into consideration the interaction between US trade politics and Chinese trade politics. Finally, I conclude by discussing the implications of this case study for international cooperation and for the integration of transition economies into the world trading system.

Regime type and credibility in international relations

Many empirical studies of international cooperation (Cowhey, 1993; Fearon, 1994; Gaubatz, 1996) argue that characteristics typical of democratic systems advantage these states in making credible international commitments. This is so for a number of reasons. In the first place, it has been argued (Leeds, 1999) that for leaders of democracies, a change in policy becomes undesirable once a public commitment has been made. Leaders of democratic states may experience audience costs in not following through on a planned course of action. As a result, not only are they more likely to enter into secure agreements, their commitments are also more likely to be credible. Similarly, Lisa Martin (2000) finds that Congress plays an active and positive role in promoting international cooperation. The institutionalized legislative participation process in democracies enhances the credibility of international cooperation through a number of mechanisms, in particular through the signaling mechanism. Institutionalized legislative participation provides the executive branch and other states with better information about legislative and societal preferences, thereby reducing the chance of reneging. It also creates institutional obstacles to changing policies and thus improves the stability of existing policies. Finally, in addition to the domestic oversight capacity, there is the penalty concern. International agreements are legal documents and, as a result, states that breach their obligations face potential legal consequences (Simmons, 2000). International agreements therefore constrain state behavior by enhancing the credibility of commitments.

If democracies are both more cautious about entering into agreements with others and more capable of guaranteeing their future behavior, then what about the compliance behavior of transition economies whose domestic political institutions function very differently from those of democracies? Four questions arise in this regard. First, in the absence of domestic institutional and normative constraints, are non-democratic transition economies less credible with their commitments? Second, are democratic regimes likely to be more cautious in forming agreements with non-democratic transition economies? Are international agreements reached between a pair composed of a democratic and a non-democratic state less likely to be secure? Third, to what extent do the preferences of domestic industries influence commitment compliance? Fourth, do international regimes alter governments' interests and behavior? These are all important questions relating to the prospect of international cooperation and the efficacy of international institutions. Although it is impossible for a case study like this to provide comprehensive answers to these questions, this chapter nevertheless aims to shed light on these critical issues.

WTO rules designed for China's accession

The GATT/WTO is more than a simple club of trading partners. The GATT/WTO is a postwar institution founded around the free market principle and designed primarily to promote free trade among Western democracies. The norms and rules of the organization were geared towards ensuring the maintenance of an open and nondiscriminatory market in which government intervention is minimized and in which tariffs and market prices guide the decisions of private firms. Given the liberal orientation of the organization, participation of non-democracies and/or non-market economies poses an anomaly for the GATT/WTO for two reasons. First, the commitments of non-democracies tend to lack credibility to others since national leaders can easily change their course of behavior without the effective supervision of the legislative branch. Second, in planned economic systems, decisions about resource allocations and imports and exports are administratively determined by the government. Tariffs and prices have little or no influence over decision-making. The domestic economic practices of non-market economies therefore contradict the free market principles of the GATT/WTO.

The participation of East European countries in the GATT during the Cold War era provoked much controversy as it raised questions about the compatibility of these economies with the principles of the GATT and their ability to comply with their GATT obligations. Nevertheless, for the most part Western governments were not constrained by the concern that the membership of Poland, Romania and Hungary would erode the GATT regime.[1] On the one hand, the membership application of these countries was viewed as an East–West issue and political and security considerations predominated. On the other hand, the participation of smaller economies, even though planned ones, was not deemed to pose a big threat to the regime. Furthermore, while Hungary requested that its tariff concessions be accepted as a legitimate price it had to pay for entry, Poland and Romania agreed to implement a quantitative quota system in the accession negotiation. In other words, Poland and Romania were not expected to meet the requirements of trade liberalization for market economies but only committed to opening their domestic markets for a certain amount of imports. Obviously the latter was less likely to dilute or erode the market-oriented rules of the neoliberal trade institution. Even so, the accession agreements in all three cases included a special discriminatory safeguard clause that would provide mechanisms for ameliorating the impact of possible dumping from these countries. The rationale behind these exclusive safeguard mechanisms was that these countries are the so-called "non-market economies". As noted in the Working Party Report with respect to the accession of Poland, rather than the customs tariff being the effective instrument of Poland's commercial policy, the foreign trade of Poland was conducted mainly by state owned enterprises and the Foreign Trade Plan.[2]

China's WTO accession negotiation caused more skepticism among Western countries about its compliance. As one of the major trading powers in the world, China's commitments with regard to tariff reduction, market access and other issues were far reaching. Indeed, they exceeded those made by any other member that has joined the WTO since 1995.[3] However, the scope and depth of China's commitment were accompanied by deep-rooted skepticism about whether the country would honor its commitments. Both China's compatibility and credibility were questioned during the negotiation process and these issues became one of the biggest stumbling blocks for the accession agreement (e.g. Holton and Lin, 1998; Cai, 1992). In the end, China agreed to bind itself to more strict and onerous rules so as to offset the distrust shared by WTO members, particularly in areas such as antidumping, safeguards and annual review.

China began its pro-market economic reform in 1978 and has claimed itself a "socialist market economy" since 1992. Today more than 96 percent of Chinese commodities are priced on the basis of market mechanisms. Russia was granted full market economy status by both the European Union (EU) and the US years ago. However, in terms of the index of economic freedom, the Heritage Foundation and the Fraser Institute put China 10 to 15 notches ahead of Russia.[4] Article 15 of the Document on China's Accession to the WTO conditionally defines China as a non-market economy (NME) and this status is to last 15 years after its WTO accession. Consequently, antidumping cases involving China would be resolved not on the basis of market-determined prices in the country but on production costs in "comparable market economies". Such treatment is highly disadvantageous to China. However, without this commitment WTO members would have significant concerns about the uncertain impact of China's entry on international trade. As the President of the Semiconductor Industry Association (SIA) put it, "this commitment was a vital part of China's overall accession package, and was central not only to industry support for accession and Permanent Normal Trade Relations (PNTR) but was also of paramount importance to lawmakers who voted in favor of the deal."[5] In other words, industries as well as governments regarded China's commitment to maintaining its NME status as an implicit regime constraint on the country's future trade behavior.

Safeguard clauses are the most direct and useful tools to prevent the dumping of products from transition economies. Under certain conditions set forth in the WTO Agreement on Safeguards, a country may impose quantitative restrictions on imports. Since this is a major departure from the most basic WTO principles of eliminating all quantitative trade restrictions, the conditions that must be fulfilled before a country imposes import quotas are rather rigorous. The country imposing restrictions must demonstrate that increased imports have caused or threaten to cause serous injury to domestic firms producing similar or competitive products. Most importantly, restrictions on imports imposed under safeguard measures must be applied on a most favored nation basis, that is, proportionately on all suppliers. In contrast, under the terms of the transitional product-specific safeguard clause in China's protocol of accession to the WTO, it will be easier for WTO members to impose restrictions on goods imported from China. The injury standard is low: market disruption, rather than serious injury.[6] In particular WTO member countries can impose quotas or other restrictions solely on products from China, even when imports of the same products from other countries have experienced a similar increase.[7] The US Trade Representative General Counsel refers to this as the "China-specific" feature of the transitional safeguard because it was solely designed for China.[8] According to the United States Trade Representative (USTR) Charlene Barshefsky, this unique and "WTO-unfriendly" clause China has agreed to "exist(s) for no other country in the world".[9]

Directly addressing their concern about China's credibility, WTO members designed a China-specific transitional review mechanism. Under this transitional review mechanism, China would be subject to an unprecedented annual review for the first eight years of membership. A final transitional review would be scheduled for the tenth year, after which China would be subject to the ordinary trade policy review. Not only was China's transitional review to be far more frequent, it was also to be more intrusive. It would involve 16 subsidiary bodies of the WTO,[10] each of which would review China's compliance with its commitments in the area of that particular body's mandate. In contrast, the normal trade policy review is conducted by the staff in the Trade Policy Review Division of the WTO Secretariat.[11]

In the United States, China's accession to the WTO raised questions from the Congress, the government and the private sector about the prospects that China would comply with WTO rules and its market access commitments. For example, government agencies such as the State Department, the USTR, the Department of Commerce (DOC), the United States–China Economic and Security Review Commission, the Government Accountability Office (GAO), major think tanks and industry associations have prepared the review of China's WTO compliance annually since its accession in 2001. Multilaterally, an annual WTO review of China's progress has also been done through the Transitional Review Mechanism (TRM). In 2003, 11 out of a total of 148 WTO members participated in the TRM of China's trade commitment implementation. These members participated by submitting written questions to China prior to meetings of the 16 WTO subsidiary bodies with a role in the TRM or by raising issues verbally with China during these meetings which took place between September and December 2003. Specifically, seven WTO members, including the US, EU, Japan, Chinese Taipei, Australia, Canada and Mexico, submitted written questions and discussed issues verbally in some of the TRM meetings. Four other members – Brazil, Korea, Norway and Pakistan – only participated verbally during some meetings. The US was the most active member in the TRM, participating one or both ways in 14 of the 16 subsidiary bodies.[12] The Chinese government has taken the US domestic and the WTO multilateral annual review of China's compliance seriously. In order to better accommodate the new international setting, China's Ministry of Commerce made a series of administrative reorganizations by creating and consolidating several departments and bureaus to deal with China's WTO affairs.[13] To policymakers in Beijing, China's WTO compliance has broader implications beyond the economic sphere. This rationale to a large degree affected Beijing's position and strategy in the case involving its semiconductor VAT rebate policy.

The case background

In March 2004 the US filed a WTO complaint regarding China's tax refund policy for integrated circuits. The US case was the first against China since it joined the WTO in December 2001. As mentioned above, since its entry into the WTO, the enforcement of China's accession commitment has been a great concern to many parties. In other words, the controversy over China's membership has continued and skepticism about China's organizational behavior has never been muted. As regimes are created to constrain and influence state behavior, the semiconductor case directly raised questions about China's willingness to comply with WTO rules.

China applied a VAT of 17 percent on sales of imported and domestically-produced semiconductors. However, in June 2000, China's State Council announced that all integrated circuits manufactured in China would receive a VAT rebate in excess of six percent of the company's tax burden (Circular No. 18).[14] The policy was amended in September 2001, when Beijing announced that integrated circuits built in China would be eligible for a VAT rebate in excess of three percent (Circular No. 70). In October 2002, the Ministry of Finance (MOF) and the State Administration of Taxation (SAT) jointly issued a new circular that reinforced Circular No. 18 and mandated that the 14 percent VAT rebate be enforced.[15] Another circular extended the six percent applied VAT to integrated circuits (IC) designed in China but produced overseas.[16] According to these circulars, the VAT rebates must be applied to research and development or capital expenditures within China. Clearly, the differential treatment of domestic and imported semiconductor products represented a measure taken by the Chinese government in order to promote its infant semiconductor sector.

Article III of the GATT on National Treatment prohibits a WTO member country from engaging in activity that treats domestic producers and products more favorably than imported products. Specifically, the second paragraph of this article states that a WTO member cannot impose taxes on imported products that are greater than those imposed on domestic products. The Chinese implementation of its VAT rebate policy puts pressure on foreign semiconductor producers to design and manufacture their products within China, or face a costly penalty. The WTO does not allow countries to eliminate tariffs on the one hand, and arbitrarily impose a tax that applies differently to domestic and foreign producers on the other. While China does provide benefits to both domestic and foreign-owned facilities in China, the different treatment of domestic production and foreign imports allegedly amounted to a violation of its national treatment commitment.[17]

Semiconductors as a strategic sector

In spite of growing frictions in various issue areas, the United States, the EU and Japan have refrained from taking any formal WTO action against China since 2001. The question then is why did the US government choose to take the semiconductor case to the WTO instead of other disputes that took place in the bilateral trade relationship? What made the semiconductor industry so unique and sensitive? What was the policy goal of Beijing's VAT rebate policy? What was the real concern of the US government?

A careful examination of China's VAT rebate policy suggests that the policy allows for rebate to both Chinese and foreign manufacturers in China. In fact, according to statistics released by the Ministry of Information Technology in China, in the first half of 2004 only 20 enterprises were eligible for a VAT rebate and the total amount of VAT rebates paid was $13.8 million. Half of the 20 enterprises that received a VAT rebate involved foreign companies such as Intel, Motorola, Texas Instruments and AMD; only two Chinese firms enjoyed the same rebate.[18] Both the small size of the subsidies and the fact that foreign-owned enterprises captured the bulk of the funds suggest that the purpose of this policy was to promote foreign investment and local production. The policy did not discriminate against foreign-owned manufacturers in favor of Chinese companies but discriminated against imports in favor of domestic production.

Semiconductors are the building blocks for American competitiveness in a broad range of high technology goods such as computers and medical technology. Semiconductors represented the second largest US export to China and China's number one import.[19] Today China is the third largest market in the world for semiconductors. It also enjoys the world's highest growth rate in this industry. It was predicted that China would be the world's second largest market for semiconductors by 2010, behind only the US. China's semiconductor market growth is occurring within the context of significant growth in China's computer and telecommunications markets. The demand for microchips is driven by China's increasing role as an electronics manufacturing hub, producing everything from personal computers (PCs) and cellular phones to flat panel displays, digital cameras and DVD players. China is already the world's largest mobile phone market and second largest PC market. Currently domestic Chinese production, including production by foreign-owned facilities in China, represents about 15 to 20 percent of China's market demand, with the remaining 80 to 85 percent of the demand met by imports.[20] Semiconductor exports to China in 2003 amounted to $2.4 billion, making semiconductors the second largest manufactured exports from the US to China. Moreover, even this figure may have under-reported the full value of US semiconductor exports to China as assembly and final testing in third countries were not captured in the US export figure.[21] Whatever the method of calculation, the US semiconductor industry enjoyed the biggest share in the Chinese market. In addition, while US policy encouraged and promoted exports of low-end semiconductor products to China, exports of semiconductor equipment as well as high-end semiconductors were subject to export control.

China has become the third largest trading partner of the United States after Canada and Mexico and its second largest source of imports. Interestingly, never in the post-war era has the US had such an important economic partner that was neither a close friend nor ally. In increasingly complex ways, China is an economic partner and an economic competitor at the same time.[22] The policy dilemma here is that on the one hand, the US would like to export more semiconductor products to the Chinese market, which would in turn require China to further eliminate its protectionist measures. On the other hand, however, Washington was constrained by its security needs to implement export control and technology transfers in high-end semiconductor products. As stated by the US Under Secretary of Commerce for Industry and Security Kenneth I. Juster, "the US government very much wants to support economic opportunities for the (domestic) semiconductor industry", but it is also aware that "some of these opportunities in China also raise potential security concerns, because advanced semiconductors are at the heart of today's advanced weapons systems".[23] While the US no longer controlled the export of general purpose chips or microprocessors to civil end-users in China, the equipment used to manufacture sophisticated semiconductors remained tightly controlled. Under US export control policy, license applications for semiconductor manufacturing equipment and technology were reviewed on a case-by-case basis by the Departments of Commerce, Defense, State, Energy and the intelligence community. The review process was thorough as the interagency vet the end-user to mitigate concerns that the technology would be diverted.[24] For example, in 2001 the Shanghai-based Semiconductor Manufacturing International Corp (SMIC), the biggest of its kind in China, faced problems when it tried to import two sets of semiconductor equipment from US equipment vendor Applied Materials, finding that the export license for one batch of the equipment was being suspended by the US Government. SMIC finally gave the order to a Swedish company after several months of fruitless waiting.[25]

Since the 1990s, China's efforts to improve its semiconductor manufacturing capability have narrowed the gap between the US and Chinese semiconductor manufacturing technology from between seven and ten years to just two years.[26] China's most advanced commercial manufacturing facilities can produce chips that are only one generation behind current, commercial state-of-the-art technology. China has made improving its semiconductor manufacturing capability a priority for national and economic security reasons and plans to build as many as twenty multibillion-dollar manufacturing facilities over the next five to ten years with substantial levels of foreign investment. In early 2002, the General Accounting Office (GAO) prepared a report for the US Senate entitled "Rapid Advances in China's Semiconductor Industry Underscore Need for Fundamental US Policy Review". In light of China's emerging semiconductor market and its growing manufacturing capacity, the report stated the US goal of keeping China at least two generations behind global state-of-the-art semiconductor manufacturing capabilities. The report also emphasized the need for the government to review current policies and further strengthen its export and investment control.[27]

In October 2003 the SIA issued a study entitled "China's Emerging Semiconductor Industry" which found that the country's discriminatory VAT rebate scheme distorted trade and investment and imposed a cost penalty for semiconductor producers trying to compete for sales in China.[28] This dilemma in semiconductor policy was reinforced by the fact that since 2001 the US had cut back nearly three million manufacturing jobs and endured forty-two consecutive months of economic decline in the manufacturing sector.[29] It was also exacerbated by the growing US trade deficit with China. Mounting protectionist pressure from the Congress created imperatives for the US government to take some action on this issue. Thus, China's VAT rebate policy was chosen as the target of a WTO complaint both because of the strategic importance of this sector and strong industry pressure.

China's domestic trade politics

Chinese semiconductor manufacturers worked closely with the government both during US–China bilateral negotiations and in the formulation of alternative government policies. This is a new development in China's trade policy since its WTO accession. In the past, the private sector tended to be excluded from the policy-making process. For example, when President Jiang Zemin announced Beijing's decision to join the Information Technology Agreement (ITA) upon accession in 1997 at his APEC summit with President Clinton, Chinese enterprises were shocked with this decision. Phasing out tariffs on semiconductors, computers, telecommunications equipment and semiconductor manufacturing equipment, as required by the ITA, would have had a great impact on China's infant high-tech industries. However, these industries did not have any channel to convey their policy preferences at that time. They were not even informed when the decision was made.[30]

In contrast, in the semiconductor case, Chinese enterprises, especially their industry association, the CSIA, were actively involved in the policy process. After the issue was first raised by the US, domestic enterprises were invited to several meetings for policy consultation. Bound by both the WTO regime obligation and the US bilateral pressure, Beijing was prepared to make concessions at the beginning. This time they informed the domestic enterprises in advance so they could make timely adjustments. In addition, the industrial sector's dissatisfaction with the current rebate policy also helped facilitate the conclusion of the negotiation. Most importantly, semiconductor manufacturers had the opportunity to provide their policy suggestions and to participate in alternative policy formulation.

Overall, Chinese semiconductor manufacturers were not strong advocates of the VAT rebate policy. First, China's policies regarding value-added tax rebate on semiconductors have not brought substantial financial benefits to domestic Chinese manufacturers. Compared to the semiconductor output value of $4.6 billion in 2003, the tax rebates amounted to only $138 million, which was insignificant to many semiconductor companies in China. Richard Chang, chief executive officer of the Semiconductor Manufacturing International Corporation (SMIC), the biggest Chinese manufacturer, estimated that the elimination of the tax rebate policy would cause $1.7 million of losses for his company in 2004, as compared to $221 million of revenues of the SMIC in the second quarter of 2004.[31] Many smaller enterprises were not even eligible for the tax rebate because their average tax burden was about or lower than three percent. Dawei Mo, a senior industrial expert, said that according to a survey conducted by official agencies before Circular No. 18 was issued, the tax burden for large-scale domestic semiconductor companies was about six percent, so they would get three percent of VAT rebates at most.[32]

Second, the small size of the subsidies also pointed to the inability of the Chinese state to implement its policies effectively. Since March 2002, the State Council shifted the role of determining the eligibility for VAT rebates from the Ministry of Information Industry (MII) to the Taxation department. However, local taxation departments were not capable of fulfilling this responsibility and delayed the whole tax rebate process. On many occasions the VAT was not fully rebated because provincial and local authorities refused to rebate VAT charges collected by another jurisdiction within China. As a result, although the planned rebates should have totaled 14 percent of domestic production, the actual subsidies represented less than one-third of one percent of domestic semiconductor production.[33]

Third, Chinese enterprises were hoping to substitute this VAT rebate policy with other WTO-compliant government policies that could benefit the semiconductor sector as a whole. There was certainly no lack of feedback from the industry. The current policy was not widely understood, and actually benefited fewer than 20 companies, most of which were large, capital-intensive manufacturers such as SMIC and Huahong-NEC. Many small companies said they never saw a nickel. The industry began to lobby for new government policies that would emphasize infrastructure improvement, general research and development (R&D) and easy access to capital. According to Elton Zhuo, an official with the Beijing Semiconductor Industry Association, "A lot of little companies were waiting for the new policy, hoping to receive some real benefit. The old system was not running so well, so maybe you paid the whole tax and never saw the rebate."[34]

The negotiation process

The US government filed the complaint to the WTO on 23 March 2004. This was an unexpected move as the dispute had existed for years. Right after the issuing of Circular No. 18 by the State Council, the US Semiconductor Industry Association (SIA) communicated with China's Ministry of Foreign Trade and Economic Cooperation (MOFTEC, now the Ministry of Commerce) at the end of 2000. In December 2001, one month after China joined the WTO, the SIA complained that Circular No. 18 and the following Circular No. 70 had violated the nondiscrimination principle of the WTO. In June 2002 government officials and industry representatives from these two countries had their first face-to-face discussions at the International Semiconductor Forum held in Beijing. The intergovernmental talks began in 2003. After the USTR put this issue in its 2002 Report to Congress on China's WTO compliance, Beijing began to take it seriously. A research group was created that included officials from six relevant ministries, including the Ministry of Finance, the State Administration of Taxation and the Ministry of Commerce, to work on new WTO-consistent industrial policies.[35]

By the time the US filed a formal complaint to the WTO, the US and China had had bilateral communications on this issue for over three years and the Chinese research group had already finished its policy report. Chinese negotiators felt that the gap between the two sides had been narrowed.[36] Chong Quan, spokesman of the Ministry of Commerce, said in a statement that China and the US had already held some rounds of bilateral talks on the issue of a VAT for integrated circuits, and had made some progress. The Chinese side expressed complete bafflement at the sudden US demand for consultation through the dispute settlement mechanism of the WTO at a time when bilateral consultations were continuing: "In the normal course of bilateral consultations, the US side suddenly raised a request under the WTO dispute resolution mechanism. China really does not understand this."[37]

However, the US side seemed to have a different story. Citing unidentified US officials, the *Financial Times* reported that the office of the US Trade Representative Robert Zoellick planned to delay a filing until after the fifteenth US–China Joint Commission on Commerce and Trade (JCCT) meeting involving top economic officials from China and the US in Washington on 19 April, but then changed that plan after the Chinese government told a US trade official in Beijing a week before that there was no chance of dropping the tax at the meeting.[38] Instead, China chose to make concessions on its controversial WLAN Authentication and Privacy Infrastructure (WAPI) standard for wireless networking and the third generation telecommunication standard TD-SCDMA (also known as the 3G standard) at the JCCT meeting.

On 27 April 2004 the US and China held consultations in Geneva. The EU, Japan and Mexico participated in the consultation as interested third parties. Further bilateral negotiations were held in Beijing on 27 May and 1–2 July, and in Washington, DC on 15 June. The two sides reached consensus for the most part in a Memorandum of Understanding (MOU) and the formal agreement was signed on 14 July. The negotiation only took 123 days and the dispute was resolved before moving to the next step of the dispute settlement procedure – the establishment of a dispute settlement panel – to consider whether China was acting in accordance with its WTO obligations. According to the MOU, effective immediately, China would cease to certify any new semiconductor products or manufacturers for VAT refund eligibility and would no longer offer VAT refunds that favored semiconductors designed in China. Beijing also agreed to stop providing VAT refunds for Chinese-produced semiconductors to current beneficiaries by 1 April of the next year.

Compared to many other WTO cases, this negotiation was not complicated. As mentioned above, the semiconductor sector bears strategic importance and the Chinese government has made it a national strategy to promote China's overall competitiveness in the innovation, design and production of semiconductors. Furthermore, given that the WTO legal process could last for years, some WTO members, which carry out WTO-incompatible industrial policy at home, have chosen to go through the WTO dispute settlement process in order to obtain some extra time for their domestic infant industries. The question, then, was why did Beijing decide to quickly wrap up a deal with Washington at the consultation stage while the two countries had been unable to settle the dispute bilaterally in the past three years?

The reasons are threefold. First, with a number of regime constraints written into China's WTO accession protocol, many believed that these "China specific" arrangements would effectively limit China's full integration into the WTO until 2013,[39] when the said mechanism would terminate. For any rule-related trade dispute, any explanation or justification provided by Beijing would be considered weak when the country was still classified as a non-market economy. For dumping disputes, Beijing's position would be diluted both by its non-market economy status and by product-specific safeguard clauses. Most importantly, the pressure of the annual review meant that Beijing would need to maintain constructive relationships with all of its trading partners. Within this context, Beijing was not confident about its capacity to fully defend its domestic industrial policy. As one Chinese negotiator put it, "from the first day of negotiations we knew we had to make concessions. In other words we knew the negotiation outcome even before it started. But this does not mean that negotiation was unnecessary".[40]

Second, many inside the government felt that it was always bad to be sued, as it would bring China a bad image. The more time Chinese negotiators would spend in the WTO depute settlement panel, the more criticisms China would receive regarding its capacity and willingness to honor its WTO commitments. More importantly, this skepticism would have spill-over effects on China's political image. This reputational concern was closely related to the regime constraints Beijing agreed to accept upon accession. The message from the central leader to the negotiator was clear: try to resolve the dispute at the consultation stage and keep it low-key.[41]

Third, as a new WTO member, Beijing was still engaged in the process of institutional learning. As Beijing became a major trading state, it started to confront growing trade disputes, particularly with the US with which China enjoyed a tremendous trade surplus. However, China was still more used to negotiating trade disputes bilaterally. Since China's entry into the WTO, Beijing has negotiated bilateral agreements with Washington over beef, soy beans, furniture, TV, auto financing, textiles and IPR protection, among other issues. Dispute settlement at the WTO represented a negotiation forum that Beijing was yet unfamiliar with. That is why MOFCOM hired a large number of foreign legal experts to work on this issue. Such an institutional learning process thus in part explains Beijing's willingness to concede at an early stage of the dispute settlement process.

Conclusion

The effect of international regimes on state behavior is a central concern of the study of international relations. The efficacy of international institutions is vital to international cooperation in the contemporary world. To many transition economies, accession into international institutions is the very first step of their integration into the international community. The commitment compliance of these transition economies in turn has significant consequences for global governance. This case study explores the impact of the extra set of rules written in China's accession protocol on its policy choices. The study shows that China has been more willing to address the concerns that the US raised through multilateral, rather than through the bilateral venues. For four years Washington and Beijing had been engaged in negotiations over China's semiconductor VAT rebate policy but were unable to reach any agreement. After Washington formally filed the complaint to the WTO, Beijing quickly wrapped up a MOU with Washington by committing to terminate its VAT refund policy. Thus the dispute was solved at the consultation stage, before it moved to the next stage of the dispute settlement procedure. The negotiations suggest that the reputational concerns of the Chinese government have exerted a constraint on its behavior. Consequently this case shows that multilateral negotiations have been more effective than bilateral efforts in eliciting Chinese cooperation.

This tentative finding has important and broader implications for studies of the integration of transition economies into international institutions. As norms and regime rules have positive influence over states' institutional behavior and as institutional learning is possible, the future accession of transition economies and/or non-democratic states would not necessarily pose a threat to rule-oriented regimes. Most importantly, concerns about the possible abuse of regime norms and principles by new and existing members can be muted by carefully designed regime constraints.

This does not necessarily mean that there will be no compliance problems in the future. In fact in China there has been an undercurrent of concern over the ability of Chinese industries to compete in an open home market with the WTO rules put in place. In the semiconductor VAT rebate case, the policy preferences of the CSIA overlapped with those of the US constituents. The passive stance of the CSIA in part helped to put the dispute to an end. It is possible that a more assertive industry posture could greatly complicate negotiations on other issues in the future.

Indeed, the involvement of domestic sectoral interests is a new development in China's trade politics and represents a promising direction for future research. To what degree can industry interests influence China's trade policy and its negotiation position in trade disputes? Will the Chinese government be able to balance the constraints imposed by the WTO and domestic industry needs when the two are in conflict? These questions can be answered by further studies of China's trade dispute settlement at the multilateral level.

Notes

1   Haus (1991: 169).
2   GATT BISD (15th Supp.) 109 at 110 (1966–67). Poland's GATT Accession Protocol, available at www.wto.org.
3   Lardy (2002: 10).
4   Fraser Institute (2006).
5   SIA (2004).
6   WTO, Accession of the People's Republic of China (Decision of 10 November 2001), WT/L/432, available at www.wto.org.
7   For the complete document on the protocol and working party report on China's accession, see www.wto.org.
8   Davidson (2001).
9   Testimony of Ambassador Charlene Barshefsky before the House Committee on Ways and Means on China's WTO Accession and PNTR, 3 May 2000.
10   They are the Council for Trade in Goods, the Council for Trade Related Aspects of Intellectual Property Rights, the Council for Trade in Services, the Committee on Balance of Payments Restrictions, the Committee on Market Access, the Committee on Agriculture, the Committee on Sanitary and Phytosanitary Measures, the Committee on Technical Barriers to Trade, Subsides and Countervailing Measures, the Committee on Antidumping Measure, the Committee on Customs Valuation, the Committee on Rules of Origin, the Committee on Import Licensing, the

Committee on Trade Related Investment Measures, the Committee on Safeguards and the Committee on Trade in Financial Services.

11   WTO (undated).
12   GAO (2005).
13   Examples included the creation of the Department of WTO Affairs and the Bureau of Fair Trade.
14   State Council Document number 18.
15   MOF and SAT Circular No. 70 (2002).
16   MOF and SAT Circular No. 140 (2002).
17   Hatano (2002).
18   Zhong (2004).
19   Testimony of Anne Craib, Director of International Trade and Government Affairs, SIA, before the US–China Economic and Security Review Commission, Hearing on China's WTO Compliance and US Monitoring Efforts, 5 February 2004.
20   Hatano (2002).
21   Scalise (2005: 3).
22   Gill and Tay (2004).
23   Juster (2003).
24   Lichtenbaum (2005).
25   GAO (2002).
26   Ibid: 3.
27   Wen (2004).
28   SIA Press Release. Available at: http://sia-online.org/pre_release.cfm?ID=287.
29   Kerry (2005).
30   Interview, summer 2006.
31   Xing Jing Daily (2004).
32   China Daily (2004b).
33   Fuller (2004).
34   Clendenin (2004).
35   Zhong (2004).
36   Ibid.
37   Dickie (2004: 2).
38   China Daily (2004a).
39   Spadi (2002: 421).
40   Interview, June 2006 in Beijing.
41   Interview, August 2006 in Beijing.

References

Cai, W. (1992) "China's GATT membership: selected legal and political issues", *Journal of World Trade*, 26 (1): 35–59.

China Daily (2004a) "China puzzled over US tax complaint at WTO", *China Daily*, 19 March. Available online: www.chinadaily.com.cn/english/doc/2004–03/19/content_3316453.htm.

—— (2004b) "Semiconductor sector shake-up", *China Daily*, 9 September. Available online: www.china.org.cn/english/BAT/106487.htm.

Clendenin, M. (2004) "China mulls new aid to chip makers", *EE Times*, 1 November. Available online: www.eetimes.com/issue/mn/showarticle.jhtml?articleID=51201468.

Cowhey, P. F. (1993) "Domestic institutions and the credibility of international commitments: Japan and the United States", *International Organization*, 47 (2): 299–326.

Davidson (2001) Statement by General Council Davidson to US–China Security Review Commission, US–China Security Review Commission Hearings on Bilateral Trade Policies and Issues between the United States and China, 2 August.

Dickie, M. (2004) "China 'baffled' by US charge at WTO", *Financial Times*, 20 March.

Fearon, J. D. (1994) "Domestic political audiences and the escalation of international disputes", *American Political Science Review*, 88: 577–92.

Fraser Institute (2006) *Economic Freedom of the World 2006* Annual Report, The Fraser Institute. Available online: www.freetheworld.com/2006/EFW2006complete.pdf.

Fuller, D. (2004) "Time for new thinking on China trade", *Boston Globe*, 24 August. Available online: http://web.mit.edu/ipc/www/pubs/articles/fuller_globe.pdf.

GAO (2002) "Rapid advances in China's semiconductor industry underscore need for fundamental U.S. policy review", GAO Report to the Ranking Minority Member, Committee on Governmental Affairs, US Senate, April.

—— (2005) "U.S.–China Trade: Summary of WTO TRM for China", GAO Report. Available online: www.gao.gov/new.items/d05209r.pdf.

Gaubatz, K.T. (1996) "Democratic states and commitment in international relations", *International Organization*, 50 (1): 109–39.

Gill, B. and Tay, S. A. (2004) "Partners and competitors: coming to terms with the U.S.–China economic relationship", Center for Strategic and International Studies, April.

Hatano (2002) "China's compliance with WTO commitments",Testimony of Daryl G. Hatano, Vice-President of Semiconductor Industry Association before the Office of the USTR, 18 September.

Haus, L. (1991) "The East European countries and GATT: the role of realism, mercantilism, and regime theory in explaining East–West trade negotiation", *International Organization*, 45 (2): 163–82.

Holton, R. H. and Lin, X. Y. (1998) "China and the World Trade Organization: can the assimilation problems be overcome?", *Asian Survey*, 38: 745–62.

Juster (2003) "Commerce's Juster Discusses China, Taiwan on Export Controls", Under Secretary of Commerce, 15 September remarks, available online: http://canberra.usembassy.gov/hyper/2003/0923/ef204.htm..

Kerry, J. (2005) "CAFTA is a giant step backward". Available online: http://kerry.senate.gov/v3/cfm/record.cfm?id=240185.

Lardy, N. (2002) *Integrating China into the Global Economy*, Washington, DC: Brookings Institution Press.

Leeds, B. A. (1999) "Domestic political institutions, credible commitments, and international cooperation", *American Journal of Political Science*, 43 (4): 979–1002.

Lichtenbaum, P. (2005) Testimony of Acting Under Secretary for Industry and Security Peter Lichtenbaum before the US–China Economic and Security Review Commission Hearing, 23 June. Available online: www.bis.doc.gov/news/2005/USChinaReview.htm.

Martin, L. (2000) *Democratic Commitments: Legislatures and International Cooperation*, Princeton, NJ: Princeton University Press.

Scalise (2005) "China's High-Technology Development", Testimony of George Scalise, President of SIA, before the US China Economic and Security Review Commission, 21 April.

SIA (2004) "China as a Market/Non-Market Economy for Purpose of the U.S. Antidumping Law", SIA report, 19 May 2004. Available online: www.sia-online.org/pre_stat.cfm?ID=241.

Simmons, B. A. (2000) "International law and state behavior: commitment and compliance in international monetary affairs", *American Political Science Review*, 94 (4): 819–35.

Spadi, F. (2002) "Discriminatory safeguards in the light of the admission of the People's Republic of China to the World Trade Organization", *Journal of International Economic Law*, 5 (2): 421–43.

Wen, D. (2004) " US policy impedes healthy trade relations", *China Daily*, 21 April, Available online: www.chinadaily.com.cn/english/doc,2004-04/21/content_325184.htm.

WTO (Undated) "Trade Policy Reviews", World Trade Organization, Available online: www.wto.org/english/tratop_e/tpr_e.htm.

Xing Jing Daily (2004) "Elimination of VAT rebate will result in the termination of the common practice in semiconductor sector to cheat for export tax rebate", *Xing Jing Daily*, 16 July.

Zhong, Z. (2004) "China-US semiconductor dispute – an uncomplicated lawsuit", *Internet Weekly* (Hulianwang Zhoukan), 28 July.

7 State, business interests and China's use of legal trade remedies

Ka Zeng

The emergence of China as a major global trade and manufacturing center has resulted in growing trade confrontation between that nation and advanced industrial states in recent years. Not only have Chinese firms been subject to a large number of antidumping actions from abroad, but Beijing has also increasingly had to respond to trade challenges from its old and new rivals alike over an expanding array of trade issues.[1] While bilateral negotiation approaches remain a policy option for Beijing, China is increasingly turning to other legal trade remedies, such as antidumping duties, safeguard measures and the dispute settlement procedures of the World Trade Organization (WTO) to address its trade grievances. If, in the past, China has primarily pursued a diplomacy-negotiation-oriented approach to dispute resolution, responding unilaterally to foreign demand for trade liberalization,[2] it is now increasingly able to resort to its own domestic legal trade remedy laws and the rules of the WTO to settle trade disputes. Indeed, China's use of fair trade laws is starting to resemble their use by other major users of these tools. The growing frequency with which Beijing utilizes legal trade remedies therefore represents an important departure from China's traditional reliance on the diplomatic route to trade dispute resolution and promises to have a major impact on China's interactions with its trading partners.

This chapter explores the motivations, manifestations and implications of China's turn toward legal trade remedies by examining a few recent developments in China's foreign trade policy, including, specifically:

- China's antidumping actions
- China's reactions to the US steel safeguard measure, and
- the China–Japan safeguard dispute over textiles.

It will be argued that at the level of the state, the move toward the utilization of legal trade remedies has been driven by a desire to use the institutionalized rules and procedures provided by law to restrain the United States' unilateral exercise of power and to retaliate against perceived unfair foreign trade practices against Chinese firms. But while the Chinese government has played a major role pushing for the turn toward such a trade strategy, domestic industries have largely shaped the pattern in which such remedies were deployed. Importantly, while import-competing chemical and steel industries, which have both experienced significant import surges in recent years, have been active users of legal trade remedies, the preferred policy instruments of these two industries have differed as the chemical industry has resorted to antidumping measures far more frequently than the steel industry. This chapter argues that the contrasting responses of the steel and chemical industries can be explained by the different market conditions confronted by firms in these two sectors. Factors such as profitability and the structure of imports and exports may differently affect the tendency of the chemical and steel companies to seek trade protection.

Industry conditions also influence the resolution of China's antidumping disputes. While Chinese industries have won most of the AD cases,[3] foreign firms have also obtained favorable outcomes in cases under several situations:

- where downstream users of the dumped products lodge complaints against the AD duties due to the higher input prices the duties incur
- where the foreign firm has substantial investment in China and hence possesses greater bargaining leverage *vis-à-vis* the Chinese authorities; or
- where the buyers of the products engage in export processing and hence are exempt from the import duties.

Under these circumstances, the case outcome favors foreign firms as the final rulings often yield no evidence of dumping by foreign firms or only result in minimal dumping margins. Consequently the linkages created by China's increasing enmeshment in the world economy have created forces in favor of openness in trade disputes, reducing the effectiveness of trade protection the state provides to domestic industries.

To support the above contention, this chapter examines a couple of substantive issue areas that have captured the spotlight in China's foreign trade policy in the past few years, such as antidumping (AD), and China's reactions to the US steel safeguard action. The legal trade remedies this chapter examines include not only the rules of the WTO but also China's domestic trade remedies (such as antidumping and safeguards) that Chinese authorities have more recently incorporated into their trade policy arsenal. The first section of the chapter provides an overview of China's use of legal trade remedies and argues that Chinese authorities have come to view the use of legal trade instruments as a way of constraining the United States' unilateral exercise of trade power during the era of bilateral negotiations. The subsequent sections argue that even though the state has consciously pushed for the use of legal trade remedies, the actual pattern of the deployment of these remedies is highly influenced by business actors. Specifically, by examining the heavy concentration of China's AD duties in the chemical sector and the outcomes of the settlement of AD cases, this part of the chapter points to the growing influence of business interests on China's use of legal trade remedies. The chapter concludes by discussing the implications of such an emerging trade strategy based on the use of legal trade remedies for China's trading partners.

The state and the turn toward the use of legal trade strategy

This section makes the argument that the Chinese state has played an important role in the decision to pursue the legal route to trade dispute resolution which has come to be viewed as offering several advantages over the *ad hoc*, bilateral route to dispute resolution. Indeed, most of the trade negotiations between China and the United States during the 1980s and 1990s were carried out either through bilateral talks or under the framework of Section 301 of US trade law.

The Chinese leadership's inability to pursue dispute resolution under other fora, such as dispute resolution under the WTO, substantially constrained Beijing's room for maneuver, leaving *ad hoc* diplomatic negotiations as Beijing's primary means for dealing with its trading partners. However, such a diplomatic route to dispute resolution allowed the United States to unilaterally shape the negotiation agenda and challenge Chinese policy. While Beijing did not always make the concessions demanded by the United States during these negotiations, it neverthe-less found itself in a very disadvantaged position, having had to respond to US demands on an *ad hoc* basis. For example, the United States challenged Chinese textile policies that led to the surge of low-cost Chinese textile products in the US market, culminating in a move to unilaterally impose quota restrictions on textile imports from China. The United States also exerted pressure on China under Section 301 of US trade law, threatening to impose sanctions on Chinese products unless that country modified its practices hindering US producers' access to the Chinese market. Finally, the United States threatened to revoke China's Most-Favored-Nation (MFN) status unless Beijing removed its market access barriers and enhanced its protection of US intellectual property rights (IPR), in addition to improving its human rights practices.[4]

In part due to the perceived disadvantages of diplomatic routes to dispute reso-lution, legal trade remedies, including the rule-based WTO multilateral forum, have come to be viewed by Chinese leaders as offering a viable alternative to bilat-eral negotiations with the United States. In particular, legal trade remedies were seen to offer several advantages over the bilateral route of dispute resolution.

First, resort to legal trade remedies offers the prospect of restraining the unilateral exercise of power by more powerful countries. Importantly, the option to resort to legal trade remedies allows a developing country such as China to force its more powerful trading partners to come to the negotiating table and discuss issues of interest to itself. As such, it prevents more powerful countries from dominating the discussion agenda, allowing China to operate on a more level playing field with its trading partners.[5] Moreover, compared to the bilateral approach, the legal route to dispute resolution has the advantage of adjudicating disputes on the basis of a set of relatively standard and clear rules and criteria. For example, the dispute settlement process of the WTO brings to bear on the parties in dispute a set of impartial stan-dards and rules that are accepted by all member countries. Negotiations conducted within an institutional context therefore privilege legal over political criteria. Addi-tionally, joining a multilateral trade organization and acquiring the ability to file a legal WTO complaint provides a state with a distributive tactic it otherwise does not have as a non-member. The underlying goal of the WTO dispute settlement system is to encourage the parties to negotiate solutions between themselves. Turning the dispute over to a neutral arbitrator in Geneva can therefore be considered as a move in a bilateral dispute negotiation, or a distributive tactic intended to worsen the defendant's alternative to agreement and force unilateral policy changes from the defendant. In this sense, the dispute mechanism of the WTO presents an alternative course of action in case of the failure of bilateral negotiations.[6]

Indeed, Beijing's decision to pursue entry into the WTO clearly reflected the Chinese leadership's desire to operate in a rule-oriented environment and on a level playing field with the United States. The rhetoric of Chinese officials indicated that even though Chinese leaders were clearly aware of the constraints that WTO entry would place on China's autonomy and policy choices, they nevertheless recognized that WTO entry, by offering an institutionalized form of cooperation, would allow them to effectively and legitimately defend China's economic interests. For example, in his comments on the effects of multilateralism in 2004, Chinese Vice Foreign Minister Wang Yi noted that "multilateralism ... is an important means to resolve international disputes ... . It is also the best way to promote democratic and law-based international relationships."[7] Similarly, in his speech to the United Nations General Assembly in 2003, China's Foreign Minister Li Zhaoxing stated that "multilateral cooperation ... should become the principal vehicle in the handling of international affairs."[8] These pronouncements clearly indicate that Chinese leaders have come to view multilateralism as an effective means for advancing China's interests in both the security and the economic realms.

Second, the multilateral forum would allow Chinese leaders to achieve their objective of domestic economic reform. As the country became closely integrated with the world economy, Chinese leaders have come to see multilateral policy-making as a means of preventing other countries from adopting policies that may negatively affect the Chinese economy or of binding themselves to market liberalization. In particular, the multilateral framework often allows countries to make cross-sector linkages for trade liberalization. It could invoke reputational and normative pressures to bear on countries that fail to live up to their obligations,[9] in addition to having the potential of binding the Chinese leadership vis-à-vis their domestic constituencies and encouraging recalcitrant ministries and officials to engage in reforms that they otherwise would be unwilling to undertake.

In addition, the resort to legal trade remedies could be viewed as part of China's domestic legal reforms. Since the early 1990s, the Chinese government has sought further reform of its domestic legal structure to emphasize the rule of law. Just as in other policy areas, Chinese leaders have come to see attempts to engage in institutionalization of domestic rules and procedures as part and parcel of the reform of the domestic legal system.[10]

Thus, embracing legal trade remedies could be viewed as a conscious choice of Chinese leaders. Indeed, the Chinese government has undertaken institutional reforms so as to harmonize China's domestic political institutions with the requirements of the WTO. For instance, the WTO Affairs Section was established under the Ministry of Foreign Trade and Economic Cooperation (MOFTEC), now transformed into the Ministry of Commerce (MOFCOM), to handle WTO-related issues. The Chinese government also devoted substantial monetary and human resources to beef up the institutional capacity of that agency. Along similar lines, Beijing has paid greater attention to developing greater familiarity with the rules of the WTO and, as will be detailed below, instituted an antidumping regime so as to better defend the interests of Chinese industries. These institutional changes formed the organizational foundation for Chinese leaders' pursuit of a rule-oriented trade strategy.

Business interests and the emerging pattern of trade protection in China

While the Chinese state was favorably disposed toward the use of legal trade remedies, it will be argued that sectoral interests have largely shaped the way in which China's legal trade remedies were deployed. This section presents evidence of the influence of domestic industries on China's trade policy. It argues that China's use of legal trade remedies largely reflected the ability of China's large import-oriented and exporting industries to influence the policy process as large, heavily concentrated industries such as steel and chemicals have dominated China's use of antidumping measures. In addition, the steel industry has been an active user of China's newly developed safeguard provisions. In other words, even though Beijing has played an important role in promoting the shift from bilateral negotiation approaches to a rules-based negotiation approach, business interests have greatly influenced the pattern of the deployment of legal trade instruments in China. This section highlights the influence of sectoral interests in China's trade policy both by examining the sectoral incidence of China's AD actions and China's use of safeguard measures. It also considers the channels through which business interests managed to influence the government's trade policy.

An important manifestation of China's emerging trade strategy revolving around legal trade remedies is its increasing invocation of antidumping duties against foreign firms. A number of studies (e.g. Huang, 2002; Messerlin, 2004; Kennedy, 2005a) have provided detailed accounts of the development of China's antidumping regime. Most of these studies suggest that like many other developing countries which adopted AD laws in part to retaliate against the rising incidence of AD petitions by foreign countries, China implemented its own antidumping regulations out of a desire to defend the legitimate interests of Chinese industries. These studies (e.g. Kennedy, 2005b) also suggest that even though China's antidumping regime has a number of deficiencies (such as using the concept of the "major proportion" of the industry as the threshold for accepting complaints, the lack of transparency of the AD investigation procedure and the privileged position domestic applicants enjoy over foreign respondents, etc.), it nevertheless has increasingly come to resemble AD systems in advanced industrialized states.[11]

Of particular interest to this study is the sectoral pattern of AD initiations in China. As will be shown below, while China's antidumping measures closely mirror foreign AD actions directed against Chinese firms, they were also tilted disproportionately in favor of China's heavily concentrated, import-competing industries such as the steel and chemical industries.

Several characteristics of the AD suits initiated by China are noteworthy. First, most of the petitioners in these suits are domestic firms instead of foreign-invested ones, and state-owned enterprises have been disproportionately favored. For example, of the 34 AD suits China initiated between November 1997 and November 2004 for which the identity of the petitioners is known, only three involve joint ventures.[12] In 1999, together with several other domestic chemical companies, DuPont Foshan Hongji filed an antidumping suit against polyester film imported from South Korea. In 2001, a new Sino-American joint venture, Zhanjiang Xinzhongmei Chemial Co., Ltd., participated in an antidumping suit against polystyrene from South Korea, Japan and Thailand. In the same year, a Japanese-invested company, Sichuan Ajinomoto Co., and another Hong Kong invested firm, Fujian Quanzhou Daquan Lysine Co., joined several other Chinese firms in an antidumping suit against lysine imported from the United States, South Korea and Indonesia. The last two cases were dismissed as Chinese authorities only found evidence of dumping, but not of injury by the alleged foreign firms.

Second, and more important, the major sectors in which the Chinese government has initiated antidumping suits pertain to chemicals and steel, two industries that have also become the prime targets of antidumping investigations from abroad. Between the initiation of the antidumping law in 1997 and 2006, the Chinese government launched 45 antidumping investigations against a broad array of foreign products, including newsprint, cold-rolled silicon steel sheets, polyester films and acrylates. Table 7.1 presents the sectoral composition of China's AD cases. It shows that industries such as chemical, steel and paper have dominated the use of the AD instrument in China. The chemical industry, in particular, has taken up the lion's share of China's AD duties, accounting for two-thirds of all AD initiations in China.[13]

The initiation of AD duties in the chemical and steel industries can in part be

Table 7.1 Sectoral composition of China's antidumping duties

Sector	Count	Percentage (%)
Chemical	30	67
Paper	5	11
Steel	3	7
Textiles and apparel	3	7
Light industry	2	4
Electronics	1	2
Pharmaceuticals	1	2
Total	45	100

explained by the high level of import competition both industries have been confronted with in recent years. As both industries have a strong domestic orientation and lack competitiveness internationally, import competition in recent years has posed a major challenge. Tables 7.2 and 7.3 present the percentage change in exports and imports of China's key industrial sectors. As the data illustrate, annual percentage change in imports in the steel industry ranged from 20.87 percent to 67.85 percent between 1999 and 2003 and from 5.36 to 71.58 percent in the chemical industry during the same period. While industries such as automobiles and electrical machinery are similarly characterized by import surges, increases in imports in these industries were matched by reasonably strong growth in exports, which arguably dampened the tendency of these industries to seek trade protection. The steel and chemical industries' domestic orientation and lack of export competitiveness therefore reinforced both industries' vulnerability to import penetration.

Indeed, China's steel industry has experienced major difficulties in recent years. Even though China was one of the world's major producers of steel, it has had to import the high-grade steel it cannot produce domestically. China's increasing domestic demand for steel products, fueled by its economic development, had resulted in rising imports. While China primarily exported low-grade steel to the world market, its low-grade steel exports were not competitive internationally. As Table 7.2 shows, the annual percentage change in steel exports has fluctuated greatly since the mid-1990s. Indeed, between 1996 and 2000, China's steel imports amounted to over 1,000 tons per year. While China's imports of steel products increased by 7.87 percent and 70.64 percent between 2000 and 2001, China's steel exports dropped by 23.6 percent and 46.37 percent during the same period.[14]

In light of rising imports and a bleak export outlook, the steel industry had taken the initiative to urge the Chinese government to relieve the industry's plight. Large state-owned enterprises were by far the most vocal actors in this effort. In terms of domestic policy measures, the steel industry has for a long period of time pushed

Table 7.2 Annual percentage change in exports of key sectors, 1995–2003

Year	1996	1997	1998	1999	2000	2001	2002	2003
Chemical	0.05	11.48	2.74	3.68	16.34	9.93	14.22	66.29
Paper	−12.57	23.92	−1.00	−6.57	16.11	−38.36	15.17	35.01
Auto	1.53	26.08	21.39	2.91	41.86	0.49	12.42	47.82
Steel	−35.52	24.07	−37.93	−13.90	75.64	−37.66	3.08	48.11
Footwear	6.62	20.17	−1.69	3.42	13.49	2.50	9.85	16.82
Textiles	−2.54	23.55	−6.27	1.92	19.65	0.93	16.08	26.79
Electrical machinery	12.28	23.18	14.01	19.38	39.93	16.47	36.55	48.67

Source: *China Statistical Yearbook* (various years)

Table 7.3 Annual percentage change in imports of key sectors, 1995–2003

Year	1996	1997	1998	1999	2000	2001	2002	2003
Chemical	0.10	−1.07	7.20	27.31	28.73	5.36	−2.85	71.58
Paper	27.99	16.42	4.16	10.49	−0.48	−7.90	13.34	6.19
Auto	−0.28	0.09	4.39	7.53	6.11	57.06	14.99	52.00
Steel	15.61	−10.69	−3.75	22.57	33.59	14.47	20.87	67.85
Footwear	4.40	0.56	−18.72	5.15	4.58	2.81	−7.60	23.03
Textiles	5.47	3.18	−16.39	−3.27	18.97	−1.84	4.51	13.53
Electrical machinery	4.32	−4.66	8.91	23.89	35.05	13.23	30.01	39.89

Source: *China Statistical Yearbook* (various years)

for reform of China's import regime, which allowed certain importers to get away from nominal tariffs under pre-specified conditions. At the same time that they sought to halt imports through domestic policy instruments, steel companies resorted to legal trade instruments to address their concerns. While China's entry into the WTO and the tariff reductions associated with it increased the competitive pressure faced by the steel industry, it nevertheless allowed national governments to engage in contingent protection in case of import surges caused by unfair foreign trade practices.

The antidumping statute provided another avenue for steel companies to address their concerns. Between 1999 and 2002, the steel industry initiated three dumping charges. In 1999, Wuhan Iron and Steel filed an AD suit against Russian steel companies for dumping silicon steel in the Chinese market. Also in 1999, Taiwan Iron and Steel, Shanghai Pudong Iron and Steel and Shaanxi Jingmi (Precision) Group initiated an AD investigation into stainless steel from Japan and South Korea. Baoshan Iron and Steel, one of China's major steel producers, reportedly weighed in on behalf of the complainants due to its growing stainless steel production.[15] In the third case, three powerful steel companies, Baoshan Iron and Steel, Anshan Iron and Steel and Wuhan Iron and Steel launched an AD complaint against cold-rolled steel coils and strips imported from Russia, South Korea, Ukraine, Kazakhstan and Taiwan.

China's first action in the WTO, the steel safeguard trade dispute, provides another illustration of the influence of the steel industry on China's trade policy. Just as the utilization of antidumping measures was a relatively recent development in China's foreign trade policy, China has only more recently resorted to the use of safeguard measures. Prior to its entry into the WTO, China lacked its own safeguard regulations and an internationally accepted instrument against import surges, even though it was able to undertake retaliatory actions in response to safeguard measures directed against Chinese imports.[16] It has only been since its entry into the WTO that China had been required to abide by the

WTO's detailed procedures governing consultations and dispute resolution over safeguards. Indeed, China did not introduce its operational legislation as required by Article 32 of its Foreign Trade Law until 31 December 2002, shortly after the country's accession into the WTO (Jung, 2002: 1039–40).

At first glance, China's safeguard regulations seem to closely follow the language of the WTO's Safeguard Agreement. However, legal scholars (Jung, 2002: 1041) suggest that a closer examination of China's safeguard procedures would indicate that the Chinese regulations are both less detailed and more vaguely worded, which provides the relevant authorities with greater discretion in terms of investigation procedures and transparency. In terms of the administration of safeguard measures, China follows a dual-track enforcement system in which the jurisdiction over examination of the existence of the increased quantities of imported products resides with the MOFTEC, now being amalgamated into the Ministry of Commerce, whereas primary statutory authority over the determination of injury is vested with the State Economic and Trade Commission (SETC).

It is noteworthy that even though its safeguard regulations have been in place for only a relatively short period of time, the Chinese government has proceeded quickly to invoke safeguard procedures. The event leading the Chinese to undertake their first provisional safeguard measure was a decision by the United States to impose safeguard measures on 14 imported steel products on 5 March 2002, a decision undertaken in an effort to aid the troubled US steel industry. As the US action generated substantial opposition from its trading partners, leading many nations to respond in kind by raising their steel tariffs, China, too, joined the chorus and on 26 March 2002, just a few months after its accession into the WTO, lodged a complaint against the United States with the WTO's Dispute Settlement Body (DSB).

While Beijing's swift move to file a WTO complaint may be explained by its large market size which afforded it sufficient economic leverage to withstand the effect of counterretaliation or by China's desire to use trade policy instruments to address perceived unfair foreign trade practices targeted at Chinese firms, it could be argued that the Chinese government's invocation of the safeguard measure in the steel case again reflected the ability of the steel industry to lobby the government for trade relief. As mentioned above, China was one of the world's largest producers of steel, trailing only the European Union and the United States. But although imports amounted to only 17.8 percent of China's domestic demand in 2001, steel imports in the first quarter of 2002 nevertheless surged by 34 percent relative to the same period in the previous year. Confronted with such a sharp increase in imports, the Chinese steel industry, spearheaded by the China Iron and Steel Association (CISA) and leading Chinese steel companies such as Baoshan Iron and Steel and Anshan Iron and Steel, subsequently made strong demands that the government take appropriate trade policy measures in response to the United States' institution of "safeguard" tariffs (Jung, 2002: 1042). In addition to the CISA, the China Chamber of Commerce similarly joined this effort to push for more action.

It was against this backdrop that the Chinese government moved swiftly to resort to the rules of the WTO to protect the interests of its key domestic industries.

Invoking its rights provided for by the WTO's Safeguard Agreement, the Chinese government announced its intention to retaliate against the United States. On 17 May 2002, China, along with the European Union, Japan and Norway, preliminarily notified the Council for Trade in Goods that it would retaliate against certain steel products should the US safeguard measure fail to maintain a substantially equivalent level of concession. According to the Chinese notification, since the US safeguard measure affected $395 million in Chinese steel exports and the tariffs collected for these goods would have amounted to $95.5 million, China's proposed retaliatory tariffs were intended to affect roughly the same amount of US exports.[17] Shortly after this move, on 21 May 2002, MOFTEC announced that it would impose a provisional safeguard measure in the form of tariff quotas on certain steel imports in order to ameliorate the repercussions that the ongoing global steel trade war has had on the Chinese steel industry.

Essentially, China invoked a two-pronged strategy in imposing the safeguard measure. First, China argued that its steel safeguard measure was largely a response to the United States' repeated invocation of protectionist trade measures against steel imports between 1998 and 2001, which constituted "unforeseen developments". According to the Chinese, the US action not only resulted in an increase in US steel imports, but also led China's trading partners such as the European Union to impose safeguard measures against steel imports. Unlike the EU's claim that the surge in EU imports could be directly attributed to the reduction in US imports, the Chinese could plausibly argue that China had become the only remaining market with the ability to absorb a sufficient amount of steel imports due to the safeguard measures imposed by the US and the EU. In this sense, then, even though just like the EU, China has used "unforeseen development" as a justification for its safeguard measure, its legal ground may be even stronger than that of the European Union (see Jung, 2002: 1050).

With regard to the requirement regarding "import increase" for the imposition of a safeguard measure, China argued that its total imports of the steel products in question had grown sharply by 24.48 percent between 1999 and 2000, and 24.16 percent between 2000 and 2001. If evaluated against the stipulations of the appellate body that the surge in imports should be "recent enough, sudden enough, sharp enough, significant enough, both qualitatively and quantitatively" to meet the requirement with regard to "import increase", then China's affirmative finding of import increase would appear to have considerable validity.[18]

Nevertheless, regardless of the legality of the measures China undertook in response to the US safeguard measure, China's rule-oriented approach poses a clear challenge to the conventional wisdom that, given the substantial adjustment period necessary for implementing the new commitments accompanying a WTO membership, a country that has only very recently acceded to that organization ought to be more prudent in invoking its trading rights conferred by the WTO agreements.[19] As emphasized earlier, one cannot fully understand the Chinese government's invocation of the safeguard measure without also understanding its desire to shield the import-competing sectors of its economy from trade challenges from abroad. Given that many of China's domestic industries have yet to confront the challenges of market liberalization, there is every possibility that the Chinese leadership may continue to engage both its domestic rules and the rules of the WTO to defend its own economic interests.

In short, the above discussion of the sectoral pattern of China's AD activities reveals the growing ability of heavily-concentrated state-owned enterprises in import-competing sectors to influence the pattern of China's AD initiation in a way that would help to ward off foreign competitive pressure. The Chinese government's increasing willingness to come to the defense of such industries as chemicals and steel is therefore indicative of the increasing bias that Chinese foreign trade policy has displayed toward large and heavily concentrated import-competing enterprises.

Advancing the interests of export-oriented industries in China: China–Japan trade disputes

In contrast to the above discussion of China's antidumping regime which reflects the Chinese government's desire to defend key import-competing industries, the Japan–China trade disputes that occurred in 2001 over Welsh onions and towels illustrate the Chinese government's increasing willingness to engage legal rules to safeguard the interests of export-oriented interests in China. The dispute started in late 2000, during the last phase of the negotiations over China's accession into the WTO, and was settled in late 2001, soon after China became a member of that organization. Therefore, almost throughout the course of the dispute, the rules of the WTO were not applicable in a strictly legal sense. Nevertheless, even prior to becoming a fully-fledged member of the WTO, the Chinese government showed a willingness to engage the rules of that organization so as to protect its export-oriented industries from what were perceived as unfair foreign trade practices directed against Chinese exports.

The China–Japan trade spats could in large part be traced to the incompatibility of economic interests in both countries. As the surge in Chinese agricultural and textile exports began to threaten the interests of the farm lobby and the textile interests in Japan, Japanese agricultural interests and towel manufacturers applied steady pressure on the government for import relief and subsequently obtained such trade protection.

Thus, beginning in early 2001, as Japan and China were still embroiled in disputes arising from China's antidumping investigations against Japanese products, agricultural producers in Japan had begun demanding import protection. On 22 January 2001, in response to rising pressure from domestic producers hard pressed by imports, the Japanese Ministry of Agriculture, Forestry, and Fisheries (MAFF), in what would herald a generalized turn toward protectionism in Japan, announced that it would launch investigations into the import levels, market shares and profitability of nine agricultural products in Japan. Then, on 22 February, 2001, in a separate move, the Japan Towel Industrial Association filed a petition with the Ministry of Economy, Trade and Industry (METI) requesting that the Japanese government impose safeguard measures against Chinese products.[20] While Japanese officials sought to convey to their Chinese counterparts the rationale for the investigations over Chinese agricultural products during bilateral meetings, the agriculture, finance and trade ministries, along with LDP officials, simultaneously began deliberations on Chinese eels and seaweed out of electoral concerns. It should be noted that although METI has traditionally set very high standards for the invocation of safeguard measures and has thereby largely avoided their use, pressure from distressed domestic industries nevertheless led Japanese officials to more seriously entertain the possibility of invoking safeguard measures and to actively engage the rules of the WTO in order to hold out the process of trade liberalization.[21] Largely as a result of such intense domestic pressure, Japan announced in April 2001 that it would invoke safeguard actions against three Chinese agricultural products, specifically spring onions, shiitake mushrooms and igusa rushes. This action, slated to take effect on 23 April, would raise tariffs of up to 266 percent on $100 million worth of trade in the three agricultural goods for a period of 200 days.[22]

Not surprisingly, the Chinese government criticized these measures as unilateral moves that not only violated rules of fair competition, but would also undercut Sino-Japanese trade relations in the long run. Indeed, on the Chinese side, too, the agricultural and textile industries have contributed significantly to China's phenomenal export drive and economic growth in the past decades.[23] These industries were also confronted with the challenge of adjusting to the changes that WTO entry would have entailed.[24]

Table 7.4 and Table 7.5 illustrate the share of the textile industry in China's total employment and exports, respectively. As these data suggest, the textile industry is one of the largest employers in China. With about 30 million employees, it constituted about eight percent of China's total workforce. The textile industry was also a

Table 7.4 Sectoral employment (as percentage of national total)

Sector	1994	1995	1996	1997	1998	1999	2000	2001
Textiles	10.50	10.18	9.83	9.59	8.27	7.97	7.97	7.83
Printing	1.50	1.47	1.49	1.45	1.45	1.45	1.41	1.34
Ferrous metal	5.25	5.23	5.22	1.58	1.77	1.87	1.95	2.06
Chemicals	6.16	6.23	6.31	6.31	6.40	6.36	6.19	5.98
General machinery	6.72	6.13	6.54	6.48	5.79	5.62	5.41	5.30
Transportation machinery	3.54	3.69	3.66	3.65	3.58	3.57	3.53	3.57
Electrical machinery	2.48	2.60	2.53	2.65	2.82	3.00	3.36	3.72

Source: *China Statistical Yearbook* (various years)

Table 7.5 Sectoral share of China's total exports, 1995–2003

Sector	1995	1996	1997	1998	1999	2000	2001	2002	2003
Chemical	5.66	5.58	5.14	5.25	5.13	4.67	4.81	4.49	5.55
Paper	0.62	0.53	0.55	1.45	1.45	1.45	1.41	1.34	0.53
Auto	2.77	2.77	2.88	3.48	3.38	3.75	3.53	3.24	3.56
Steel	3.21	2.04	2.09	1.29	1.05	1.44	0.84	0.71	0.78
Footwear	4.48	4.70	4.67	4.57	4.45	3.95	3.79	3.41	2.96
Textiles	24.11	23.15	23.63	22.04	21.17	19.82	18.73	17.77	16.74
Electrical machinery	18.60	20.57	20.93	23.75	26.72	29.25	31.90	35.60	39.33

Source: *China Statistical Yearbook* (various years)

key export sector in China as its share of China's total exports has ranged from 17 to 24 percent (see Table 7.5). Despite the proliferation of small and medium-sized enterprises (SMEs) in China since the 1980s, State Owned Enterprises (SOEs) still accounted for over 60 percent of China's textile and clothing exports and it was estimated that about 41 percent of China's state-owned enterprises were loss-making in 1999.[20] What is most noticeable from Table 7.5 is that even though the textile industry is a leading exporter in China, its share in China's total exports has undergone a steady decline, from 24 percent in 1995 to 16.74 percent in 2003.

In light of the textile and clothing industry's importance in terms of total output and exports, the fact that the industry has been hard hit by Japanese import restrictions only increased the attractiveness of engaging WTO rules and using trade remedy laws as a means of safeguarding the interests of key export-oriented industries in China. Not surprisingly, then, when confronted with the Japanese safeguard measure, China quickly moved to challenge the Japanese measure head on.

Essentially, the Chinese government's response to Japan's safeguard measure was two-pronged. On the one hand, and most importantly, Beijing sought to couch its response to the Japanese safeguard measure on the basis of China's domestic laws and actively engaged WTO rules to challenge the legality of the Japanese action. As mentioned earlier, since the rules of the WTO were not entirely applicable during the course of this dispute, Beijing based its legal strategy primarily on Chinese domestic rules. On the other hand, when it became clear that such a strategy had failed to defuse Japanese protectionist pressures, Beijing quickly moved to invoke retaliatory tactics by imposing its own restrictions against a range of Japanese products.

To challenge the legality of the Japanese safeguard measure and defend the lawfulness of its retaliatory measures against Japanese products, Beijing insisted throughout the course of the negotiations that the Japanese provisional safeguard measure constituted a discriminatory trade restriction against China. Specifically, Chinese officials asserted that the Japanese action constituted discriminatory measures against China in that of the six products that the MAFF requested for investigation, safeguard measures had been imposed only on those three products for which the Chinese share in the Japanese market reached 90 percent. The other three products (tomatoes, green peppers and onions) had been left out because other WTO member countries commanded significant market shares in these products in Japan too. According to the Chinese, such a selective application of safeguard measures meant that the Japanese action was in clear violation of the principle of nondiscrimination, one of the basic principles of the WTO.[26]

Alternatively, to defend the legality of its countermeasure, Beijing invoked Article 6 of its Regulation on Import and Export Duties, which empowers Chinese authorities to impose special customs duties on imports originating in a country that applies "discriminatory rates of duty or other types of discriminatory treatment" to Chinese products.[27] In other words, China has sought to justify its countermeasure under its domestic law, and has by and large dismissed the Japanese argument about the lawfulness of its safeguard measure under international law.

It is not entirely clear if the Japanese safeguard measure does indeed violate WTO principles of nondiscrimination, in part because it is difficult to verify the factual basis of the Chinese argument as no systematic data are available on those three products excluded from the investigation. Nevertheless, regardless of the lawfulness of the Chinese argument, to the extent that the Chinese government did actively engage the rules of the WTO and used WTO principles to back up its argument, it could be argued that the Chinese actions clearly indicate the Chinese government's willingness to resort to legal remedies to advance its key economic interests.

The second prong of the Chinese response to the Japanese safeguard measure was to invoke retaliatory strategies when it became clear that negotiations had failed to make any inroads. On 9 February 2001, separate from the safeguard investigations, the Chinese government announced that it would conduct an antidumping investigation against polystyrene products from Asian countries, including Japan, Thailand and Korea. At the same time, although China continued to hold talks with Japan in an attempt to convey its displeasure with the Japanese emergency safeguard action regarding agricultural products, it moved to retaliate in other sectors too. In early June, China threatened to impose restrictions on imports of Japanese automobiles. By 20 June, it had moved to place punitive tariffs of 100 percent on such Japanese imports as cars, mobile phones and air conditioners worth approximately $500 million.[28] China's retaliatory move was greeted with criticism by Japanese officials who, in line with a trade strategy based on the WTO, urged the Chinese to follow WTO-consistent measures in the future.

China's retaliatory strategy eventually paid off. In July and August 2001, when two sets of talks failed to resolve the trade disputes, Japan was already considering a move to compensate Japanese companies affected by the Chinese import restrictions by the end of August. At the same time, however, Japan also undertook some conciliatory moves, such as delaying its decision regarding import restrictions on towels from China on the grounds that import levels had stabilized, in an attempt to improve the atmosphere of impending public- and private-sector trade talks between the two countries aimed at finding a resolution to the ongoing safeguard dispute. By 8 November, the deadline for Japan to decide whether to renew the controversial import tariffs on Chinese agricultural goods for up to four years, it had become clear that the talks had failed to achieve any breakthrough. When confronted with China's refusal to consider the Japanese proposal for "orderly trade", Japan could only agree not to invoke full-scale import curbs on farm products from China and to put off extending the four-year limit to 21 December 2001.

In short, the Sino-Japanese safeguard trade disputes may only herald the beginning of even more agricultural and industrial disputes between the two countries in the future. The fact that the Chinese have invoked the WTO principle of "nondiscrimination" to question the legality of the Japanese safeguard measure suggests that China may increasingly resort to the rules of that organization to settle disputes with its trading partners. Like Japan which has recently begun to use the rules of the international trading system in an instrumental fashion,[29] China, while still a newcomer to the WTO, seems to be increasingly engaging WTO rules and resorting to its domestic laws in defense of the interests of its key industries in the world marketplace. As will be emphasized in the conclusion, such an emerging trend in China's foreign trade policy ought to offer important lessons for its main trading partners such as the United States, because it suggests that it may no longer be adequate for the US to resort solely to a bilateral approach in dealing with China.

Explaining the dominance of the chemical industry in China's AD initiations

As mentioned above, even though both the chemical and steel companies have been confronted with a high level of import increases in recent years, the responses of the two industries to import penetration were nevertheless somewhat different. As mentioned earlier, even though both the chemical and steel industries were main users of China's AD statutes, the chemical industry has nevertheless dominated China's use of the AD instrument, accounting for two-thirds of all AD cases initiated by China. The question that merits further investigation, then, is why the chemical industry has resorted to antidumping duties far more frequently than a similarly capital-intensive and concentrated industry such as steel. The following discussion suggests that the answer to this question may be found in different industry conditions. Specifically, the chemical industry differs from the steel industry not only in terms of profitability, but also in terms of the structure of exports and imports.

First, one plausible argument about the concentration of AD actions in the chemical industry is the possible concentration of AD duties in such "antidumping intensive" sectors worldwide. Previous research (e.g. Messerlin, 2004) suggests that such industries as chemicals, metals, machinery and electrical equipment can be considered as "antidumping-intensive" sectors with a relatively high frequency of AD initiations as they are not only characterized by oligopolistic market structures and relatively standard products, but also constitute key sources of export growth for many rapidly developing countries. The concentration of AD duties in a few "antidumping-intensive" sectors worldwide may therefore reflect the trend toward the segmentation of the world market whereby firms with sufficient oligopolitic power lodge similar complaints in several key industries.

Indeed, while the chemical industry has initiated the most AD duties in China, it also happens to be the largest target of AD suits directed against China by foreign firms. For instance, in terms of the sectoral incidence of US AD actions against China, the chemical industry represented one of the largest initiators of AD suits against Chinese firms. Of the 56 AD suits the United States launched against Chinese exports between 1983 and 1995, 19 (or 32 percent) were targeted at the chemical sector. Out of 56 cases, 16 were directed at the metals industry.[30]

Similarly, the chemical industry was one of the primary targets of EU anti-dumping actions against China. Although the main focus of EU antidumping actions against China has shifted from chemical, mineral-ores and machinery sectors in the earlier 1980s to electronics (such as microwave ovens, color televisions and cathode-ray color television tubes) and mechanical goods (such as bicycles and parts, ring binder mechanisms, roller chains and photo albums) in the late 1990s, cases involving exports of Chinese chemicals and ores still amounted to about half of the total AD actions the EU took against China. Moreover, as the most frequent initiator of AD suits against China, the chemical sector alone accounted for 37.8 percent of total EU antidumping cases against China between 1979 and 2000.[31] To the extent that about 70 percent of China's total imports happen to fall within the top antidumping-intensive sectors (i.e. metals, chemicals, textiles and plastics), this ought to have increased the pressure faced by Chinese authorities from both domestic firms and joint ventures to initiate antidumping disputes.[32] Indeed, the rapid growth in foreign AD actions against China in the chemical industry has led officials of the China Chamber of Commerce of Metals, Minerals and Chemicals Importers and Exporters (CCCMC) to warn that foreign dumping measures toward China would likely "paralyze the nation's burgeoning petrochemical sector", which was still in its infancy.[33] A trade lawyer in China similarly commented that the surge in foreign AD actions against China has increased the incentive of local chemical companies to "resort to legal means to fight the intended dumping in order to defend their legitimate interests".[34]

But while explanations emphasizing the influence of "antidumping-intensive" sectors in China's AD petitions are plausible, they still cannot help us understand why the chemical and steel industries, which are both antidumping intensive sectors, have nevertheless demonstrated very different propensities with regard to the use of the AD instrument. The following section tentatively proposes that, in order for us to explain this puzzling pattern, one may have to take into account the different structures of these two industries in terms of ownership and market segmentation.

First, even though both the chemical and steel industries are predominantly controlled by the state, there is nevertheless a greater number of state-owned enterprises in the chemical industry. In addition, the chemical industry has a greater number of employees and more of the state-controlled enterprises in this sector are experiencing financial losses. According to statistics published by the National Bureau of Statistics of China, there were 2,084 firms in the chemical materials and manufactured products industry in 2004 that were either controlled by the state or had state shareholding. Of these firms, 597 were reported to be loss-making, with a total loss of 4.62 billion yuan. In comparison, in the same year there were about 579 firms in the ferrous metals industry. One hundred and eighteen of these firms were reportedly loss-making, with a loss of 0.98 billion yuan.[35] Moreover, chemical industry production often requires even heavier investment than steel production. Therefore the vested interests of bureaucratic actors in the chemical sector are arguably even more overpowering than those of the bureaucratic actors in the steel sector. An interviewed official from the Ministry of Commerce suggests that the chemical industry and its representative bureaus and agencies have effectively tapped on the privileged position the industry enjoyed during the era of centralized planning and avail of existing institutional channels to influence China's AD process.[36] In other words, while China's AD process has become more open, transparent and institutionalized, the process nevertheless advantages Chinese industries that have experienced financial difficulties in recent years.

Second, while both the steel and chemical industries have experienced strong import penetration in recent years, the steel industry nevertheless has a higher degree of reliance on imported products, especially in the high-end category. As mentioned above, even though China is a large exporter of low-grade steel, it cannot produce the high-grade steel it needs at home and hence has had to rely on imports to satisfy its domestic demand in those areas. Especially with regard to certain specialty steel, China still needs to satisfy its own domestic demand for imports. The greater demand of the steel industry for specialty steel which China cannot produce at home could therefore have reined in the temptation of the industry to seek trade protection. And even in the safeguard case where China did impose its own tariffs on foreign products, opposition from China's steel importers and large downstream users of these products against the sharp rise in production costs has led the Chinese government to scale back the number of products targeted by the initial AD action.[37] Hence even in a sector such as steel where the state presumably has a strong interest in protecting the domestic industry, domestic producers' reliance on those products that China cannot produce efficiently may have tempered the industry's aggressive behavior.

In short, this section tentatively proposes that industry conditions are relevant for understanding the pattern of China's AD initiations. In particular, the number of state-owned enterprises in a sector, the financial situation of an industry, or the patterns of trade in a sector may be associated with the probability that an industry will seek trade protection through China's newly acquired legal trade instruments. Future research could probe even further into these questions and develop more systematic accounts of how industry-related variables affect an industry's propensity to seek trade protection via the legal route.

Business influence on the settlement of China's AD cases

Kennedy (2005a) suggests that the AD investigations initiated by China have not always led to an outcome favorable to the domestic industry, even though the procedures for AD investigations in China presumably favor the domestic industry. While Kennedy identifies downstream users of the products under AD investigation as an important ally of foreign respondents and hence a source of openness in trade disputes, its appears that foreign investment or the tax exemption status of the end-users of the products targeted by AD actions also play an important role in explaining the varying degree of Chinese producers' success in AD cases. The next question this chapter addresses is why some antidumping cases have ended with only minimal dumping duties charged on the foreign producer or were eventually withdrawn by the Chinese authorities. In doing so, it presents several scenarios in which the case outcome has not necessarily tilted in favor of Chinese firms.

First, in line with the findings of Kennedy (2005a), downstream users of the products under AD investigation often stand to lose from the higher prices that the dumping margins would induce and, as a result, have voiced opposition to imposing AD duties on foreign products. The case involving acrylates was relevant in this respect. In this case, Chinese downstream users opposed the rise in the price of key products as the dumping margins would substantially increase the costs of their inputs. According to an interview source, due to its high absorption rate, acrylic acid has often been used in the production of disposable diapers. Diapers made with acrylic acid in them not only more quickly absorb waste products, they also help to lock them in place until the next diaper change. The antidumping charge therefore raised the price of key inputs for diaper producers and led them to oppose the dumping charges. Hence, once the proposed AD duties were announced, downstream users in the diaper industry maintained that the duties were unduly high and that the industry was unreasonably hurt by the rise in price of their key inputs. Diaper producers, through organizations such as the China Association of Textile Industry, which represents producers of industrial textiles, subsequently lobbied the Ministry of Commerce against the increase in the price of their key inputs. According to officials of a major association representing the chemical industry, opposition from producers and their representative associations played a key role in explaining the final case outcome.[38] Thus, when downstream users of a product lodge opposition to the dumping margins, the case outcome is less likely to be tilted in favor of domestic firms.

Third, China's AD actions are also often influenced by the political clout of the foreign firm named in the AD petition. Given the importance of foreign direct investment for economic development and the damage that a high-profile trade dispute could potentially exert on an important bilateral relationship such as US–China trade relations, Chinese authorities have sometimes balked at imposing AD duties on firms with sufficient political or economic clout. While the influence of firms with investment in China does not dictate the outcome of a case, it nevertheless has an important bearing on how the case is handled by the authorities.

The literature on the influence of foreign direct investment postulates that global capital flows can be a source of openness in the international political economy. The literature on "quid pro quo investment", (e.g. Bhagwati *et al.*, 1987; Blonigen and Feenstra, 1997), for instance, suggests that foreign direct investment, by creating employment and income in the host country, may appease host country firms and governments, thereby reducing the probability that domestic firms may seek trade protection. The literature on the bargaining relationship between multi-national corporations and developing countries suggests that the leverage of a foreign firm vis-à-vis the host country government could be dependent on the size of the host market, the need of the developing country for advanced technology and the specific character of the foreign investment undertaken. In the Chinese case, while the Chinese government has incentives to protect its own domestic industry, the need to attract foreign investment, especially in sectors where nascent industrial capabilities are insufficient and where the infusion of foreign know-how and technology would benefit local industrial development, may have necessitated a more generous treatment of the foreign firm.

The optical fiber case involving Corning nicely illustrates such a dynamic. In July 2003, two Chinese companies, Yangtze Optical Fiber and Cable Company Ltd. and Jiangsu Fasten Photonics Co. Ltd. initiated an AD petition against foreign optical fiber produces such as Corning, Samsung and a number of smaller companies from Japan and the United States, alleging the latter dumped single-mode optical fiber products in the Chinese market. However, the fact that Corning accounted for over 30 percent of China's domestic optical fiber market and that optical fiber was the most technologically advanced product targeted by China's AD suit soon elevated this case to a major trade dispute between China and the United States. While Corning reportedly provided Chinese authorities with detailed information and cooperated in the AD investigation, an official involved in the AD investigation hinted that considerations about the impact that a hefty dumping margin would have on an already highly contentious US–China relationship had influenced the final AD decision.[39] In the end, while Corning was ruled to have dumped in the Chinese market, the company received a minimal antidumping tax of 1.5 percent on the grounds that the dumping volume was small. Other named foreign companies did not fare nearly as well as Corning and were assessed dumping duties ranging from 7 to 46 percent.[40] The result disappointed domestic producers and representatives of the optical fiber industry association, who argued that the final decision did very little to stave off imports or protect the industry from foreign competition.[41] It also "prompted suggestions that the central government was 'selling out' to US interests".[42]

Finally, the effectiveness of the AD duties could also be reduced due to the tax exemption status of enterprises engaged in export processing. Many buyers of chemical products qualify for special duty concessions as they sell their products to manufacturers who engage in processing of raw materials for exports to the world market, or what the Chinese call *sanlai yibu*. As they were already exempt from import duties and so would not be affected by the increase in tariffs, the dumping margins consequently had very little impact on these firms and on market equilibrium. Consequently, in some sectors, even though AD duties were initially proposed or even imposed, the duties have turned out to have negligible impact on the domestic industry. In these cases, while China might have won a legal victory against foreign respondents, the AD duty has done very little to alter industry conditions. For instance, in the synthetic resins and synthetic fibers sector, only about 30 percent of China's imports bear full chemical import duties as a result of tariff concessions.[43] Thus, in December 2002, Beijing went ahead and announced its decision to impose antidumping duties on imports of acid ester from Singapore, South Korea, Malaysia and Indonesia. While the dumping margins amounted to as much as 46 percent, only a portion of the targeted companies exporting to China were affected as their customers in China use imported acrylate to produce goods for export and, as a result, qualify for special duty exemptions. For example, representatives of one of the companies hit by the proposed AD duty, Singapore Acrylic Ester, commented that the duties would impact only a small share of the company's sales to China.[44] In part given the lack of substantive effect the AD duties had on the Chinese market, MOFCOM lowered the AD duties from 11 to 3 percent in 2005, three years before the duties were set to expire. Consequently, even though in this case China imposed antidumping margins on the foreign firm, the AD duties produced few benefits for the domestic industry. In other words, even though Chinese firms are considered to have won a legal victory, the substantive results of the implementation of the AD ruling indicate that China's domestic industry may have received few tangible benefits from trade protection.

In short, the above discussion suggests that the final outcome of China's AD investigations was not always tilted in favor of Chinese firms, albeit for very different reasons. Lobbying by downstream users, the clout of the foreign firm and the importance of its foreign investment to the Chinese economy, or the special tax exemption status of many Chinese users have heavily influenced the way through which AD duties were deployed. Hence, the increasingly open nature of the Chinese economy has provided points of leverage for foreign respondents, in some cases reducing the effectiveness of protection provided by the Chinese state to struggling domestic industries.

Conclusions and policy implications

As the above analysis of the recent trade actions undertaken by China has shown, China's trade diplomacy is undergoing a subtle shift from one based on power to one oriented toward legal rules. Beijing has invoked both its domestic laws and the rules of the WTO to protect Chinese industries from the vicissitudes of the international marketplace. Moreover, China's large, concentrated state-owned enterprises in import-competing industries have availed of China's newly acquired trade instruments to lobby for trade protection. These actors were able to influence China's trade policy-making process due to the strong ties with the state they developed during the era of centralized economic policy-making and their importance to the Chinese economy.

Moreover, it should be noted that domestic industries have largely shaped the way in which the AD instrument has been deployed. While China's large and heavily concentrated import-competing industries have dominated the use of such instruments, their choice of policy instruments nevertheless differed. As the above analysis shows, the chemical industry, which has experienced greater financial losses, has tended to resort to the AD instrument to a much greater extent than industries similarly confronted by import competition, such as the steel industry. The analysis therefore suggests that industry-level variables matter, and that industries that enjoy considerable political clout, or are considered important to the future development of the national economy, or occupy a privileged position within the domestic political economy, will increasingly seek trade protection.

Finally, it should be noted that the previous discussion suggests that in terms of the settlement of antidumping disputes, China's AD rulings have not always resulted in outcomes favorable to domestic producers due to opposition from (both domestic and foreign) downstream users, the importance of the foreign firm's investment in the Chinese market, or the tax exemption status of the buyers of the targeted products. Such a changing trend therefore suggests that one has to find the sources of trade policy in China's increasing integration into the world economy.

In terms of the implications of this study, it should be noted that in spite of its more recent embracement of legal tactics, China's more active use of legal remedy laws may signal an important change in the basic orientation of Chinese trade policy. Beijing's imposition of the steel safeguard measure and the increasing frequency of its AD imposition suggest that China may indeed resort to the rule-oriented rather than the power-oriented negotiation approach more frequently in the future.

Such a changing trend of China's trade diplomacy ought to offer some important lessons for China's trading partners. In particular, China's active engagement with the AD statute and the rules of the WTO suggests that it is increasingly using these legal trade remedies to protect its domestic industries. Regardless of whether China will win a WTO suit with its trading partners in the future, such an active embracement of legal trade remedies is likely to exert a positive effect both on China's social and legal systems and on the international community. Domestically, such aggressive legalism may enhance the participation of legal scholars and the participation of the policy and academic communities in the interpretation of legal rules and principles, including the rules of the WTO and, consequently, facilitate compliance with and honoring of legal norms and principles governing trade relations.

Internationally, since China can now legitimately question the legality of the trade actions of other countries before the WTO and therefore evade unilateral market-opening pressure from foreign countries, it is important that China's main trading partners such as the United States recognize that a bilateral approach for dealing with China may no longer work as effectively as it had in the past. Instead, they will increasingly have to adjust to this emerging trend in Chinese trade diplomacy and adopt corresponding measures to deal with the Chinese over such disputes as antidumping or safeguards. Moreover, to the extent that China can now provide legal justifications for the challenges it mounts to foreign trade measures, it is equally important that China's major trading partners come up with adequate legal defense for their actions. Continuing to pursue the WTO's legalized route to dispute resolution may provide a valuable service in this respect because the trade dispute resolution mechanisms of the WTO ought to offer enhanced legitimacy to the trade actions of major players, allowing them to better defend their economic interests and deflect criticism of uneven-handedness in dealing with rapidly growing countries such as China. In this sense, a more legalistic approach may also work to the benefit of China's major trading partners by prodding China to uphold its commitments without increasing the risks of full-scale trade wars.

Acknowledgements

I would like to thank Barry Naughton, Judith Goldstein, and participants at the Conference on Chinese Trade Policy at the University of California, San Diego (UCSD) for their comments on an earlier draft of this chapter. I am solely responsible for any errors that may remain.

Notes

1   In recent years, China has had to respond to either restrictive trade measures imposed by its trading partners (such as Japan's imposition of safeguard measures against Chinese agricultural and textile products in 2001) or trade complaints filed against it within the context of the World Trade Organization (such as a case brought by the United States against China regarding the latter's value-added tax on integrated circuits in early 2004). Other countries, such as Brazil and the European Union, have also threatened to take trade disputes with China to the WTO. See, for example, ABC (2004); EU Business (2004).

2   For example, most US–China trade negotiations prior to China's accession into the WTO were conducted on a bilateral basis or under Section 301 of US trade law. The trade disputes that took place prior to China's entry into the WTO therefore relied primarily on the use of diplomatic routes to dispute resolution.

3   See the chapter by Scott Kennedy in this volume for an elaboration of this point and for a detailed list of China's AD case outcomes.

4   For a detailed account of US–China trade negotiations in the 1980s and 1990s, see Zeng (2004).

5   On this point, see Davis (2006).

6   Ibid.

7   People's Daily (2004).

8   Li (2003).

9   Keohane (1984); Haas (1980).

10   Author's interview.

11   See Kennedy (2005a).

12   For a list of cases between 1999 and 2004, see China Trade Remedy Information available at: www.cacs.gov.cn/DefaultWebApp/index.htm.

13   "The Effect of the Implementation of Trade Remedy Measures in China," (*Woguo shishi maoyi jiuji cuoshi xiaoguo qingkuang*), released by the Industry Injury Investigation Bureau and the Fair Trade Bureau, Ministry of Commerce, 3 July 2006, available at: www.cacs.gov.cn/DefaultWebApp/showNews.jsp?newsId=300080000017.

14   Han (2003: 149).

15   Kennedy (2005b: 86).

16   For example, in the Korea garlic dispute, in response to the announcement in May 2000 that South Korea would adopt definitive safeguard measures on garlic imports from China, China's MOFTEC retaliated against imports of Korean mobile telephones including vehicle mobiles sets and polyethelene as of June 2000.

17 Jung (2002: 1043).
18 Ibid.
19 For instance, up until the late 1980s, Japan has chosen to bypass the rule-oriented approach based on WTO norms and instead relied on a bilateral case-by-case approach in dealing with its trading partners. In fact, Japan has rarely resorted to the GATT dispute settlement mechanism to resolve disputes with its trading partners.
20 Hijino (2001).
21 Pekkanen (2002: 581).
22 Tanikawa and Kirk (2001).
23 Even though agricultural products account for only 10 percent of China's total exports, China nevertheless ranks among the world's top 15 agricultural exporters, accounting for about three percent of world agricultural exports in 2001 (WTO Trade Statistics, 2002. Similarly, China was already the world's largest producer and exporter of textile and apparel products at its accession to the WTO. Several studies have shown that with the liberalization and elimination of quotas constraining Chinese exports following the country's accession into the WTO, China's world market share of these products is likely to experience even more rapid increases. Lardy (2002: 109–10, 123–8).
24 On the impact of WTO membership on China's agricultural and textile industries, see Lardy (2002: 123–5).
25 Yeung and Mok (2004: 943–4).
26 "Japan's Discriminatory Curbs Oppose WTO rules" (2001).
27 See Nakagawa (2002: 1031).
28 Times Union (2001).
29 See Pekkanen (2001).
30 Compiled from statistics published by the United States International Trade Commission.
31 Liu and Hylke (2002: 1130–2).
32 See Messerlin (2004: 111–14).
33 "Dumping Hits China's Petrochemical Sector" (2005).
34 Ibid.
35 *China Statistical Yearbook* 2005.
36 Interview with an MOFCOM official, June 2006.
37 See the Kennedy chapter in this volume.
38 Interview with representatives of the China Petroleum and Chemical Industry Association, 30 May 2006.
39 Author's interview, June 2006.
40 SinoCast (2005).
41 Liang (2005).
42 Shih (2005).
43 Chemical News (2001).
44 Divyanathan (2002).

References

ABC (2004) "Brazil may take trade dispute with China to WTO", ABC Radio Australia, 21 June.

Asia Pulse (2005) "Dumping hits China's petrochemical sector", *Asia Pulse*, 24 March.

Bhagwati, J. N., Brecher, R, Dinopoulos, E. and Srinivasan, T. N. (1987) "Quid pro quo foreign investment and welfare: a political-economy-theoretic model," *Journal of Development Economics*, 27: 127–38.

Blonigen, B. A. and Feenstra, R. C. (1997) "Protectionist threats and foreign direct investment", in Feenstra, R.C. (ed.) *The Effects of U.S. Trade Protection and Promotion Policies*, Chicago, IL: The University of Chicago Press: 69–76.

Chemical News (2001) "Is all the China WTO excitement justified?", *Chemical News and Intelligence*, 29 November.

China Statistical Yearbook (various years) Beijing: National Bureau of Statistics of China. Available online: www.stats.gov.cn/tjsj/ndsj.

Davis, C. L. (2006) "Do WTO rules create a level playing field? Lessons from the experience of Peru and Vietnam", in Odell, J. S. (ed.) *Negotiating Trade: Developing Countries in the WTO and NAFTA*, Cambridge: Cambridge University Press, 2006: 219–56.

Divyanathan, D. (2002) "China hits firm with anti-dumping tariffs", *Straits Times*, 6 December.

EU Business (2004) "EU warns WTO action imminent unless China lifts coke restrictions", *EU Business*, 14 May.

Haas, E. B. (1980) "Why collaborate? Issue-linkage and international regime", *World Politics*, 32 (3): 357–405.

Han, Z. (ed.) (2003) *WTO Accession and China's Metallurgical Industry* (*Jiaru WTO Yu Zhongguo Yejin Gongye*), Beijing: Metellurgical Industry Publishing House.

Hijino, K. (2001) "Tokyo may restrict China imports", *Financial Times*, 26 February.

Huang, T. W. (2002) "The gathering storm of antidumping enforcement in China", *Journal of World Trade*, 36 (2): 255–83.

Jung, Y. (2002) "China's aggressive legalism: China's first safeguard measure", *Journal of World Trade*, 36 (6): 1037–60.

Kennedy, S. (2005a) "China's porous protectionism: the changing political economy of trade policy", *Political Science Quarterly*, 120: 407–32.

Kennedy, S. (2005b) *The Business of Lobbying in China*, Cambridge: Harvard University Press.

Keohane, R. (1984) *After Hegemony: Cooperation and Discord in the World Political Economy*, Princeton, NJ: Princeton University Press.

Lardy, N. R. (2002) *Integrating China into the Global Economy*, Washington, DC: Brookings Institution Press.

Li, Z. (2003) Speech to the United Nations General Assembly, 24 September.

Liang, R. (2005) "Anti-dumping fails to protect China's optical fiber industry", *China Economic Net*, 19 April. Available online: http://en.ce.cn/Insight/200504/18/t20050418_3633707.shtml.

Liu, X. and Hylke, V. (2002) "European Union anti-dumping cases against China: an overview and future prospects with respect to China's World Trade Organization membership", *Journal of World Trade*, 36 (6): 1125–44.

Messerlin, P. A. (2004) "China in the World Trade Organization: antidumping and safeguards", *World Bank Economic Review*, 18 (1): 105–30.

Nakagawa, J. (2002) "Lessons from the Japan–China 'Welsh Onion War' ", *Journal of World Trade*, 6 (6): 1019–36.

Pekkanen, S. M. (2001) "International law, the WTO, and the Japanese state: assessment and implications of the newly legalized trade politics", *Journal of Japanese Politics*, 27 (1): 41–80.

—— (2002) "Japan's legal actions in the GATT/WTO system", *Journal of World Intellectual Property*, 5 (4): 1747–96.

People's Daily (2004) "Full text of Chinese Foreign Minister's press conference", *People's Daily*, 6 March.

—— (2001) "Japan's discriminatory curbs oppose WTO rules", *People's Daily*, 27 June.

Shih, T. H. (2005) "China shows mettle in trade tiff", *South China Morning Post*, 5 January.

SinoCast (2005) "Corning wins antidumping case in China", SinoCast China IT Watch, 7 January.

Tanikawa, M. and Kirk, D. (2001) "Mushrooms with garlic and tariffs", *New York Times*, 17 April.

Times Union (2001) "A WTO prelude? China's tariff tiff with Japan bodes ill for future trade showdowns", *Times Union*, 28 June.

Yeung, G. and Mok, V. (2004) "Does WTO accession matter for the Chinese textile and clothing industry?", *Cambridge Journal of Economics*, 28 (6): 937–54.

Zeng, K. (2004) *Trade Threats, Trade Wars: Bargaining, Retaliation, and American Coercive Diplomacy*, Ann Arbor: University of Michigan Press.

8 The impact of the World Trade Organization on China's trade policy

A case study of the telecommunications sector

Yuka Kobayashi

China … will join the community governed by the rule of law … it is also the best way to promote reforms in China and stability in the region.[1]

> Charlene Barshefsky, former US Trade Representative, on
> approval of China's permanent normal trade relations

Using telecommunications services as a case study, this chapter assesses the impact of accession into the World Trade Organization (WTO) on China's trade policy. Since the telecommunications sector was one of the most difficult areas for the Chinese to open up to trade, this case study illuminates the extent of the WTO's impact on Chinese trade policy-making. Prior to WTO accession, trade in this sector was prohibited. However, since China opened up the telecommunications sector after WTO accession, policy-making in this sector has become more complicated.

Since the ministries related to trade and foreign affairs took the lead in the negotiations leading to China's WTO accession, the ministries related to telecommunications services had only limited involvement in trade policy-making before China became a member of the WTO. However, following China's WTO accession, the telecommunications-related ministries have become more involved in trade policy and this has greatly complicated the generation of trade policy in this sector. The complication of the decision-making process led to near breaches of China's WTO commitments that were resolved through diplomatic means without making it to the WTO dispute settlement mechanism. These cases show that the coordination of trade policy became more problematic after WTO accession. While China's WTO commitments provided the basis for a more transparent trade regime, trade policy in telecommunications services has come to involve more operators and a more diverse range of trade and telecom-related ministries. The pluralization and decentralization of the policy-making process in this sector thus create a formidable challenge to China's WTO compliance.

This chapter is in four sections. The first section provides a background to the WTO and China's telecommunications sector. The second section examines China's WTO accession negotiations, focusing on how bureaucratic turf wars and center–local relations play out during the negotiations. The third section turns to China's compliance with its WTO commitments, suggesting that growing bureaucratic involvement and conflict in this sector may dim the prospect of policy implementation in line with China's WTO commitments. The chapter concludes by discussing the policy implications of its findings.

This chapter draws on WTO documents, government reports and the author's own fieldwork to support its contentions.[2] It shows that turf wars inherent in this sector have created serious difficulties for policy implementation and, as a result, there have been many near breaches of the WTO agreements. The case studies therefore illustrate how trade policy following WTO accession has become a more complicated and fragmented process.

The WTO and China

On 11 December 2001, China officially became a member of the WTO. China's accession negotiations represented the longest and most protracted accession negotiation in the history of the General Agreement on Tariffs in Trade (GATT) and its successor, the WTO. Once a WTO member, China had to find a way to comply with the WTO commitment package that it had signed up to. WTO membership called for considerable reform in trade policy, particularly in formerly closed sectors such as telecommunications.

Between 1949 and 1978, China had kept its borders tightly closed and many of its trade policy practices ran counter to the principles of the GATT/WTO. It was not until 1978 that Deng Xiaoping, the successor to Mao Zedong, finally decided that it was necessary to introduce greater competition to the Chinese economy and started to advocate the Open Door Policy.[3] But even then, China continued to protect its infant industries and prohibited trade liberalization in its most underdeveloped and non-competitive sectors such as telecommunications, banking and insurance. As Long Yongtu, the Vice Minister of the then Ministry of Foreign Trade and Economic Cooperation (MOFTEC, currently MOFCOM) and China's chief negotiator for GATT/WTO accession, points out, "countries with planned economies have never participated in economic globalization".[4] As it brings many reforms to trade policy, WTO entry is likely to exacerbate domestic conflicts over trade policy in a transitional economy such as China.[5]

The WTO is a forum for member countries to engage in rules-based negotiations and to adopt approaches necessary for trade liberalization. Although China has been undergoing extensive economic reform, change occurs only gradually. According to Greg Mastel (2000: 25–6), even the enforcement mechanisms of the WTO will not be sufficient to help China address its "complex and opaque system of bureaucrats, provincial governments, and state-owned enterprises combined with its lack of rule of law".[6]

A key hurdle for China's WTO membership is the fact that China is a "socialist market economy", not the type of the market economy envisioned at the time the GATT was founded.[7] As such, China must implement extensive reforms in its trade policy. The GATT/WTO is based on the theory of comparative advantage and operates on the assumption that trade liberalization – that is, minimizing governmental interferenced with trade flows – would benefit all nations.[8] The main purpose of the GATT/WTO is to act as a forum to reduce obstacles to trade by lowering tariffs and removing non-tariff barriers so as to ensure the smooth, predictable and free flow of trade. The rationale is that such a system would increase the demand for foreign goods, thereby increasing international trade and ultimately improving the welfare of member countries. However, China's foreign trade regime was in conflict with the GATT/WTO's principle of free trade as its imports were traditionally constrained by the state plan. Moreover, licenses, along with foreign exchange, remained under the control of the government, a practice that again contradicted the WTO's principle of free trade.[9] Even John Jackson, one of the more optimistic of WTO scholars, acknowledges that assimilating China into the WTO is a "formidable task".[10]

China's national security interests and protectionist practices designed to help its internationally non-competitive telecommunications sector made it difficult for foreign companies to access China's telecommunications market. The challenge of complying with China's commitments in the telecommunications sector is further exacerbated by the bureaucratic tussles that intensified following China's accession into the WTO. The difficulties in compliance in the telecommunications sector in turn indicate that China's existing trade environment is far from the ideals of the WTO.

This chapter engages in a case study of the telecommunications sector since it is widely considered to be one of the most difficult sectors for China to liberalize. Selecting one of the most contentious sectors as a case study will allow for the coverage of the full extent of the impact of the WTO on trade policy. The telecommunications sector is "the digitized information processing, storage and transmission sector that is the emblem of modern technology and the largest and fastest growing industrial sector and trade category".[11] It is defined to include telecommunications equipment production, telecom services and Information Technology (IT) industries. This chapter examines telecommunications services as defined under the General Agreement on Trade in Services (GATS).

The telecommunications sector in China

The Chinese telecommunications market is the fastest growing in the world and is quickly becoming the largest for mobile telephone usage (136 million subscribers) and telephone-paging services (50 million subscribers).[12] When one considers that China has only a penetration ratio of 9.2 percent, compared to 40 percent and 50 percent in the US and Europe respectively, the Chinese domestic market has huge potential.[13] Thus, it is not an exaggeration to say that in the context of telecommunications, it is as much about "the WTO joining China" as it is about "China joining the WTO". In other words, the impact of the WTO on the telecommunications sector in China is as significant as the impact of China's telecommunications market on the global community.

Traditionally, the global telecommunications market has been dominated by state monopolies. Many countries have historically kept the telecommunications sector public and under government control because of national security. In addition to providing a country's population with telephone lines, telecommunications supports a nation's military and national security networks. Since the 1980s, starting with AT&T in the United States, developing countries have begun a process of deregulation in order to encourage domestic competition in the telecommunications sector. With globalization and improved transportation systems, the global telecommunications sector has made significant headway in international competition and trade liberalization. Furthermore, the telecommunications industry is a capital-intensive industry that thrives on economies of scale and professional expertise. Having reached a development level ripe for trade liberalization and possessing a comparative advantage, developed countries have taken the lead in trade liberalization in the telecommunications sector. Naturally, developing countries with infant industries have been slow to follow this trend.

Nevertheless, the liberalization of the telecommunications sector has been a sensitive issue in every country. Not only does this sector have strong links to national security and hence is of strategic importance, it is also a lucrative sector that constitutes a major source of governmental revenue in many countries.[14] In the case of China, telecommunications liberalization is particularly difficult as telecommunications operators have traditionally occupied a protected status. Domestic telecommunications companies are still comparatively weak and are unable to compete with foreign entrants at the same level. Moreover, communications services have traditionally been an area of great importance since there is extreme sensitivity to the control of information. In addition, as communications channels are closely linked to the military, relinquishing control of telecommunications lines has been seen as endangering state secrets.[15]

Indeed, in China the concern for national security has resulted in telecommunications being kept under strict government control, with little opportunity for direct foreign investment. National security and national sovereignty are of vital importance to the Chinese government as articulated in the "Five Principles of Peaceful Co-existence".[16] In order to ensure that these principles are abided by, China's domestic laws and rules in the telecommunications sector remained obscure, non-transparent, and in many cases secretive.[17] This lack of transparency allowed the Chinese to keep telecommunications a matter of state security under government control.[18]

The Chinese were reluctant to open their telecommunications sector also because the penetration rate was extremely low and China's telecommunications market still had much potential to be tapped. The Chinese telecom market is the second largest telecommunications network in the world, and the fastest growing one. By 2002, China's telecommunications exchange capacity had reached 201 million [lines], and mobile switching capacity amounted to 235 million [lines]. The total number of telephone subscribers had grown to 350 million, with 188 million fixed users and 162 million mobile users, making China's network the largest in the world in terms of size and subscribers.[19] In order to keep this lucrative sector with immense market potential to their domestic players, the Chinese adopted protectionist policies which ran counter to the principles of the WTO.

Telecommunications service providers in China were traditionally state-owned enterprises (SOEs).[20] Since it was primarily a government dominated sector, there used to be no need for telecommunications laws or a regulator. Telecommunications was subject to overall planning and industry administration under the Information Industry Department of the State Council. The strong link with industrial policy meant that telecommunications was considered in relation to the overall plan for the development and construction of the information industry, which in turn took into account the development goals of the national economy and society.[21]

The telecommunications sector's strong linkages to national security and the legacies of state planning, compounded by the non-transparent nature of Chinese politics and legal regime, results in a complex web of overlapping interests. At the central level there exist many ministries with varying interests.[22] At the local level, the fact that the telecom industry constitutes the source of much local revenue means that the central and local governments often have divergent preferences regarding this industry. The complex bargaining among various interest groups and bureaucratic agencies in the telecom sector consequently has yielded unexpected policy outcomes in the past.[23]

In light of this historical background, it becomes clear that complying with China's WTO commitments in the telecommunications sector would likely entail considerable challenge. Prior to accession, China's trade policies were coordinated and unified by MOFTEC (currently MOFCOM). However, membership in the WTO has resulted in an increase in the number of players in trade policy-making, including more ministries and private entities, thus making it difficult for MOFCOM to live up to its responsibilities.

China's WTO commitments in the telecommunications sector

As mentioned earlier, China's WTO accession represented the longest accession negotiation in the history of the GATT/WTO. The prolonged nature of the negotiations was due in large part to the legal, political and ideological conflicts between the Chinese trade regime and the principles embodied by the GATT/WTO. Telecommunications was one of the last sectors in which an agreement was reached. The difficulties the Chinese government would have in implementing its WTO commitments were also anticipated in the early stages of the accession negotiations.

China's Accession Package is the lengthiest legal document in the history of the WTO.[24] China's relative importance in trade conferred on the country great responsibility to implement a tough accession package.[25] China's commitments under the WTO are comprised of the following (see Table 8.1):

- China's Protocol to Accession (main text of 11 pages) and its nine Annexes

- Schedule of Commitments (annexed to the Protocol: China's Goods and Services Schedules), and
- the Working Party Report (WPR), part of which was incorporated into the Protocol. These incorporated provisions of the WPR acquire the same binding force as those in the main text of the protocol.

The WTO and GATS agreement with regard to telecommunications requires that China abide by the following principles following WTO accession:

- market access (geographically and periodically phased in as shown in Figure 8.1)
- national treatment
- most-favored-nation treatment, whereby China should treat all other members equally for market access in telecommunications services
- transparency and uniform application.

The Annex of Telecommunications (para 5(a)) requires "access to and use of public telecommunications transport networks and services on a *reasonable* and *non-discriminatory* term and conditions for the supply of service included in its Schedule". It also calls for progressive trade liberalization, removal of technical barriers to trade and the creation of a competitive, independent and transparent regulatory regime. In addition, China's WTO commitments call for changes in market structure (i.e. the number of service suppliers and the extent of foreign ownership); services and facilities; and regulatory principles as found in the Reference Paper.

In short, China's WTO commitment called for substantial opening of the tele-communications market to foreign companies.[26] In the past the Chinese government had prohibited foreign investment in the operation and management of the telecommunications businesses.[27] However, once a member of the WTO, China had to reform the laws to comply with its commitments to liberalize this sector.

China's commitments in the telecommunications sector also required significant institutional transformation in the Chinese regulatory environment. These commitments called for reform of SOEs, fair competition and increased foreign presence in the telecommunications sector. Composed mostly of SOEs, the telecommunications sector traditionally had no need to regulate or to have any legislation. It was only in

Table 8.1 The basic structure of China's commitments in services

	Services
Basic principles	GATS
Additional details	Services Annexes (e.g. Reference Paper)
Market access commitments	China's Schedules of Commitments

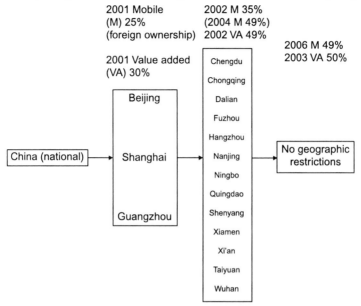

Figure 8.1 China's commitments in the telecommunications sector under the GATS agreement

preparation for WTO accession that telecommunications legislation had come to be discussed publicly. According to China's accession agreement, Beijing must implement fundamental legislative measures, eliminate long-standing discretionary administrative practices and replace them with "independent, transparent, and prudential" regulations.[28] The country was expected to have competitive safeguards to ensure that appropriate measures are in place to prevent anti-competitive practices.[29] In addition, interconnection procedures and licensing criteria were expected to be made publicly available and transparent and dispute settlement mechanisms were to be established.[30] While China did not agree to full market access to foreign investors in any of the telecommunications sectors, it had agreed to partial liberalization implemented over several years depending on the nature of the services and the geographic region.

The periodic and geographic phase-in approach taken in the commitments reflects the power of trade-related ministries during the accession negotiations. The Chinese telecommunications commitments do not make sense from the point of view of the telecommunications sector. However, from the perspective of economic development, the phase-in approach was the ideal way to facilitate China's integration into the global telecommunications market.[31] Developing countries generally tend to prefer to have foreign investors assist in the costly construction of the telecommunications network. From this point of view, it would be sensible to have foreign investment in those regions where telecommunications networks are not well developed. The Chinese negotiation team, which was primarily made up of trade specialists, felt that gradually opening up telecommunications services in areas where the domestic incumbents were more competitive would be the preferred approach. This is a typical economics-based argument in which the trade negotiators were better versed. The telecommunications commitments therefore represent the telecommunications specialists' lack of influence during the accession negotiation.

While the nature of China's commitments seems compatible with other member states, when one takes into consideration the history of protectionism in the telecommunications sector in China, the commitments that seem modest *prima facie* prove revolutionary. As one official of the United Nations Conference on Trade and Development (UNCTAD) suggested, the Chinese commitments in services clearly went beyond those anticipated in the negotiations, and were much more ambitious when compared with other developing countries.[32] Not only are China's infant industries unable to withstand the competition from telecommunications companies in the developed world, the telecommunications industry in China has traditionally been a protected industry with strong links to national security. With this consideration in mind, increasing market access in basic telecommunications up to 49 percent and that in value-added services up to 50 percent to foreign providers can be said to be quite a leap forward.

When former Vice-Premier Zhu Rongji visited former President Bill Clinton in Washington DC in April 1999, China's intention of opening its telecommunications sector was leaked to the press.[33] This was of course kept secret from the heads of the telecommunications-related ministries. Once former Minister Wu Jichuan of the Ministry of Information Industry (MII) heard of this news through the foreign press, he threatened to resign, making deregulation of the telecommunications sector a hot topic in China.[34] This incident illustrates the extent to which telecommunications-related ministries were excluded from trade policy-making prior to accession. Much of the policy-making in the telecom sector during the accession negotiations was left to the trade-related ministries. As such, former Minster Wu only found out about the commitments he would have to implement through the US media.

These turf wars between the pro-WTO forces (i.e. the trade ministries) and the anti-WTO forces (i.e. the telecom-related ministries) within the Chinese government were contained before accession. However, once China became a WTO member, the telecommunications ministries gained greater influence in trade policy, and, as a result, there have been more heated debates between the conflicting parties. These conflicts resulted in near breaches of the WTO rules as covered in a subsequent section of this chapter.

The telecommunications ministry and actors in China

The institutional structure

The telecommunications sector in China has the contradictory goals of complying with the competitive principles of the WTO, maintaining state control over basic telecommunications services and keeping its public network secure. The Chinese government being the key investor with the majority of the property rights in this sector further complicated the pursuit of these objectives. In the early 1990s, Minister Yang

Tianfang and Minister Wu Jichuan repeatedly stressed the need to strengthen administrative planning and control of telecommunications so as to protect China's domestic industries.[35] As exemplified by the battles between former Premier Zhu Rongji and former Minister Wu Jichuan on whether to open up the telecommunications sector, the State Council has traditionally been more liberal towards China's telecommunications reform while the MII has been more conservative. However, in preparation for its WTO entry, China's protectionist policies for the telecommunications sector have been gradually moderated, and in 2003, the conservative Minister Wu was replaced with the more liberal Minister Wang Xudong.

Although the Chinese government has taken actions to liberalize the telecommunications market, the industry remains a key sector and has been identified as a major driver of economic growth in both the Ninth (2001–2005) and Tenth (2006–2010) Five Year Plans. Although the state is gradually relinquishing its control and introducing greater competition to this sector, these changes are only being implemented slowly. In other words, the state continues to retain administrative management of this sector.

In April 1998, the State Council merged the former Ministry of Post and Telecommunications (MPT) with the Ministry of Electronics Industry (MEI) and parts of the Ministry of Radio, Film and Television to form the Ministry of Information Industry in an attempt to develop the state's telecommunications services in a coherent manner. The MII became the sole industry watchdog for the IT sector. In addition to establishing telecommunications-related policies, laws and regulations, the ministry was charged with negotiating with foreign enterprises. The MII is composed of several departments. The departments most closely related to telecommunications services are the Policy and Legislation Office, the Executive Management Office, the Economic System Reforming and Management Office and the Telecommunications Management Office. The MII has wide discretionary powers to formulate regulations and apply them. Only important strategic policy decisions have been approved by the State Council. It was hoped that bringing the management of the IT industry under one ministry would strengthen the bureaucracy's effectiveness.

However, regulation of telecommunications in a broader sense is shared by the MII and many other governmental actors, and this makes the regulation of telecommunications in China particularly problematic. The responsibility for the regulation and surveillance of the content is spread across many actors, ranging from the Party to various ministries and state agencies. In terms of security, the Public Security Bureau and the Ministry of State Security deal with state security and encryption; the press, publications and propaganda authorities are mostly interested in content. As for functionality, the MII, the Ministry of Railroads and the Ministry of Energy are concerned with telecommunications competition; the State Administration of Radio, Film and Television (SARFT) is responsible for the cable business; and the Ministry of Finance and major banks have primary interests in E-business.

Since telecommunications is considered a key industry, the regulation of this industry also involves the planning and development agencies.[36] As stipulated in

Article 3 of the *Telecommunications Regulations*, the State Council's department in charge of information industry is responsible for the general supervision and administration of China's telecommunications. The State Council supervises the MII, makes important policy decisions and enacts important regulations. It also has the authority to determine pricing. While local pricing standards are set locally, often specific approval from the national authority is needed.[37] The SARFT succeeded the Ministry of Radio, Film and Television (part of which was subsumed under the MII in 1998). While the agency lost ministerial status in the 1998 reforms, it retained regulatory control over broadcasting and cable. The convergence in telephony (telephony and broadband/media) also gave the SARFT regulatory responsibilities.[38] As convergence in functionality and bandwidth takes place in telephony and broadband/media, the MII and SARFT have had continuous conflicts over regulatory issues.

This complexity in the web of actors is only exacerbated by WTO accession. The existence of many actors with different institutional interests makes it difficult for China to implement the WTO telecommunications agreement.

Telecommunications operators

Prior to 1993 the Ministry of Post and Telecommunications (MPT) was the sole provider of telecommunications and China Telecom dominated China's telecommunications market. It was only in 1994, with the introduction of China Unicom, that the Chinese government made clear its policy towards telecommunications competition. In that same year, China Telecom's monopoly was broken up into a duopoly with China Unicom entering into the fixed line market. Furthermore, China Telecom was separated from the Ministry in 1995. Competition was enhanced by China Mobile dividing off from China Telecom in April 2000. By 2001 there were four new companies in basic telephony. These actions signaled that China was moving telecommunications from the state to the market to increase competition.

There are currently four major telecommunications providers:

- China Telecom[39]
- China Network Telecom (China Netcom) which handles fixed line telephony
- China Mobile, and
- China Unicom which handles mobile telephony.[40]

The market share of these companies in total telecommunications service revenue in basic telecommunications services is as follows:

- China Telecom 52.4 percent
- China Mobile 37.6 percent, and
- China Unicom 9.6 percent.[41]

For local, domestic and international long-distance fixed telephony, China

Telecom and China Unicom take up 87 percent and 13 percent of the market share respectively. For IP telephony, the breakdown is as follows:

- China Telecom 75.6 percent
- China Unicom 18.4 percent
- China Jitong 3.6 percent
- China Netcom 1.5 percent.[42]

The Ministry of Railroads has the second largest telecommunications network next to China Telecom. In 2000 the Ministry was licensed by the MII to provide local fixed-line telephone service, domestic long distance fixed-line service, data transmission, internet related services, and IP telephony. However, while both the Ministry of Railways and China Jitong Telecom (Jitong) have market presence, they are far behind the four major providers.

The MII was the majority shareholder in China Telecom and China Mobile. Prior to the establishment of the MII, the MEI was the majority shareholder of Unicom and Jitong. However with the MEI coming under the MII, Unicom and Jitong became MII-majority owned. The Ministry of Railroads also holds a significant number of shares in Unicom and is the majority owner of Railcom. Netcom was established by the Chinese Academy of Science and the Ministry of Railways, SARFT and Shanghai Municipal Government. In February 2001, Netcom had its first initial public offering (IPO) for 12 percent of shares with investment from News Corp, Goldman Sachs, the Bank of China and the Construction Bank of China. China Telecom did a similar IPO in 2002 which turned out to be the cause of the interconnection crisis.

While considerable competition has been introduced into the telecommunications market, the market is still managed by the MII. As the MII is able to influence the market with its controls over China Telecom, China Mobile and China Unicom, there is the lack of a clear break between the regulator and the operators. Moreover, China Telecom has a virtual monopoly over fixed line services. Other areas of telecom such as long distance calling have duopolies, but the incentive for market entry by foreign businesses is low. It is only in value-added services where there is low risk and fewer monopolistic incumbents that market opportunities for foreign entrants exist.

Despite the reforms mentioned above, the ambiguities inherent in the regulatory structure have only been improved slightly since WTO accession. While government endorsements of state protection of telecommunications were less frequent than in the past and while once prohibited foreign investment in the telecommunications sector has now been opened up with WTO entry, problems still remain. For example, the *Telecommunications Regulations* require all telecommunications companies in China be majority (i.e. 51 percent) state-owned. In reality, however, non-state domestic investors have equity in the market and there are also public market shares available. Consequently, although foreign investors are legally allowed 49 percent ownership, it has not always been feasible.[43] As most of the telecommunications companies are owned by government agencies such as the

MII, the Ministry of Railways and SARFT, this poses a serious challenge as the regulator (the state) and the majority owner (the state) are the same. This condition is exacerbated by the conflicts between the telecommunications-related ministries and the trade-related ministries, which have very different agendas. As will be described below, such conflicts create significant impediments for international competition as required by the WTO.

The impact of the WTO on trade policy-making in telecommunications

The impact of the WTO on China has been significant. One Western observer suggests, "engagement with China … is actually causing the political changes that the proponents of engagement have predicted."[44] However, as a US Congressional analyst argues:

> WTO obligations have often been hampered by resistance to reforms by central and local government officials seeking to protect or promote industries under their jurisdictions, government corruption, and lack of resources devoted by the central government to ensure that WTO reforms are carried out in a uniform and consistent manner … [45]

Structural changes have taken place in the bureaucracy to facilitate trade policy coordination following China's entry into the WTO. As previously discussed, the bureaucratic restructuring in 1998 in preparation for the WTO brought together the Ministry of Post and Telecommunications and other ministries related to telecommunications. The MII and its provincial branches became the primary regulators and policymakers for the telecommunications sector. The MII is responsible for regulatory planning, distribution and allocation of nationwide public telecommunications resources. The telecom administration authorities of the provinces, autonomous regions and municipalities refer to the telecommunications regulatory bureaus in the respective jurisdictions.[46] The MII supervises and administers the telecommunications industry at the national level, and the provincial regulatory bureaus supervise and govern the telecommunications industry in their respective regions under the direction of the MII.[47]

Prior to WTO accession, the MII and its local counterparts were also the practical service providers in the sector. However, under these kinds of circumstances, as the service providers were also SOEs which were directly linked to the government, it was more difficult to abide by the nondiscrimination principle. The Reference Paper requires China and MII to become independent as the regulator cannot be both the regulator and service provider at the same time.[48] However, while the MII is *de jure* structurally and financially separated from all telecom operators and providers, the *de facto* situation is that there is still strong linkage between the two. AT&T in its testimonial to the USTR contests that MII has a dual role as both the industry regulator and protector of SOEs.[49]

Another difficulty China faced in fully implementing its WTO agreements is that it has negotiated as one country, with MOFCOM (then MOFTEC) as the lead ministry. Participation by other relevant government agencies such as the Ministry of Foreign Affairs (MOFA) was limited. Most decisions were made by MOFTEC, now MOFCOM, with trade and economic considerations playing the most important role. However, once a member of the WTO, the emphasis shifted from negotiation to implementation and compliance. This means that MOFCOM has played a less prominent role and the responsibilities for implementation and compliance have been shifted to the ministries in charge of the relevant sectors. Consequently the number of ministries taking part in trade policy-making has increased enormously and the level of participation by other related ministries at the domestic level has been magnified. The conditions for implementation seemed somewhat improved with the bureaucratic streamlining. However, the conflicts between the trade ministries and the telecommunications sector only intensified after accession as the telecommunications-related ministries have become increasingly involved, with more say in the direction of telecommunications trade policy.

In addition, the involvement of the newly privatized telecommunications operators such as China Telecom further complicated trade policy-making. Since telecommunications was a lucrative sector, the telecommunications operators had considerable influence over trade policy in the sector. Consequently, trade policy after China's WTO accession has come to involve both governmental and nongovernmental entities with conflicting interests and this has further exacerbated the problem of generating a uniform trade policy.

In short, the above discussion suggests that trade policy has become a complicated process with China's accession to the WTO. This is exemplified in the following three cases: the CCF case, the MII vs. SARFT case and the 750 percent increase in fees in the interconnection case. While not a direct breach of WTO agreements, and resolved outside of the WTO dispute mechanism, these actions

Figure 8.2 A simplified organizational chart of the ministries related to China's WTO implementation in the telecommunications sector

illustrate the extent of intensified turf wars and conflicting interests both in the events leading up to and after WTO accession.

The China–China–Foreign (CCF) model of investment

Prior to its WTO accession, China had significant non-transparent, anti-WTO practices in the telecommunications sector. The China–China–Foreign (*Zhong-Zhong-Wai*, hereinafter CCF) enterprises are ones in which foreign telecommunications companies are licensed to operate in telecommunications services using a loophole in trade legislation (see Figure 8.3 for an illustration of the CCF Model).

The lucrative Chinese market lured foreign investors even when foreign participation in telecommunications was forbidden under the MOFTEC Investment Catalogue (the Catalogue for short). Legal uncertainty that existed in China prior to its WTO entry produced considerable grievances for many foreign investors since the "green light could turn red the next day".[50] However, while this ambiguity created problems, it also provided opportunities for many foreign companies. In particular, as China Unicom was having great difficulty developing its networks and was confronted with fierce competition from China Telecom, the lack of domestic funding made the company turn to foreign investors. Consequently the China–China–Foreign investment model was devised.

Article 4 of the Enforcement Ordinance of the Foreign Capital Enterprise Law prohibited foreign investment, but the CCF joint venture model was devised to circumvent the regulations. Before China's WTO entry, foreign investment in the Chinese economy was divided into either "encouraged", "discouraged" or "forbidden" categories. Telecommunications fell under the "forbidden" classification under the catalogue.[51] Section VII, Part of the Prohibited Foreign Investment Industries Chapter expressly prohibited foreign investment in the management of telecommunications business. Since telecommunications services support the national communication line and have strong links to national security, the Chinese government has sought to shelter telecommunications from foreign competition.[52] This

Telecom in China Pre-WTO

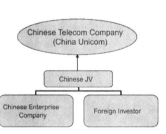

- MOFTEC catalogue prohibited investment in Telecom
- Closed eye to CCF financing mechanism
- 45 projects between Unicom and 20 firms (Sprint, NTT, Bell Canada, and Cable & Wireless HKT) totaling US$1.4 billion
- MII suddenly announced September 1999 that it was irregular and should be prohibited

Figure 8.3 The China–China–Foreign model of investment

became incompatible with the development in telecommunications liberalization in the Uruguay Round and the GATS.

The CCF was not a financial scheme unique to the telecommunications sector, but included some important joint ventures in telecommunications services. The CCF would involve three parties: two Chinese companies and one foreign company. The foreign company would form a joint venture with a Chinese company in the non-prohibited sector, and this China–Foreign (CF) joint venture would invest in a Chinese company which operates in a foreign prohibited sector. The money from the foreign company would be funneled through the CF company to finance projects in the second joint venture company which would be formed with the Chinese partner in the prohibited sector. The foreign company would get the returns from such projects through the two joint venture companies.[53]

Joint ventures with foreign and Chinese companies made investment contracts with Unicom. The joint ventures were used as a channel for foreign investment, and foreign companies were prohibited from owning and operating telecommunications networks and participating in business management with the exception of indirect methods such as through separate agreements on technology cooperation.

About 39 companies came to be involved in the CCF scheme.[54] These companies believed that by taking part in the CCF, they would have "one foot in the door" if and when China liberalized its telecommunications market.[55] The CCF presented a means for the weak telecommunications industries to absorb foreign funds and technology. It is in a developing country's interest to attract foreign capital at low interest rates to build its networks. This desire to attract foreign investment overlapped with the desire of telecommunications companies in developed countries to enter into a lucrative market such as China. The overlap of foreign telecommunications companies and Unicom's respective interests brought forth the CCF.

The MII initially turned a blind eye to the CCF financing scheme. However, the ministry started to tighten control when it turned out that enough technology and funds were transferred to the Chinese companies.[56] Although there was tacit consent, at the end of 1998 the MII declared them "irregular" and said that they must be "rectified". While the MII declared the model "irregular", implying that it was problematic and had to be addressed, it never stated that it was "illegal". In June 2000, when MII cancelled all CCFs, the settlements were confidential: investors were given back their initial investment plus interest on Chinese bank terms.[57] This left many foreign telecommunications companies unhappy as their administrative expenses were not refunded, which meant that foreign investors would suffer considerable economic damages.

The CCF case, among many other incidents, illustrates that bureaucratic conflicts over the telecommunications industry intensified both prior to and after WTO accession. Once a member, China was required to have consistent trade policy: as such, the MII would be responsible for the implementation of telecommunications trade policy. The CCF case shows that MII was more concerned about protecting the domestic industry and gaining comparative advantage, rather than keeping foreign investors content. Once foreign funds and know-how had been absorbed, MII felt it was time to clamp down on the CCFs. While this action created uniform practices in the telecommunications industry, the sudden shift in policy came without much warning. Such practices in China were therefore far from the predictable and transparent system of operations envisioned by the WTO.

The CCF case also illustrates how different ministries within the Chinese government have different interests. While bureaucratic conflicts did not have any direct impact on trade policy prior to China's entry into the WTO as the trade ministry was the leading agency, they have translated into more heated debates or conflicts after accession as the actors involved in implementation became more diverse and took on increasingly divergent interests.

The MII and SARFT

According to Lardy, "In its WTO negotiations, China's MOFTEC negotiators made commitments in services without sufficiently consulting with the relevant domestic regulators."[58] As mentioned earlier, Zhu Rongji made concessions in the telecommunications sector without consulting MII minister Wu when he visited Clinton in April 1999.[59] Since he only found out about the concessions when the news was leaked to the press, Wu objected in a dramatic manner, and threatened to resign. Zhu, then head of the State Council, adopted a more flexible approach to telecommunications liberalization compared to the MII, which was more conservative in orientation. Moreover, compared to the MII, which was looking after the interests of one sector, the State Council as an organ was more willing to make tradeoffs between different sectoral interests. The concessions made by Zhu were seen by the telecommunications-related ministries as too much, and once Zhu returned home, the Chinese negotiation team backed off on its concessions. Such divergent interests with regard to the telecommunications sector bred turf wars and departmental politics. These battles were intensified as the telecommunications-related ministries gained more voice after WTO accession.

Such intensified bureaucratic conflicts following China's WTO accession were reflected in the struggle for telecommunications legislation. Each ministry, commission and department of the State Council has the power to legislate laws in its particular issue area. Any rules issued at below the ministry level are called *tiaoli* (regulations) instead of *falu* (law). In addition, local governments are vested with law-making powers: provincial People's Congresses and their standing committees and the provincial governments have the power to issue local regulations and rules.[60]

Authorities with overlapping legislative rights have had intense conflicts. For example, the State Administration of Radio, Film and Television (SARFT), the management authority for cable networks, and the Ministry of Information Industry (MII), the management authority for telecommunications, have disputed over the legislative rights for cable telephony.[61] Due to convergence in telephony, radio/television and telephone technologies are increasingly coming closer, adding tension to the turf wars between the SARFT and MII.

For example, cable networks have broader bandwidth than the telecommunications network, and can provide better services in Internet access, video-on-demand and interactive shopping. Since neither ministry had any incentive to compromise, the turf wars have become heated, pushing ministries to self-destructive measures.[62] SARFT and the MII were both jeopardizing their own long term interests by waging a lengthy turf war. Each authority was employing hidden strategies to weaken the other ministry's authority.[63]

This extensive turf war was resolved with the intervention of the State Council: television transmission was excluded from the authority of the MII, but telecommunications networks and radio and television transmission networks remained under the MII.[64] It was decided that the production and broadcasting of radio and television programs would be regulated by the SARFT, and network and transmission would be operated by telecommunications companies and regulated by the MII.

With the SARFT and MII turf war being resolved by the State Council, some local cable broadcasting companies have started trial operations in telecom businesses supervised by the MII in cooperation with SARFT. One such example is internet access via the cable network.

These tensions at the horizontal level of the central government also existed vertically between the central and local governments. The central–local communication channels were particularly difficult, and in services, there existed many interested parties in different ministries and localities. Such conflicts in center–local relations further complicated trade policy at the national level. Local governments were most interested in what would be beneficial to their respective jurisdictions, so implementing and complying with the WTO was not of the foremost concern to them. As the turf wars at the central level are exacerbated by conflicts in center–local relations, they are likely to generate WTO-related disputes in the future.

Interconnection

The WTO Reference Paper requires interconnection with an incumbent carrier to be available to competitors at any technically feasible point in the network upon request. The interconnection should be timely, cost-based, transparent and non-discriminatory. This was reinforced in the *Mexico – Measures Affecting Telecommunications Services* case (Telmex Case for short), where MCI and AT&T, who were respectively partial owners of Alestra and Avantel, lobbied the US government to claim Telmex in breach of the GATS Reference Paper.[65]

In the Telmex Case, the panel found that Telmex's interconnection rates for the US telecommunications suppliers were not "cost-oriented" and that Mexico should have provided interconnection to the US on a facilities basis under cost-oriented rates. The Telmex case attests to the progressive development of international telecommunications regulation, and shows that the GATS and the Reference Paper are becoming utilized to define the practices in telecommunications. Indeed, interconnection is fast becoming one of the most problematic areas for trade in telecommunications services.

According to the Chinese representative in the 2002 Trade Review Mechanism (TRM), the Chinese interconnection settlement standards were to be based on cost. It was intended to have interconnection fees comply with international practices. The Chinese also signaled their willingness to strengthen cooperation with other members and share their successful experiences with respect to interconnection cost and settlement standards.[66]

According to the *Telecommunications Regulation of the PRC* and the *Regulations on Interconnections between Public Telecommunications Networks*, leading telecom operators should develop rules on interconnection and report them to the MII for approval prior to implementation.[67] In the *Telecommunications Regulations of the PRC*, dominant telecommunications carriers established interconnection rules and procedures, guided by the principles of nondiscrimination and transparency. Leading telecom operators were required to provide interconnections within the specified time limit. They were not allowed to deny requests for interconnection from other telecom operators and private network operators nor were they permitted to freely restrict the right of users to choose the telecom services provided by other operators.[68]

Leading telecommunications operators were required to ensure that the quality of the inter-network connection service they provided to other telecommunications operators was the same as they provided within their own networks or to their subsidiaries or branches. The dominant carriers had the obligation to adopt the necessary technical measures to ensure that consumers enjoy their network call functions.[69]

In offering inter-network connections to other telecom operators, the service quality of leading operators was required to be as good as that of like services within their own networks or that of like services supplied to subsidiaries or branches. Leading telecom operators had an obligation to coordinate with users acquiring telecom network code number resources in order to realize the function of the resources.[70]

Interconnection agreements between public telecommunications networks and between public and specific telecommunications networks were concluded on the basis of consultations between the parties and according to the *Administrative Regulations on Networks Interconnection*. Such agreements were subsequently filed with the MII.[71]

In October 2002, China Telecom increased its interconnection rates by 750 percent overnight.[72] The MII sent a confidential circular advising China Telecom to raise its interconnection charges so that its profits would improve in preparation for the company's IPO on the Hong Kong and New York stock markets.[73] Following this move, foreign telecommunications companies also raised their international call rates to China in order to remain profitable. As foreign companies sought to limit their access to China in order to generate a profit, there was a two-week period where making international phone calls to China became very difficult.[74]

This 750 percent increase in interconnection charges was a clear breach of the WTO telecommunications agreements, particularly the Reference Paper. While the MII believed that this move would make China Telecom a more desirable company, this action only attracted criticism from other WTO members. This incident illustrates the extent to which the MII is still strongly linked to China Telecom. While the Chinese government takes the stance that the MII is an independent regulator, it is still indirectly dictating how China Telecom should be managed. The MII is independent on paper and in the law. However, if the MII were truly independent, it should not take an interest in how China Telecom conducts its IPO. The mere fact that the MII was interested in making China telecom's IPO successful shows that the relationship between the MII and China Telecom is still strong and that the MII is far from an independent regulator.

This case illustrates that the WTO's impact on China's existing telecommunications regime is divided. The WTO commitments require China to effectively break its monopoly and deregulate the telecommunications sector. However, the relationship between the MII and China Telecom is very close. In the short term, this can translate into non-WTO compliant behavior as seen in the sudden increase in interconnection fees. As conflicts of interest exist not only among government organizations but also between government and non-government entities (such as between the MII and China Telecom), this may complicate the environment for China's implementation of its WTO commitments in the telecommunications sector.

Conclusion

WTO membership calls for a new wave of trade-related reforms. However, implementation of WTO-related reforms promises to be a drawn out process for many countries. For China, WTO membership creates an impetus for trade liberalization and the opening up of traditionally closed sectors such as telecommunications. While WTO-related reforms were initially introduced to enhance the uniformity of the country's trade policy, the environment for trade policy-making has become more diverse and complicated.

Prior to WTO accession, the decisive powers were in the hands of MOFTEC (now MOFCOM), the ministry in charge of trade. While other ministries participated in policy-making, they did not have much say in the direction of China's trade policy. In terms of the telecommunications sector, this resulted in China signing onto an agreement which was difficult for the telecommunications ministry to implement. While the agreement made sense in trade and economic terms as it promised to gradually open up the telecommunications sector in those areas in which the country has a competitive advantage, the reforms called for by the agreement are impractical given the nature of the telecommunications bureaucracy.

Moreover, once China had joined the WTO, the responsibilities for policy implementation shifted from the trade ministry, MOFTEC/MOFCOM, to the telecommunications ministry, the MII.[75] This was compounded by privatization in the telecommunications sector as the entities involved in telecom trade policy included not only the trade and telecom ministries but also the newly independent operators such as China Telecom. The aforementioned cases of near breaches of

WTO agreements (the CCF, the MII vs. SARFT and the 750 percent increase in interconnection fees) show that trade policy after China's WTO accession was more complicated, involving an increasing number of ministries and private entities. As China is still represented at the WTO by MOFCOM, with MOFA and the State Council following closely behind, WTO trade policy now includes all these entities with conflicting interests.

In short, the above examination of the case of telecommunications illustrates that Chinese trade policy following its accession into the WTO is a more fragmented and complicated process. Despite all of the reform efforts, the environment remains inhospitable to the implementation of China's WTO commitments.

Notes

1 Declaration by USTR Barshefsky after the US Senate voted to approve Permanent Normal Trade Relations (PNTR) for China. See Nichols and Cox (2000).
2 The findings are primarily based on fieldwork: I conducted 130 interviews in Geneva, Beijing, Shanghai and Guangzhou. Interviewees included officials, govermental advisors and professionals involved in the implementation of WTO agreements in China. These were in-depth, qualitative interviews, ranging in length between 1.5 and 3 hours, and were combined with participant observation in some cases.
3 See Fairbank and Twitchett (1978). The Open Door Policy was articulated in the December 1978 Third Plenum communiqué and followed up by a decision in 1979 to expand foreign trade and allow foreign companies to invest in China. This represented an attempt to open China to the global economy as well as to accelerate the country's modernization. See Shirk (1993: 47).
4 In this chapter, I take a functional definition of trade policy – in this case how China's interests are represented in the WTO.
5 See Lardy (2002a).
6 Mastel (2000).
7 As Douglas Newkirk, former Assistant United States Trade Representative states, "[t]he GATT wasn't written with a socialist market economy in mind", quoted in Bhala (2000).
8 "Comparative advantage" is a concept developed by Ricardo which posits that free international trade increases the opportunities and profits available to economic actors. Actors may increase their welfare gains when they specialize in the skills they are best at. See Trebilcock and Howse (1999:5).
9 Lovelock (1999: 301).
10 Jackson is one of the more optimistic scholars of the benefits of expanded membership of the WTO. He is also enthusiastic about the prospect of China being a responsible member of the WTO. Jackson (1999: 291). See also Kennedy (1994) for a commentary on Jackson's work.
11 See Borrus and Cohen (1997).
12 BBC (2001); Groombridge and Barfield (1999:36).
13 Harwood (2002).
14 This was illustrated in the Deutsche Telecom case where the FCC tried to stop Deutsche Telecom from investing in the US telecommunications company VoiceStream. Eventually the FCC had to allow Deutsche Telecom to invest as they had already allowed NTT to do so. Moreover, the proposed restriction would also be in breach of MFN. The Deutsche Telecom case illustrates the extent to which foreign investment in telecommunications sector can be problematic, even in a developed country where telecommunications companies are well established and have a competitive advantage.
15 Fieldwork at WTO, 2002–2003.
16 The "Five Principles of Peaceful Co-existence" include mutual respect for sovereignty and territorial integrity; mutual nonaggression; non-interference in each other's internal affairs; equality and mutual benefits; and peaceful coexistence. Kong (2000: 656).

17   Even in 2000 when China was beginning telecommunications reform in preparation for WTO entry, the MII was not forthcoming in giving out information about its laws and regulations to Chinese legal practitioners. Interview with ex-MII official, summer 2001.

18   Interview with MII officials in Beijing and Hong Kong, July 2001.

19   MII statistics as of April 2002. Available online: www.mii.gov.cn/mii/hyzw/tongjiziliao200203.htm.

20   Most telecommunications technology came from the military, and the telephone lines were the lifeline to security in China. In any country, there is general mistrust of allowing foreign entrants into the more important areas of telecommunications services such as fixed-line service.

21   Para 72 China Trade Review Mechanism (TRM) 2002 S/C/M/63, which is an official document of the WTO.

22   Lieberthal and Lampton (1992); Shirk (1993).

23   For a good analysis of the bargaining over telecommunications policy, see Lovelock (1999).

24   Most other Protocols of the newly acceding countries only have 2-page main texts while China has an 11-page long main text.

25   Paragraph 9 of the Working Party Report does state that "Some members of the Working Party indicated that because of the significant size, rapid growth and the transitional nature of the Chinese economy, a pragmatic approach should be taken in determining China's need for recourse to transitional periods and other special provisions in the WTO agreements available to development country WTO Members".

26   This will be elaborated in detail in the following section on CCF. Previously, foreign direct investment was carried out through the Chinese–Chinese–Foreign investment model. However, this was not binding, as MOFTEC declared foreign investment in this sector illegal, and MII stated that they were "irregular" and must be "rectified". See Chuang (2000).

27   The restrictions are detailed in the Foreign Investment Catalogue of the former Ministry of Foreign Trade and Economic Cooperation (MOFTEC) and several of the older laws and regulations. See Eichelberger and Allen (2002).

28   China has geographic restrictions and a phase-in period of six years for the telecommunications sector. See discussions in Janda and Jing (2002).

29   Baker and McKenzie (2001).

30   Interconnection refers to the phenomenon where two means of communications link up at one point. For example, when mobile phones call another country, they go through cells that connect mobile phones in the country of origin, and then use land lines in another country's communication system. This connection between the cell and the landline is called interconnection, and requires the mobile company to pay interconnection fees to the landline company. How these interconnection fees are set and their fairness is one of the central topics in the WTO Reference Paper. WT/MIN(01)/3/Add.2, p.49.

31   Interviews at WTO, 2002.

32   Whether or not China was a developing country was a contentious topic in the accession negotiations. However, by the time China joined in 2001, the WTO has been established for six years and most of the benefits accorded to developing countries were already phased out, so the issue of developing country status was no longer relevant. Interviews at UNCTAD, Geneva, September 2001.

33   Interview with WTO delegation member, summer 2001.

34   Interview with WTO delegation member, summer 2001.

35   DeWoskin (2001).

36   The former State Development and Planning Commission played a decisive role as a result of the legacy of the command economy, but this has changed with the 1998 governmental reforms.

37   DeWoskin (2001: 645).

38   "Convergence refers to the coming together of several formerly distinct services and industries. Whereas audio, video and data services were once distinct offerings, provided by companies in distinct market segments, those services have been rapidly converging into a single, digital marketplace. Wire and wireless telephone companies, cable companies, broadcasters, satellite operators, and even utilities increasingly are competing in the provision of a common service: the

transmission of bits of digital information. Once in digital form, audio, video and data can be transmitted by a single infrastructure and received by a single device." William T. Lake, Lynn R. Charytan, and Matthew A. Brill, "Telecommunications Convergence: Implications for the Industry and for the Practicing Lawyer", (March 2000) 597 PL19 at 9.

39   China Telecom Hong Kong Ltd. (CTHK) was established in Hong Kong on 3 September 1997 as a subsidiary of China Telecom. CTHK was listed on the New York Stock Exchange 22 October 1997 and on the Hong Kong Stock Exchange on 23 October 1997. As of 2001, CTHK became part of China Mobile, and changed its name to China Mobile (Hong Kong) Ltd.

40   In June 2000 Unicom raised $4.92 billion through its IPO on the New York and Hong Kong Stock Markets.

41   OECD figures at end of 2001.

42   OECD figures at end of 2001.

43   DeWoskin (2001: 643).

44   Kynge (2003).

45   CRSR (2003: 8–9).

46   Telecommunication service providers can only apply for a nationwide license from the MII. Para 68 China TRM 2002 S/C/M/63.

47   Para 67 China statement TRM 2002 S/C/M/63.

48   Para 28 TRM 2002 S/C/M/63 China.

49   AT&T testimonial to the USTR. See also US statement para 36 TRM 2002 S/C/M/63; Para 68 US statement TRM 2003 S/C/M/69.

50   Interview, Tianjin Morishima.

51   MOFCOM, formerly MOFTEC webpage. Available online: www.moftec.gov.cn/moftec/html/laws_and_regulations/investment25.html.

52   Communication technology is strongly linked to military technology. For example the initial trial for the mobile technology of CDMA was held inside the People's Liberation Army, and the military devised China's own version of mobile technology. Interview in Beijing.

53   "China Sets Limit on 'Unicom-Invented' Investment Model, Impact Hotly Debated at China Telecom 2000 Conference in New York." PR Newswire.

54   These companies include Sprint International, Wireless Electronique Ltd. (i.e. WelCOM), Daewoo, Bell Canada International, France Telecom, NTT and Deustche Telecom. Chuang (2000: 528).

55   Unicom was one of Chinese partner companies that was quite active in the CCF. The company managed to absorb 72 percent of its funding through the scheme. Interview in Beijing.

56   Interview with Beijing telecom companies, conducted at Telecom Expo, Beijing 2003.

57   Dean and Forney (2000: A26); Chuang (2000).

58   Lardy (2002b).

59   Tkacik (1999).

60   Working Party Report para 66.

61   Interview with MOFTEC officials and representatives of business councils, Beijing.

62   There were instances where local SARFT and MII officials were found to be pulling out each other's cables. Interview, Beijing 2002–2003.

63   For example, in 2002, local level SARFT and MII in the southern provinces were pulling out each other's cable wires. Author's interviews in Beijiing.

64   *State Council Telecommunications Regulation* (2000), Article 45, 25 September.

65   Sarooshi (2003: 16).

66   Para 71 China TRM 2002 S/C/M/63.

67   *Administrative Regulations on Public Telecommunications Networks Interconnection*, promulgated by MII on 7 September 1997. Available online: www.fjqi.gov.cn?FLFG/FL/fbzdjzf.htm. This was abolished and replaced by the *Administrative Regulations on Public Telecommunications Network Interconnection*, promulgated by the MII on 10 May 2001. Available online: www.mii.gov.cn/mii/zcfg/05-29-01.htm.

68   According to Order 291 of the State Council and its administrative regulation on interconnection of public telecommunication networks, dominant carriers referred to those who controlled the

necessary facilities of basic telecommunications and held more than 50 percent market share in the fixed local telephone business and at the level of local network, and were able to substantially influence other telecommunication carriers' entry into the market. Para 27 China TRM 2004 S/C/M/75.

69 Para 69 China statement TRM 2002 S/C/M/63; Para 27 China TRM 2004 S/C/M/75.
70 Para China 77 TRM2003 S/C/M/69.
71 China para 71 TRM 2002 S/C/M/63.
72 Fieldwork observations and interviews, 2002–2003.
73 China Telecom had its IPO for the Hong Kong and New York Stock Market in October 2002. Fieldwork observations and interviews, 2002–2003.
74 International calling companies need to pay interconnection charges to China Telecom, since they would be using the infrastructure of China Telecom to provide international calls to China. International phone calls rely on the services of several telecom companies. The international calling company rarely owns the infrastructure used to provide the service, but rather pays interconnection charges to the indigenous telecom companies and packages it as under its own brand for consumers.
75 MII shared responsibility with SARFT in areas involving cable.

References

Baker and McKenzie (2001) "China's accession to the World Trade Organization: opportunities in the telecommunications sectors", Baker & McKenzie, China Practice Group Hong Kong, November 2001.

BBC (2001) "China Telecom Splits", BBC News, 11 December. Available online: http://news.bbc.co.uk/hi/english/newssid_1703000/1703965.htm.

Bhala, R. (2000) "Enter the dragon: an essay on China's accession saga", *American University Law Review,* 15: 1469–578.

Borrus, M. and Cohen, S. (1997) *Building China's Information Technology Industry: Tariff Policy and China's Accession to the WTO,* BRIE Working Paper 105, November.

Chuang, L. (2000) "Investing in China's telecommunications market: reflections on the rule of law and foreign investment in China", *Northwestern Journal of International Law and Business* 20 (3): 509–37.

CRSR (2003) "China–U.S. Trade Issues", Congressional Research Service Report No. IB91121, 16 May.

Dean, J. and Forney, M. (2000) "Qualcomm gets good news from China – Beijing says it is closing in on a wireless network using firm's technology", *Wall Street Journal,* 11 October.

DeWoskin, K.J. (2001) "The WTO and the telecommunications sector in China", *China Quarterly,* 167: 630–54.

Eichelberger, J. and Allen, A. (2002) "A legal perspective: the impact of WTO on foreign investment in China's internet/E-commerce sector", Perkins Coie LLP. Available online: www.perkinscoie.com/resources/intldocs/twoimpact.htm.

Fairbank, J. K. and Twitchett, D. C. (eds) (1978) *The Cambridge History of China,* Cambridge: Cambridge University Press.

Groombridge, M. and Barfield, C. (1999) *Tiger by the Tail – China and the World Trade Organization,* Washington, DC: AEI Press.

Harwood, S. (2002). "China and the WTO: the net effect of accession", Available online: www.hollandandknight.com/newsletters.asp?ID=250&Article=1447.

Jackson, J. (1999) *The World Trading System: Law and Policy of International Economic Relations,* 2nd edn, Cambridge, Mass: MIT Press.

Janda, R. and Jing, M. (2002) "China's great leap of faith: telecommunications and financial services commitments", in Alexandroff, A., Ostry, S. and Gomez, R (eds) *China and the Long March to Global Trade: The Accession of China to the World Trade Organization,* London: Routledge, 66–98.

Kennedy, D. (1994) "The international style in postwar law and policy", *Utah Law Review,* 7: 7–104.

Kong, Q. (2000) "China's WTO accession: commitments and implications", *Journal of International Economic Law,* 3 (4): 655–90.

Kynge, J. (2003) "China's bold political reform", *Financial Times,* 12 January.

Lake, W.T., Charytan, L.R. and Brill, M.A. (2000) "Telecommunications Convergence: Implications for the Industry and for the Practicing Lawyer", 597 PL19 at 9.

Lardy, N. (2002a) "Issues in China's accession process", US–China Security Review Commission, 9 May. Available online: www.brook.edu/views/testimony/lardy/20010509.htm.

Lardy, N. (2002b) "Problems on the road to liberalization", *Financial Times,* 15 March. Available online: www.brook.edu/views/op-ed/lardy/20020315.htm.

Lieberthal, K., and Lampton, D. M. (1992) *Bureaucracy, Politics, and Decision Making in Post-Mao China,* Berkeley: University of California Press.

Lovelock, P. (1999) *The Evolution of China's National Information Infrastructure (NII) Initiative: A Policy Making Analysis,* Ph.D. Dissertation, University of Hong Kong, Department of Politics and Public Administration.

Mastel, G. (2000) "China and the World Trade Organization: moving forward without sliding backward", Paper prepared for Symposium: "The First Five Years of the WTO". Available online: www.law.georgetown.edu/journals/gjil/symp00/documents/mastel.pdf.

Nichols, B. and Cox. J. (2000) "Backers hope China pact will promote reform", *USA Today,* 20 September.

Sarooshi, D. (2003) "Commonwealth developing countries and the WTO communications regime", in Grynberg, R. and Turner, E. (eds), *Multilateral and Regional Trade Issues for Developing Countries,* London: Economic Affairs Division Commonwealth Secretariat, 9–21.

Shirk, S. L. (1993) *The Political Logic of Economic Reform in China,* Berkeley: University of California Press.

Tkacik, J. J. Jr. (1999) "Beijing hardliners gain stronger hand as China's WTO hopes to go up in smoke", Heritage Foundation, 11 May. Available online: www.heritage.org/Press/Commentary/ED051199.cfm.

Trebilcock, M. and Howse, R. (1999) *The Regulation of International Trade,* 2nd edn, London: Routledge.

9 Conclusion

Ka Zeng

The chapters in this book illustrate that China's foreign trade policy has undergone significant changes and the process of decision-making has become considerably more open and porous to the influence of non-state actors. Contributing authors suggest that the preferences of industries, bureaucratic actors, local governments, and even those of transnational actors, are increasingly important to the outcome of China's bilateral and multilateral trade disputes. They indicate that foreign trade policy-making in China has become more fluid and open to the influence of societal actors. Such a decision-making process represents a sharp departure from the past where policy-making remained relatively closed, with few avenues of influence by non-state actors.

Moreover, the chapters have noted the increasing legalization of China's foreign trade policy which refers to China's growing resort to antidumping duties and the rules of the World Trade Organization (WTO). In terms of the preferences of the Chinese state, the trend toward legalization was rooted in a desire to constrain the United States' unilateral exercise of power through the use of impartial multilateral rules and regulations. However, from the point of view of domestic actors, legalization serves the interests of large, concentrated state-owned enterprises in need of protection. Moreover, provincial governments and the domestic industry are increasingly driving the choice of China's negotiation forum and the resolution of trade disputes. To the extent that domestic business groups are exerting greater influence over the decision-making process, we may be witnessing a gradual "privatization" of trade policy in China.

As such, we may also see some previously implicit fissures and tensions within the Chinese governing apparatus become more pronounced and even approach the breaking point. They will have important implications for China's foreign policy behavior, particularly with regard to China's desire to act in ways consistent with liberal trade norms. This will also help us better understand China's role as a rising trading power and the nature of Chinese competition and/or cooperation. The concluding chapter identifies questions for future research, discusses the qualifications of our argument and considers the implications of the argument for China and its trading partners.

Directions for future research

While the findings reported in this project emphasize the increasing influence of sectoral, bureaucratic and transnational actors on Chinese trade policy and therefore help to advance our knowledge of Chinese trade policy in the post-reform era, there is nevertheless a disjuncture between studies of trade policy in China and the mainstream political economy literature on trade policy, the latter of which emphasizes variables such as lobbying by societal groups, political institutions, macroeconomic cycles, the rise of intra-industry trade and asset specificity, etc. This section charts a course for future research. In addition to identifying new research questions, it points out the need to bridge the gap between case studies, such as our analyses of China, and studies of trade policy as well as the need for more systematic data collection.

New research questions

An important contextual change identified in this project is China's entry into the World Trade Organization and the shift from bilateralism to multilateralism brought about by China's growing integration into the world economy. As the chapters indicate, the Chinese government and business actors are increasingly learning the rules of the global trade regime as a way of advancing China's interests. Such a move was driven by a desire to constrain the use of unilateral trade policies against China. It was also motivated by a desire to acquire the same policy instruments used by the major players in the trading system. Such a shift toward "aggressive legalism" may resemble the pattern in other countries with a non-legalistic culture such as Japan. Future research could more systematically assess the role of the WTO in constraining the use of aggressive trade policies by China's trading partners or compare China's movement toward "aggressive legalism" with the responses of similarly situated countries.

The Kennedy chapter in this volume traces the evolution of China's anti-dumping regime, emphasizing how the desire to achieve equal standing and acquire the policy instruments available to major trading countries underlies China's move to adopt AD rules. While this finding is instructive, more research is needed to deepen our understanding of China's use of the AD procedure. For example, future research could address questions such as when an industry chooses the AD route instead of other policy instruments to deal with a trade problem, the political-economic determinants of China's AD decisions, or under what circumstances an AD suit is terminated during the investigation with the industry reaching a voluntary export restraint (VER) with the foreign producer accused of dumping, and so on.

While the initiation of AD duties by China is still a relatively new phenomenon and so far the country has only initiated a rather small number of cases, China has been the target of a relatively large number of AD suits from abroad. Nevertheless, the pattern of AD initiation against China is under-studied, nor do we have much knowledge about how China responds to the proliferation of AD suits against

Chinese firms. There is preliminary evidence that the adjustment strategies of Chinese firms to AD suits have differed. A study by Liu (2001), for instance, tentatively suggests that the responses of Chinese industries to foreign antidumping actions vary depending on the extent to which Chinese firms are able to coordinate their actions and overcome free-riding problems to achieve collective action. There may be other variations across industries that could potentially help us understand the coping strategies of Chinese firms and their different ability to deal with AD suits. Hence, how Chinese industries react to the proliferation of AD suits is in need of further investigation.

Another related question that merits further analysis is forum shopping in China's trade policy. In her chapter on China–Japan trade disputes, Naoi raises the question as to what factors prompt Chinese industries to use voluntary export restraints (VERs) instead of safeguard measures. She finds that the combination of the degree of government decentralization and geographical concentration is an important factor explaining Chinese industries' choice of trade policy instruments, reasoning that the expected costs of enforcing VERs among private actors significantly influence China's preferred trade policy instrument. By systematically linking regional interests to China's choice of the negotiation forum, this chapter points out a novel direction in the study of Chinese foreign trade policy.

Indeed, the greater range of policy instruments available to the Chinese in recent years would make research about forum shopping in Chinese trade policy potentially fruitful. Questions that deserve further investigation may include why Chinese industries opt for antidumping duties, VERs, or the WTO dispute settlement system and how the interests and preferences of Chinese industries and the relevant government agencies affect the choice of these alternative negotiation fora. While Naoi emphasizes enforcement costs as a determinant of the choice of the negotiation venue and hence adopts a "top-down" view of the processes underlying dispute initiation, future studies could pursue a "bottom-up" approach and examine domestic industries' preferences and their expectations of the negotiation outcome as a parameter of China's choice of the negotiation venue.

Along similar lines, the future pattern of China's utilization of the WTO dispute settlement system would be a fascinating area of future research. Even though so far China has been a complainant in only one WTO suit (DS252 filed against the imposition of steel safeguard measures by the United States in 2002) and has been a respondent in only a small number of cases, it is likely that the growing trade tensions between China and its trading partners will result not only in more WTO trade disputes directed against China but also more WTO dispute filings by Chinese industries. China's growing involvement in the WTO dispute settlement system could allow one to address questions such as which industries China will select for WTO dispute resolution and, alternatively, how Chinese industries will respond to the growing number of WTO disputes directed against China. The sheer growth in the number of trade disputes in the future will potentially constitute a rich dataset that allows one to systematically analyze the impact of the WTO dispute settlement system on a transitional economy such as China.

The above research questions relate to the initiation, negotiation and resolution of trade disputes involving China. Another avenue of research, apart from the above, concerns China's compliance with its international commitments. While this is a relatively new phenomenon, recent studies (e.g. Mertha and Zeng, 2005; Pearson, 2004; the Kobayashi chapter in this volume) have probed this question and sought to explain how domestic politics may affect China's compliance with its WTO commitments. In particular, these studies emphasize how bureaucratic politics and changing patterns of center–local relations in China may complicate China's effort to live up to its WTO commitments. Overall, these studies are less than sanguine about the prospect of China's WTO compliance, suggesting that bureaucratic conflicts and the difficulties associated with ongoing attempts at re-centralization may diminish the chances that China will fulfill its international obligations. Future research could push this line of inquiry even further and more systematically investigate the domestic determinants of China's compliance behavior. In addition, one could take a "second image reversed" approach and examine how participation in the WTO and other international economic institutions affect business collective action, bureaucratic politics or center–local relations.

Grounding studies of Chinese foreign trade policy in the mainstream political economy literature

The chapters in this volume collectively tackle the question as to whether China has become a normal trading state. Through a series of case studies, they draw our attention to the pathways through which bureaucratic actors, regional interests, sectoral interests and transnational actors influence Chinese foreign trade policy. As such, these studies represent an important step in unraveling China's behavior in the area of international trade policy. Nevertheless, despite the contributions of this project, there remains the need to further link studies of China's foreign trade policy to the literature on international political economy and trade policy and to more systematically assess how interests, institutions and ideas inform China's behavior in the international trading system.

Standard political economy studies of trade policy emphasize the influence of interests and political institutions, among other variables, on trade policy. The society-centered approach to trade policy focuses on societal demand for trade policy and devotes considerable attention to the source, substance and organization of such demands. Previous studies (e.g. Magee *et al.*, 1989; Milner, 1988; Destler *et al.*,1987; Gilligan, 1997) have examined how interest group mobilization influences trade policy. Research (e.g. Rogowski, 1989; Hiscox, 2001) has also looked at the distinction between the sector and factor models of trade policy and the impact of factor mobility on the choice between those two models.

China could provide an interesting testing ground for these theories. The chapters in this project make the suggestion that sectoral interests matter, but more research could be conducted about how industry groups lobby the government for protection. For instance, in discussing China's first WTO dispute, the semiconductor dispute, Wei Liang notes that the lack of active support by the domestic semiconductor industry has facilitated the conclusion of a settlement in China's first WTO dispute. Similarly, the chapter by Zeng suggests that industries that are more heavily concentrated, enjoy political clout due to their size, or experience economic difficulties have had greater success obtaining trade policy protection. While these findings are interesting, they are nevertheless somewhat tentative and have yet to systematically address questions such as how industries lobby the government for protection or what exactly are the channels of industry influence. In addition to addressing the above questions, future studies could also more formally test the hypotheses advanced in the mainstream trade policy literature.

In terms of the role of political institutions, this study notes that bureaucratic politics and interministerial conflicts matter for policy outcomes. There remains the need, however, to ground analysis of China's trade policy in the political economy literature. For instance, McGillivray (2004) engages in a comparative study of redistribution politics across industries in Europe and systematically addresses the influence of electoral rules, party strength and industrial geography on redistribution policies. Other studies (e.g. Mansfield and Busch, 1995) have assessed the influence of such institutional factors as the electoral system or campaign contributions (e.g. Grossman and Helpman, 1994; Hansen and Drope, 2004) on trade policy. More recently, studies (Dixon and Moon, 1993; Mansfield *et al.*, 2000; 2002; Milner and Kubota, 2005) have examined the influence of regime type on trade policy, systematically addressing questions such as whether democracies pursue more liberal trade policies than authoritarian regimes. As China is not a democracy, it is important for us to think about how models derived from Western democracies apply to an authoritarian state such as China. As formal political institutions do not matter to the same extent in an authoritarian state as in a democracy, one may want to ask how aptly these models apply to China. Along similar lines, one could ask how the informal rules of the game affect trade policy outcomes in an authoritarian state such as China. Overall, it is important for us to think about how standard accounts of political economy can inform studies of Chinese trade policy and how studies of China can in turn contribute to the broader IR/IPE literature.

Data collection

To better address the key research questions identified in this chapter and to better bridge the gap between studies of Chinese foreign trade policy and those of trade policy in open economies, it is imperative to develop a richer dataset of Chinese foreign trade behavior.

Use of survey data on the public's attitude towards globalization and international trade could be a promising area of research. Given the divisive nature of WTO entry in China, public opinion surveys could allow us to better assess the coalitional patterns over trade issues in China and offer a richer depiction of the dynamics of trade policy. Currently surveys of public opinion are conducted either as part of a broader public opinion survey (e.g. Pew Global Attitudes Project), or are intended to tap local Chinese elites' attitude toward economic reform (Chhibber and Eldersveld, 2000) or globalization as reflected in China's accession into the WTO (Cooper and Landry, 2006). More research could be conducted along these lines.

Second, with the growth in the number of antidumping disputes, a dataset could be constructed to better capture the range of antidumping actions in China. This would allow us both to better assess the pattern of China's AD actions and to tap the factors that influence the resolution of AD suits involving China.

Third, along similar lines, one could use firm-level data to ask questions about trade policy. The World Bank, for instance, releases the World Business Environment Survey and the Business Environment and Enterprise Performance Survey which examine a wide range of interactions between firms and the state in selected transition economies. These surveys produce measurements such as corruption, lobbying and the quality of the business environment. These data could be useful not only for assessing firm performance, but may also be useful for analyzing the trade policies of firms.

Fourth, the collection of data would no doubt prove beneficial for further theory development. While China's opening to the world economy is still a relatively recent phenomenon, there has nevertheless been a growing number of disputes involving China. Data could be collected about China's use of voluntary export restraints, antidumping duty cases initiated by or targeted at China and, with the development of events, China's use of the WTO dispute settlement mechanism. Such a richer dataset could allow scholars to better assess the patterns of industry lobbying, the factors influencing how issues are brought to the WTO, choices across policy instruments, and so on. It is bound to significantly improve our understanding of the policy-making process in general.

Finally, much of the WTO- and trade-in-China literature focuses on national-level variables and processes. It almost never moves down to the subnational level except to argue that "compliance may be a problem, but … ". Mertha's chapter gives us some indication of the complexities that exist at the local level (see also Mertha and Zeng, 2005). However, such research involves types of research design and methodology that are extremely time-intensive. It requires a great deal of inquiry into sensitive structures and processes that are very difficult to uncover without the type of language and other skills necessary to undertake such research. Nevertheless, in order to answer questions regarding compliance in a credible and confident manner, much more of this type of worm's eye view research needs to be done.

Implications for the Chinese state

The findings from this project have implications for understanding the reach and capacity of the Chinese state. Proponents of the view that there has emerged a hybrid pattern of state–society interactions in China argue that the relaxation of centralized state economic and administrative controls in the reform era has created a certain amount of space for the expression and legitimation of societal interests. At the same time the state attempts to incorporate and encircle the new economic and social forces unleashed by economic reform, the state itself has been reshaped by these emerging forces. As Baum and Shevchenko (1999: 348) put it:

> While the state continues to define the terms and conditions of its engagement with society, state control is exercised indirectly – through cooptation, coordination, and "interest licensing", rather than directly, through vertical command. What has emerged, therefore, is a hybrid form of state–societal interdependence that is less firmly state-driven and state-dominated than the "organizational dependency" model of the Maoist era, but more highly regulated and regimented than the civil society model.

This research about trade policy in China lends support to such a depiction of the changing nature of the Chinese state. As the chapters indicate, marketization and decentralization have augmented the power of local agents in the pursuit of local interests, thus undercutting the hegemony of the central state. In addition, a "social space" has been opened up which allows for the expression of preferences on the part of a diverse range of social and economic actors. For instance, business and industry associations such as the Chamber of Commerce are becoming more proactive and are now actively lobbying for protection. Such societal activism is constraining the reach of the state. While far from being an autonomous civil society, it is eroding the hegemony of the central state in China.

In addition, the findings of this study ought to help advance our understanding of the overall capacity of the partially transformed Chinese state. The chapters indicate that rather than viewing state–society relations in zero-sum terms, it may be more useful for us to examine the reconfiguration of state power. Even in a political environment characterized by low levels of formal institutionalization and limited autonomy of societal forces, new social forces and organizations have emerged and have embedded themselves in the political system. As new business associations and local governments respond to central policies in different ways and assert themselves in the political process, it is likely that they will acquire increasing viability, producing diverse patterns of accommodation and adaptation in interactions with the central state. It may therefore be more useful to view the efficacy of the central state vis-à-vis civil society in a path-dependent, rather than in a dichotomous fashion.

Policy implications

Several policy implications emerge from this project. First, to the extent that China's decision-making process is becoming more pluralistic, any effort by foreign actors to engage China and to induce "cooperative" behavior from China on trade issues is bound to encounter considerable difficulties. As decisions about trade policy are no longer made in a vacuum and as societal influence over trade policy has proliferated, negotiations with China now imply bargaining with a wider range of forces within China. This is likely to reduce the policy discretion of central decision-makers. Thus, a cooperative stance from China on trade issues cannot be assumed. Even the most well-intentioned gesture of central leaders in Beijing to reach cooperation with foreign actors could be undermined by recalcitrant domestic actors.

Second, to the extent that China is now more actively pursuing negotiation routes other than bilateral negotiations and engaging the rules of the WTO, it is imperative that the United States and other major trading states continue to deal with China within the multilateral framework. Such a course of action would allow foreign players to deal with China on the basis of established norms and principles that are accepted by all WTO members. This would both allow the US and other international actors to strengthen the legitimacy of their position in the face of possible Chinese challenges and to prevent charges of unfairness in dealing with a rapidly growing economy such as China.

Third, as the Chinese trade policy process itself becomes more complex, the response of the United States and other trading partners is likely to become less sanguine to shortcomings in China's international behavior. The US preference for speed and a clear delineation between cause and effect (i.e. processes and outcomes) will certainly be frustrated as the nexus in which this takes place becomes increasingly complicated. The feedback effect of such a shift in the character of relations is likely only to exacerbate such tensions, as it provides China the negative reinforcement necessary to pursue multilateralism while also undercutting Beijing's desire to rein in its less compliant local government and other partners.

Finally, this pluralization in the policy process in China is evident in other issue areas such as hydropower (Mertha and Lowry, 2006). Thus, the findings in this volume can also be tentatively generalized to other issue areas, both domestic and international in scope. As such, the contributions to this volume ought to have broader implications for other issue areas and sectors in addition to the vitally important context of China's international trade relations.

References

Baum, R. and Shevchenko, A. (1999) "The 'state of the state'", in Goldman, M. and MacFarquhar R. (eds) *The Paradox of China's Post-Mao Reforms*, Cambridge, M.A: Cambridge University Press.

Chhibber, P. and Eldersveld, S. (2000) "Local elites and popular support for economic reform in China and India", *Comparative Political Studies,* 33 (3): 350–73.

Cooper, M. C. and Landry, P. F. (2006) "The political impact of WTO membership in urban China", in Cameron, D. R., Ranis, G. and Zinn, A. (eds) *Globalization and Self-Determination: Is the Nation State under Siege?"*, London: Routledge.

Destler, I. M., Odell, J. and Elliott, K.A. (1987) *Anti-Protection: Changing Forces in the United States Trade Politics*, Washington, DC: Institute for International Economics.

Dixon, W. J. and Moon, B. (1993) "Political similarity and American foreign trade patterns", *Political Research Quarterly*, 46: 5–25.

Gilligan, M. (1997) *Empowering Exporters: Reciprocity, Delegation, and Collective Action in American Trade Policy,* Ann Arbor: University of Michigan Press.

Grossman, G. M. and Helpman, E. (1994) "Protection for sale", *American Economic Review,* 84 (4): 833–50.

Hansen, W. and Drope, J. (2004) "Purchasing protection? The effect of political spending on U.S. trade policy", *Political Research Quarterly,* 57 (1): 27–37.

Hiscox, M. J. (2001) "Class versus industry cleavages: inter-industry factor mobility and the politics of trade", *International Organization,* 55 (1): 1–46.

Liu, W. (2001) *Zhimian fanqingxiao* (Face antidumping), Guangdong: Guangdong Economics Press.

McGillivray, F. (2004) *Privileging Industry: The Comparative Politics of Trade and Industrial Policy,* Princeton, NJ: Princeton University Press.

Magee, S., Brock, W. and Young, L. (1989) *Black Hole Tariffs and Endogenous Policy Theory,* Cambridge: Cambridge University Press.

Mansfield, E. and Busch, M. L. (1995) "The political economy of nontariff barriers: a cross-national analysis", *International Organization,* 49 (4): 723–49.

Mansfield, E., Milner, H., and Rosendorff, B. P. (2000) "Free to trade: democracies, autocracies, and international trade", *American Political Science Review,* 94 (2): 305–21.

_____ (2002) "Why democracies cooperate more: electoral control and international trade agreements", *International Organization,* 56 (3): 477–513.

Mertha, A. C. and Zeng, K. (2005) "Political institutions, resistance and China's harmonization with international law", *China Quarterly,* 182: 319–37.

Mertha, A. C. and Lowry, W. (2006) "Unbuilt dams: seminal events and policy change in China, Australia, and the United States", *Comparative Politics,* 39 (1): 1–20.

Milner, H. (1988) "Trading places: industries for free trade", *World Politics,* 40 (3): 350–76.

Milner, H. and Kubota, K. (2005) "Why the move to free trade? Democracy and trade policy in the developing countries", *International Organization,* 59 (1): 159–73.

Pearson, M. (2004) "China's WTO implementation in comparative perspective", *Review of International Affairs,* 3 (4): 567–83.

Rogowski, R. (1989) *Commerce and Coalitions: How Trade Affects Domestic Political Alignments,* Princeton, NJ: Princeton University Press.

Index

Printed in the United States
218758BV00002B/7/P

9 780415 547093